EU Foreign and Interior Policies

This book offers an innovative theoretical and empirical analysis of integration in EU foreign and interior policies across the three pillars, from the Maastricht Treaty to the Treaty of Nice.

The establishment of the three-pillar structure in the Maastricht Treaty has been one of the key transformations of European governance. This divided EU policies into three main areas: European Community, Common Foreign and Security Policy (CFSP) and Justice and Home Affairs (JHA). For the first time the two sovereignty-related areas of foreign and interior policy became part of the formal governance structure of the EU. This is the first book to offer a comparative perspective on how integration in both areas across the three pillars has contributed to the construction of a distinct sovereignty dimension of the EU. By drawing from sociological institutionalism and on the basis of the two case studies of EU Middle East and migration policies, it offers a comprehensive empirical analysis of cross-pillar policy-making dynamics in foreign and interior policies in the EU.

Offering a fresh approach to understanding and analysing policy-making in the context of an integrating EU, this book will appeal to scholars and researchers interested in International Relations, European Union Politics and Middle East Studies.

Stephan Stetter is Lecturer in Political Science and International Relations at Bielefeld University, Germany.

Routledge Advances in European Politics

EU Foreign and Interior Policies

Cross-pillar politics and the social construction of sovereignty

Stephan Stetter

Routledge
Taylor & Francis Group

LONDON AND NEW YORK

First published 2007
by Routledge
2 Park Square, Milton Park, Abingdon, Oxon OX14 4RN

Simultaneously published in the USA and Canada
by Routledge
711 Third Ave, New York, NY 10017

Routledge is an imprint of the Taylor & Francis Group, an informa business

Transferred to Digital Printing 2009

© 2007 Stephan Stetter

Typeset in Garamond by
Book Now Ltd, London

British Library Cataloguing in Publication Data
A catalogue record for this book is available from the British Library

Library of Congress Cataloging in Publication Data
A catalog record for this book has been requested

ISBN10: 0–415–41491–1 (hbk)
ISBN10: 0–415–54359–2 (pbk)

ISBN13: 978–0–415–41491–3 (hbk)
ISBN13: 978–0–415–54359–0 (pbk)

für Barbara

Contents

Illustrations

Tables

Figures

Foreword

Many of the most innovative developments in European integration since the early 1990s have taken place outside the established institutions of the European Community, in fields that had been excluded from the Commission-led process of integration because they were close to the heart of national sovereignty. Foreign policy co-operation had developed, through meetings of foreign ministers and of subordinate foreign ministry officials, from 1970 onwards, with only very limited success beyond agreeing common 'declarations'. Co-operation among interior and justice ministries, and the agencies which implemented their policies, had grown up even more informally, with far less publicity, over the same period. Since the end of the Cold War, however, the development of common policies, and institutions, in the field of Justice and Home Affairs has been impressive and remarkable. After successive setbacks, in the face of German hesitation and French and British determination to retain their freedom of action whenever they wished, the outlines of a Common Foreign and Security Policy are now appearing, with even a military staff in Brussels and significant national forces deployed in joint EU operations outside its borders.

Most studies of the second and third pillars have covered only one of the two: hardly surprisingly, since the academic disciplines that focus on policing and migration have little overlap with the study of international relations. This volume is particularly valuable because it treats both pillars as part of a broader phenomenon – of increasing co-operation among governments in response to external pressures, gradually overcoming their hesitation over integrating policies in such traditionally-sensitive fields. It argues that the 'sovereignty block' that held governments back from commitment to joint action in these policy fields is now crumbling. It shows how far European co-operation has now moved beyond the Realist image of monolithic states pursuing clearly-defined national interests. Stephan Stetter's detailed analysis shows how far different actors and agencies within national political systems pursue distinctive policies, often finding co-operation with parallel agencies within other states easier than co-ordination with other structures within their own national administration. Disaggregation of national policy-making towards other open political systems has been an observable aspect of globalization across the advanced democracies. But it has been particularly visible within the EU, in the intense trans-governmental interaction fostered by the EU's institutional framework and patterns of working.

It is a paradoxical quality of these sensitive fields for national policy-making and international co-operation that the *esprit de corps* of the professionals who devote their careers to them builds links across state boundaries. Diplomats and soldiers have long been recognized as professional cadres characterized by mutual respect for shared expertise, sometimes accompanied by shared disdain for the political 'amateurs' to whom they are formally responsible within national political systems. Police, gendarmerie, border guards and customs officers, have similar self-images as professional organizations whose work is only half-understood by outsiders. The opening of frontiers has necessarily brought these forces closer together, their shared professionalism providing a basis both for closer co-operation and for common resistance to detailed political control. Judges and prosecutors, rooted in distinctive traditions of domestic law, might have been expected to prove more resistant to the development of cross-border co-operation based on mutual trust and limited formal structures. But, as this study suggests, they too have now come to work together within the European framework far more closely than seemed conceivable 15–20 years ago.

This study also makes an invaluable contribution to our understanding of the processes of integration by demonstrating that issues of accountability and democratic control as often emerge as tensions between professionals and outsiders at all levels as battles between national and European institutions. Foreign policy, police co-operation, military exchanges, and above all intelligence co-operation, escaped scrutiny within national parliaments more easily than the common policies of the European Community; in many member states, these had long been the fields in which the executive had had most freedom of action, and parliamentary and judicial accountability the least. Governments and their agencies naturally extended these patterns of executive co-operation across national boundaries. Parliamentarians had every incentive, therefore, to co-operate in attempting to prevent this burgeoning pattern of trans-governmental co-operation from escaping further from democratic scrutiny. Part of the drive towards closer co-operation among scrutiny committees of national parliaments within the EU, which we have witnessed over the past decade, together with closer exchange of information and co-operation between national committees and their equivalents within the European Parliament, has been a response to the greater obstacles that the second and third pillars have presented, in terms of access to information and openness to scrutiny.

The pace at which governments and agencies are growing together, furthermore, is unlikely to slow in the foreseeable future. Stetter notes the significant institutionalization of common foreign and security policy over the past 10 years, with a substantial staff within the Council Secretariat, including since 1999 a military staff; the Franco-British initiative of St. Malo in November

1998 may not have led to the integrated forces and common procurement which some optimists hoped for, but has nevertheless provided a framework for closer co-operation among national militaries, and for a number of joint operations in third countries. The external pressures which drove co-operation in the third pillar from the early 1990s – the EU's permeable frontiers to the east and the south, the expansion of illegal immigration (or 'people-smuggling') through organized cross-border networks, the parallel expansion of other forms of cross-border crime, the rising pressure from desperate migrants to get across the boundary between poverty and wealth – are not diminishing. The summer of 2006 saw FRONTEX, the EU's fledgling border control agency, taking on new tasks in response to another surge of migrant boats from West Africa and across the Mediterranean. At the same time, EU governments were responding to pressures from the US Administration, the UN Secretariat, and other governments by providing forces to restore order in southern Lebanon. The number of troops from European states stationed outside the boundaries of the EU was higher in late 2006 than at any time since the withdrawal from empire 30–40 years before: in Bosnia, Kosovo, Congo, Afghanistan, Lebanon, some still co-operating with the Americans in Iraq, smaller numbers in peacekeeping operations elsewhere.

Stephan Stetter provides here a carefully-researched study of the development of this new pattern of integration, in new fields. He also helps us to grasp the similarities, as well as the differences, between developments in the second and the third pillars – both driven more by external challenges than by internal initiative or institutional design. It is unlikely in the extreme that these external challenges will weaken in the near future. The insights this book offers will thus be of relevance to a widening circle of policy-makers, as well as to those who study their actions or who seek to hold them to account.

William Wallace
September 2006

Acknowledgements

I am grateful for having had the opportunity to combine in this book my passion for the study of European integration, Middle East politics and migration policies. I would not have been able to accomplish this work without the support and help of many colleagues and friends who assisted me so generously in pursuing my research on this book. I am deeply indebted to all of them.

My greatest thanks go to my family and in particular my parents, Annegret and Franz Stetter. They have helped me in every conceivable way – emotionally, intellectually, financially and logistically – to pursue my academic interests. I would also like to thank my sisters Judith and Barbara Stetter, my grandmother Philippine Läufer and, in particular, Anna Sigl for their invaluable presence in my life. I am more grateful than words can say that you are all there.

This book builds upon my Ph.D. which I wrote at the Department of Government at the London School of Economics and Political Science (LSE). I am indeed thankful for the support I received from my two supervisors, William Wallace, from the Department of International Relations, and Simon Hix, from the Department of Government. My many interesting discussions with them have been crucial for the completion of this work. I have profited to a great extent from the comments of my two examiners, Christopher Hill from the University of Cambridge and Jörg Monar from Sussex University. I am also grateful to those organizations which have co-financed me during my studies. Most importantly, the Abteilung Studienförderung at the Friedrich-Ebert-Stiftung, and in particular Marianne Braun, have generously supported my studies in political science, sociology and history as an undergraduate and graduate student as well as during my Ph.D. I would also like to thank the Economic Social and Research Council (ESRC) for their financial support. The Department of Government at the LSE also provided important financial assistance for me to participate in several conferences and it was also a grant from the Department of Government, in the framework of the Socrates programme, which enabled me to spend a wonderful research semester at the European University Institute (EUI) in Florence in 2001.

I would like to thank in particular my friends. Tobias Werron has provided me with more support and friendship than I could possibly describe. I would also like to thank Alexandra Nocke, Barbara Lüders, René Wildangel and Rike Geisler for their wonderful friendship. With my friend Jan-Hinrik Meyer-Sahling I have had many superb discussions on political science since we both met at the LSE for our M.Sc. back in 1997. I am grateful to my friend Kostas Skordyles, not least for always offering accommodation while I was staying in London. I am deeply indebted to Armido Rizzi and Alberta Poltronieri who offered me friendship and hospitality during my research stay in Florence – when I became part of their family.

I also want to thank Klaus H. Goetz from the Department of Government at LSE for his continuous encouragement, support and friendship. 'Toda raba' to Alfred Tovias from the Hebrew University of Jerusalem, who was the first to trigger my interest in EU Middle East policies during a year of study in Jerusalem in 1996/7.

I am extremely grateful to the Department for the Middle East at the Friedrich-Ebert-Stiftung (FES). Winfried Veit and Türkan Karakurt have provided me with the incredible opportunity to learn and foster my interest and contacts in Israel and the Middle East. They, with their colleagues at the Israel and Palestine offices of the FES as well as at the Bonn and Berlin headquarters allowed me to actively engage in various projects in the Middle East, such as the Palestinian–Israeli–German 'Jerusalem–Berlin Forum' (JBF) and the 'Israeli European Policy Network' (IEPN). These projects are themselves small European contributions to the overcoming of violence and hostility in Israel and Palestine and I feel honoured to be part of them. In that context I would like to express my gratitude to Michèle Auga, Hermann Bünz, Matthes Buhbe, Raffaella A. Del Sarto, Knut Dethlefsen, Micky Drill, Rami Friedman, Andrä Gärber, Katharina von Münster, Rami Nasrallah, Roby Nathanson, Sharon Pardo, Joel Peters, Elisabeth Petersen, Dirk Sadowski, Elisabeth Schumann-Braune and Ernst Stetter as well as my friends from Team Jerusalem and Team Berlin.

I would also like to thank the officials from the European Union – in Brussels, Tel Aviv and London – which I had the chance to interview for this book. I would also like to thank my colleagues at various conferences in the EU and abroad where I received fruitful and encouraging comments which helped a lot in strengthening the arguments of this book.

Many individuals have given support at various stages of this project. I think in particular of Mathias Albert, Annegret Bendiek, Tanja Börzel, Tonny Brems Knudsen, Riad Al-Khouri, Alkuin Kölliker, Richard Gillespie, Knud Erik Jørgensen, Annette Jünemann, Tanja Kopp-Malek, Jeremy Richardson, Frank Schimmelfennig, Karen E. Smith, Nadine Stolze, Gary Sussman, Stelios Stavridis, Thomas Risse, Angelika Timm, Volker Verrel, Ramses Wessel, Jochen Walter and Antje Wiener. Special thanks go to my students in the courses I have taught at the Department of Government at the LSE and Bielefeld University. I also would like to thank my Hebrew and Arabic teachers at the Hebrew University of Jerusalem, the Landesspracheninstitut Nordrhein-Westfalen and elsewhere, who have helped in fostering my 'understanding' of

Israel, Palestine and Arab countries – and of the wonderful languages spoken there. Special thanks go to Heidi Bagtazo and Harriet Brinton from Routledge as well as Hayley Greenaway from Taylor & Francis and to Richard Cook and Frances Nugent of Book Now for their excellent and professional support in the preparation of this book. Many thanks to the four anonymous referees for their insightful and constructive comments.

I would like to thank Taylor & Francis for giving me the permission to reprint parts of my two articles 'Cross Pillar Politics: Functional Unity and Institutional Fragmentation of EU Foreign Policies', originally published in *Journal of European Public Policy*, 11(3): 720–39 and 'Democratisation without Democracy: The Implementation of EU Assistance for Democratisation Processes in Palestine', originally published in *Mediterranean Politics*, 8(3:) 153–73. In particular, Chapters 3 and 7 of this book draw from parts of these two articles. See also: www.tandf.co.uk/journals/alphalist.asp for a link to *Journal of European Public Policy* and *Mediterranean Politics*.

I dedicate this book with love to my sister Barbara Stetter.

Abbreviations

CFSP	Common Foreign and Security Policy
CIREA	Centre for Information, Discussion and Exchange on Asylum
CIREFI	Centre for Information, Discussion and Exchange on the Crossing of Borders and Immigration
COREPER	Committee of Permanent Representatives
DCT	Draft Constitutional Treaty
DG	Directorate General
EC	European Community
ECJ	European Court of Justice
EEAS	European External Action Service
EIB	European Investment Bank
EMP	Euro-Mediterranean Partnership
ENP	European Neighbourhood Policy
EP	European Parliament
EPC	European Political Co-operation
EPP	European Peoples' Party
ERF	European Refugee Fund
EU	European Union
GMP	Global Mediterranean Policy
IGC	Intergovernmental Conference
IO	international organization
JHA	Justice and Home Affairs
MEDA	*mesures d'accompagnement*
MEP	Member of the European Parliament
PA	Palestinian Authority
PES	Party of European Socialists
PKK	Kurdish People Party
PLO	Palestine Liberation Organization
PPEWU	Policy Planning and Early Warning Unit
REDWG	Regional Economic Development Working Group
RELEX	External Relations Directorate General (*Relations extérieure*)
RMP	Redirected Mediterranean Policy
SCR	Joint Service (*Service commun*)

SEA	Single European Act
SIS	Schengen Information System
TCN	third-country national
TEC	European Community Treaty
TEU	Treaty on European Union
UN	United Nations
US	United States

1   Introduction

The three-pillar structure revisited

The establishment of the three-pillar structure in the Maastricht Treaty has been one of the main transformations of European governance. Thus the Maastricht Treaty brought those parts of foreign and interior policies that hitherto had not been part of the formal Treaty structure into the 'single institutional framework' of the newly founded European Union (EU). For the first time in the history of European integration both policy areas, which are deeply linked to national conceptualizations of sovereignty, have become in their entirety an integral part of EU politics. At the same time, from an institutional perspective, foreign and interior policies were spread across all the three pillars, with some parts being located in the 'supranational' first pillar of the European Communities (EC), while others became part of the two 'intergovernmental' pillars, namely the Common Foreign and Security Policy (CFSP) and Justice and Home Affairs (JHA).

This observation brings to the fore some crucial questions that are of interest to scholars and students of EU politics in general, and EU foreign and interior policies in particular, namely: how can we account for the dynamics and limits of integration in both policy areas? What is the impact of the pillar structure on policy-making in foreign and interior affairs? Why do member states embark on integration in these sovereignty-related policy areas? And what is the impact of integration in foreign and interior policies for the political system of the EU at large?

This book sheds a new light on these crucial questions by offering a theoretically guided in-depth comparative study on the dynamics of integration in EU foreign and interior policies from the Maastricht Treaty (1993) to the Treaty of Nice (2003).[1] By drawing from the theory of sociological institutionalism, it addresses in particular the manifold cross-pillar overlaps within both policy areas and, hence, systematically identifies the functional, institutional and substantive linkages between foreign and interior policies in the 'supranational' first pillar (EC) with foreign and interior policies in the 'intergovernmental' second and third pillars (CFSP and JHA) and how these linkages affect policy-making processes in both areas. This focus on political dynamics across the three pillars directs attention towards an integrated perspective on the *functional unity* of each of the two policy areas despite remarkable *institutional fragmentation* (Wessel 2004). This approach consciously departs from a quite common trend in the literature to implicitly equate foreign policies with the CFSP and interior policies with JHA. In order to trace the functional, institutional and substantive linkages across all the three pillars, this book draws, on an empirical level, from extensive document analysis and expert interviews related to two distinct case studies from both policy areas, namely EU Middle East policies (foreign policies) and migration policies (interior policies). The empirical chapters of this book thus focus on some crucial areas in which the dynamics of cross-pillarization become visible, namely the capabilities of supranational actors, the level of substantive policies and the dynamics of policy-making between supranational actors and the Council in both policy areas.

This study not only looks at the macro-level of Treaty provisions but also addresses the dynamics of day-to-day policy-making across all the three pillars. In order to trace the cross-pillar dynamics in both policy areas on this level, it uses EU Middle East (bilateral policies towards Israel and Palestine; policies on the Israeli-Palestinian conflict; the Euro-Mediterranean Partnership (EMP) as far as this relates to Israel and Palestine) and migration policies (asylum; immigration; free movement of third-country nationals; visa and border issues) as concrete case studies. Given the centrality of these two case studies in the larger realm of EU foreign and interior policies, it could be argued that they represent rather easy targets for tracing these cross-pillar overlaps. However, such a line of argument seems untenable for two reasons. First, it overestimates the *sui generis* character of Middle East and migration policies vis-à-vis more general developments in EU foreign and interior policies. Thus EU Middle East and migration policies are linked to other issues dealt with in the wider context of EU foreign and interior policies, such as policies on conflict prevention or cross-border police co-operation, to name but two examples. Second, it draws a somewhat too harmonious picture of substantive shortcomings and institutional obstacles, which not only characterize EU policies on issues such as, for example, the war in Iraq or judicial co-operation, but also affect Middle East and migration policies. As a quick glance at the literature reveals, Middle East and migration policies are subject to similar dynamics and constraints as other issues of EU foreign and interior policies (Peers 2000; Aoun 2003).

It should be mentioned that, on the face of it, the Amsterdam Treaty of 1999 did provide for significant changes with regard to the pillar structure. This relates in particular to interior policies, since the Treaty base of EU migration policies shifted from the third to the first pillar (Title IV EC-Treaty). However, this book argues that in substance this *passerelle* did not fundamentally alter the political dynamics underlying the pillar structure in JHA prior to 1999 (Stetter 2000). Thus migration policies were not communitarized in the 'classical' sense. With regard to the 'soft law' character of substantive decisions, the overall decision-making process and judicial overview, there have only been incremental changes to the third-pillar provisions of the Maastricht

Treaty. Migration policies after Amsterdam are, thus, part of a *hybrid institutional setting* which still contains key features of the third pillar, such as unanimity requirements in the Council, a shared right of initiative of both the Commission and member states, a weak role of Parliament in the legislative process and severe restrictions to the jurisdiction of the Court of Justice (see also Monar 2001). More recent legislation by the Council has moved the pendulum further into the 'classical' EC direction. However, considerable parts of the migration policy regime, such as unanimity requirements on some crucial issues and restrictions to the jurisdiction of the European Court of Justice, still adhere to the third-pillar legacy (Maurer and Parkes 2006).

While there is no shortage of excellent publications on both EU foreign and EU interior affairs, the systematic and comparative analysis of cross-pillar politics in this book does address a significant gap in the literature (somewhat related arguments have been made by Mörth and Britz 2004; Cederman 2000; Wessel 2004). For example, there has not yet been a study which has coherently addressed the striking similarities between both policy areas, despite scattered remarks in the literature that the shared sovereignty dimension of both areas would render such an exercise a worthwhile endeavour (Wallace 2000). The lack of such a comprehensive and comparative study on cross-pillar politics might be surprising, given the aforementioned claim that the establishment of the pillar structure has indeed been one of the main transformations of European governance. Thus, as William Wallace has argued, the incorporation of all parts of foreign and interior policies under the umbrella of the 'single institutional framework' of the EU significantly increased the 'levels of politicization' within the EU (Wallace 2000: 525). While, traditionally, foreign and interior policies were regarded as core elements of an exclusively national conceptualization of sovereignty, since Maastricht the EU has been gradually emerging as a political authority for regulating sovereignty in its own right. And this remarkable development occurred despite the ongoing institutional fragmentation induced inter alia by the pillar structure. Thus, on the Treaty level, some parts of foreign policy (external economic policy and trade agreements as well as developmental aid) continue to be located in the first pillar, while others (foreign diplomatic relations, political agreements and defence policies) are still part of the second pillar. In a similar way, parts of interior policy (free movement, visa policies, internal border issues and, since the Amsterdam Treaty, migration policies) belong to the first pillar, while other areas (migration prior to Amsterdam, justice and police policies) are integrated in the third pillar.

Against this background of a formal endurance of the pillar structure, it is the main argument of this book that behind the persistence of the pillar structure on the Treaty level loom much more complex decision-making structures within and between the first, second and third pillars. A 'pillarized' perspective on both areas is, therefore, not able to detect the key substantive and institutional dynamics in both areas. What is instead required is a study that systematically addresses the manifold functional, substantive and institutional linkages of both policy areas across the three pillars and then assesses how these linkages affect the dynamics of policy-making in both areas (see also Bogdandy 1999; Wessel 2000; for foreign and interior policies see M. E. Smith 2003; Monar 2001). The comparative perspective on EU foreign and interior policies in this book not only brings to the fore the dynamics – and limits – of integration in cross-pillar politics at the EU level in each of these two areas, but also allows the detection of remarkable functional similarities between them.

In spite of the functional and institutional similarities between foreign and interior policies, i.e. their parallel integration into the Treaty framework as well as their *shared* functional features with regard to the emerging sovereignty dimension of the EU, there has until today been no study which has systematically analysed both areas from a comparative perspective. However, some scholars have pointed to these similarities and have encouraged further efforts to establish 'pillar studies' in EU research (Majer 1999; Monar 1997b; W. Wallace 2000). A word of caution is, however, advisable since, notwithstanding these structural similarities, variations in the observed patterns of policy-making in both case studies do indeed exist. Thus why were migration policies in the Amsterdam Treaty transferred to the first pillar, albeit with institutional rules, at least until 2004 (and arguably beyond) that in many ways resemble those which previously existed in the third pillar rather than those of 'traditional' first-pillar areas? Why did a similar change not occur with regard to wider Middle East and foreign policies? Why is the Council Secretariat (through the establishment of the offices of the Special Representative and the High Representative) a more active player in foreign policy than in interior policy? How can the differences in the influence of the European Parliament (EP), the Commission, the European Court of Justice (ECJ) and the Court of Auditors in both areas be accounted for? It should thus be kept in mind that while they do share certain key characteristics, foreign and interior policies are nevertheless distinct policy areas with their own 'policy histories' and actor constellations (see, for interior policies, Guiraudon 2003).

One obvious reason for this expected variation between policy areas is that from an organizational perspective there are different sets of actor constellations engaged in policy-making. This can, for example, be seen when addressing the supranational actors involved in policy-making in both areas. Thus in Middle East policies these are various Directorates-General (DG) of the European Commission with foreign policy capacities, the Foreign Affairs Committee of the EP and, since 1996, the Special Representative to the Middle East Peace Process, and after 1999 the High Representative. In migration policy responsibility rather lies with one DG, i.e. DG JHA of the European Commission and the Civil Liberties Committee of the EP. Moreover, the ECJ has made some important judgements on migration policy cases, whereas the Court of Auditors has been particularly active in the area of foreign policy. The role of the Council Secretariat in migration policy is more based on its 'traditional' function as a 'politically neutral' actor, whereas its role in foreign policy is much more proactive (Hayes-Renshaw and Wallace 1997: 101). This partially different set of actor constellations on the level of supranational actors is one of the reasons why a certain variation of patterns of policy-making between both areas can indeed be expected.[2]

Another reason for variation between policy areas relates to partially different forms of decision-making in foreign and interior policy settings. This corresponds with the observation that 'there is no single pattern of policy-making in the EU. Different modes of policy-making ... have emerged in different policy domains' (W. Wallace 2000: 524). As subsequent chapters will show in greater detail, interior policies rest to a larger extent on legislative decision-making compared with foreign policies in which executive decisions, framework decisions and budgetary decisions dominate. This argument should, however, not divert attention from a shared characteristic, namely that despite a somewhat different balance between these various decision-making procedures, both policy domains are characterized by a dominance of 'soft institutions' (H. Wallace 2000: 34). Thus even most legislative decisions in foreign and interior policies – for example, in the second and third pillars but also, to a lesser extent, in external trade and in the semi-communitarized migration policy regime after the Amsterdam Treaty – do not have the same 'hard law' character as do legislative decisions in classical first-pillar areas.[3]

This corresponds with Helen Wallace's argument that different patterns of policy-making should not prevent a combined perspective on joint structural features between policy domains. Thus foreign and interior policies have been identified as two domains which 'were among the most dynamic areas of EU policy development at the end of the 1990s'; moreover, they are characterized by a shared policy mode which allows these 'new areas of sensitive public policy' to be regarded as belonging to one policy-making type, namely 'intensive transgovernmentalism' (H. Wallace 2000: 34). This book argues from a similar point of departure that in spite of the relevance of partially different modes of decision-making, the shared functional features of both areas, namely their direct linkage with a distinct EU sovereignty dimension, does indeed provide a solid justification for a comparative perspective on both foreign and interior policies.

Sociological institutionalism and cross-pillar politics

By drawing from some major theoretical insights of sociological institutionalism, in particular the role of 'functional frames' in specific policy settings, this book shows that despite the obvious substantive differences between foreign and interior policies, policy-making in both areas relates to such a shared 'functional/cultural frame', namely the development of an EU insider/outsider distinction, which functions as a 'focal point' for the construction of a distinct sovereignty dimension of the EU (Fligstein and Mara-Drita 1996; Garrett and Weingast 1993; Christiansen, Jørgensen and Wiener 2001; see also Checkel 1999 and Checkel and Moravcsik 2001). It is with regard to these functional dynamics that integration in foreign and interior affairs must be understood as a remarkable achievement, despite often meagre substantive outcomes. Thus the gradual consolidation of this insider/outsider distinction through policy-making in EU foreign and interior policies allows the construction of the EU as a distinct 'Self' vis-à-vis 'Others': either third countries or third-country nationals (Ugur 1995; Neumann and Welsh 1991; Diez 2004). As a result, the EU incrementally acquires an external and internal sovereignty dimension. Due to this constitutive function of both policy areas for the identity of the entire political system of the EU, this book argues, on the basis of Theodore Lowi's famous classification, that they jointly constitute a distinct policy type at the EU level. This policy type is referred to here as the policy type of 'constituent policies' (Lowi 1964, 1972; Wiener 2001, 2003). As the in-depth empirical analysis in this book shows, it is these functional features rather than intergovernmental or supranational logic that spur the dynamics of integration in both areas.

This book thus argues that, notwithstanding the formal staying power of the pillar structure, these functionally induced dynamics in both areas transcend the pillar divide and have paved the way for an incremental centralization of foreign and interior policies at the EU level. Thus both policy areas across all the three pillars have become an integral part of EU politics and serve a shared function for the entire political system of the EU. Notwithstanding this argument, it is important to emphasize that because both areas lack the institutional characteristics of 'classical' first-pillar policies this centralization has not amounted to a 'supranationalization' of EU foreign and interior policies. As will be shown here in great detail, cross-pillar politics in foreign and interior affairs are characterized by the *functional unity* of foreign (EC/CFSP) and interior (EC/JHA) policies across the pillars, as well as by a high degree of *institutional fragmentation* (Stetter 2004). This institutional fragmentation can be seen when analysing the complex and cumbersome decision-making and implementation processes across and within the three pillars. Moreover, both policy areas in all the three pillars are subject to a remarkable dominance of the 'triple EU executive' (Council, Commission, Council Secretariat), while the parliamentary and judicial overview by the European Parliament and the Court of Justice is much less developed. Therefore, the centralization of foreign and interior policies must not be understood as a linear process of ever growing EU competences, but rather as the outcome of an incremental process that remains highly susceptible to institutional deadlocks and setbacks. This underlying tension between the functional unity and institutional fragmentation of cross-pillar politics also raises doubts about whether integration in foreign and interior policies at the EU level, in the specific way in which it has proceeded since Maastricht, will ultimately be able to equip the political system of the EU with a sovereignty dimension and legitimacy independent of member states.

While from an institutional and substantive perspective the pace of integration in foreign and interior policies has often been rather slow, the aforementioned sovereignty dimension of both areas on the functional level nevertheless renders it a highly significant endeavour. This political significance of foreign and interior policies for the political system of the EU is widely recognized in the literature (Geddes 1995; Walters 2002; Manners and Whitman 2003; Tonra and Christiansen 2004; M. Smith 2003; see also Stetter 2000, 2004). There is also a normative dimension to this debate, since integration in both policy areas has raised concerns about a 'securitization' of EU foreign and interior policies (Buzan, Wæver and de Wilde 1998). According to this view, securitization occurs either through processes of 'Othering' in the foreign policy realm or through building a 'fortress Europe' in interior affairs (Diez 2004; Neumann and Welsh 1991; Huysmans 2000b).

In many ways, the literature on EU foreign and interior policies has increased our understanding of key dimensions pertaining to both areas. However, the precise shape of functional, institutional and substantive cross-pillar dynamics has been addressed much less systematically (for key publications on both areas see, for example, Denza 2002; Peers 2000; Geddes 2000; Guiraudon 2003; M.E. Smith 2003; Hill 1993, 2004; Nuttall 2000). In this context, it has become commonplace to refer to the substantive and institutional overlaps in both policy areas across the three pillars. Yet, as this book argues, there is still an implicit consensus in most of the literature that, in contrast to 'classical' EC policies, foreign and interior policies are primarily characterized by intergovernmental dynamics under the guidance of (some) member states. It is quite interesting to note that in the general literature on European integration this underlying consensus on separate pillar logics and member state dominance in foreign and interior politics has even been able to bridge the otherwise deep divide between intergovernmentalist approaches on the one hand, and neo-functional or comparative politics perspective on the other (Moravcsik 1998; Garrett and Tsebelis 1996; Pollack 1997; Bulmer 1998).

While the specialized literature on foreign and interior policies has always been more cautious with regard to such far-reaching claims, there is still a tendency to focus on the intergovernmental pillars, rather than addressing developments across all three pillars. In this context Ramses Wessel (2000: 1135) has rightly noted that the pillar structure 'is often used as a justification for separate analyses of the three pillars' and that this trend has fostered the emergence of 'largely isolated research communities' in studies on the EC, the CFSP and the JHA. It is precisely this gap in the literature which this book addresses by analysing the functional, institutional and substantive cross-pillar dynamics which shape the integration of both policy areas at the EU level.

To summarize, the subsequent in-depth empirical analysis of the manifold cross-pillar overlaps in both foreign policy (EC/CFSP) and interior policy (EC/ JHA) aims to provides new perspectives on the interplay between functional unity and institutional fragmentation in both policy areas at the EU level. It thereby wishes to deepen our understanding of EU foreign and interior policies on two crucial dimensions. On a theoretical level it offers a framework of analysis to the study of both areas which draws in particular on sociological institutionalism. By addressing the impact of the 'functional frame' of an EU insider/outsider distinction and the policy type of 'constituent policies', it accounts for the way in which integration in both policy areas contributes to the construction of a distinct sovereignty dimension at the EU level. Moreover, the analysis of policy-making processes in both areas from Maastricht to Nice shows that these functionally induced dynamics form the main factor which shapes substantive and institutional developments in EU foreign and interior policies across the three pillars.

This analysis brings to the fore some of the central dynamics in the integration of EU foreign and interior policies since the Maastricht Treaty and provides for a detailed account of policy-making processes in cross-pillar politics. Through its comparative assessment on how the pillar structure has developed over time, it shows that EU foreign and interior policies should be addressed from a holistic perspective that systematically assesses developments in all three pillars, including the increasingly substantive linkages between the two policy areas, e.g. in the EMP or in readmission agreements. Seen from this perspective, it becomes evident that both areas across the three pillars have, since Maastricht, become gradually centralized at the EU level and jointly contribute to the social construction of the EU as a distinct political system.

While it is argued here that since Maastricht there has been a gradual process of merging the pillars in day-to-day policy-making, and supranational actors have had a significant impact on shaping substantive policies, it is not claimed that this development has led to a supranationalization of foreign and interior policies. Member states and the Council continue to be the central players in both areas, and the Treaties, in particular in the area of foreign policy, have codified the centrality of the (European) Council and the rotating Presidencies in the policy-making process. In fact, the price supranational actors have had to pay for shaping policies across the pillars has been the assertion by member states within the framework of the Council and the European Council that they will provide collective executive leadership – often in conjunction with the European Commission – in both areas. By doing so, member states have also embarked upon the opportunities provided for by the dynamics of cross-pillarization. Thus the inroad supranational actors have made into what are formally intergovernmental domains has been mirrored by the attempt of member states to gain more control over both the cross-pillar policy agendas in foreign and interior affairs – including erstwhile 'supranational' policy domains of the first pillar and the implementation of policies across all three pillars (Fligstein and McNichol 1998).

One of the immediate implications of the argument put forward here relates to terminology. It is based on scepticism regarding the commonplace distinction between first-pillar foreign policies and CFSP on the one hand, and first-pillar interior policies and JHA on the other hand. The strict delineation between the different parts of these policy areas as they are spread across the pillars is, according to the findings presented here, less important than suggested by a terminology that reproduces this very *pillarization* by imprecise labels such as 'intergovernmental' and 'supranational'. In particular, the interchangeable usage of the term 'foreign and interior policies' with the acronyms CFSP and JHA is rejected. Acknowledging the implications of cross-pillarization, the term 'EU foreign and interior policies' covers the whole spectrum of policies in both areas, including first-pillar provisions, whereas CFSP and JHA are not distinct policy areas but specific – and internally fragmented – domains *within* the wider realm of EU foreign and interior policies.

Referring to a centralization of both policies at the EU level does not necessarily mean that the substantive policies in both areas need to be impressive. Neither does it mean that this process has amounted to a transfer of authority to supranational actors comparable to 'classical' first-pillar areas, but rather that over time both areas have become an integral and important part of the political system of the EU. Notwithstanding the central role of member states and the Council in EU foreign and interior policies, the analysis in this book shows that policy-making processes in both areas depend on the interplay at the central EU level between the Council on the one hand, and supranational executive actors such as the Commission and the Council Secretariat on the other. Neither side of this 'triple EU executive' is, hence, ultimately able to dominate policy-making alone. These institutional features of cross-pillar politics lead to manifold power struggles and co-ordination problems in inner-executive relations which negatively affect the overall efficiency of EU foreign and interior policies.

Addressing the role of supranational actors

The focus in parts of this book on the role of supranational actors requires some additional specifications, in particular with regard to the inclusion of the Council Secretariat in the analysis. As Christiansen notes from a more general perspective:

> inclusion of the Council Secretariat may require further justification since it is usually not regarded as either 'supranational' or as an 'institution' ... However, in spite of the official nomenclature, the Council Secretariat is clearly an institution, possessing a formal structure with a set of internal rules and administrative practices which regulate the work of a body of permanent staff; and it is located at the European level, possessing a high degree of institutional autonomy and may therefore be regarded as supranational.
>
> (2002: 35)

This perspective also takes note of the observation that the functions of the Council Secretariat in the policy-making process in foreign and interior policies have gradually been extended since the Maastricht Treaty. As subsequent chapters will show in greater detail, the traditional functions of the Secretariat to support the Presidencies and being the 'institutional memory' of the Council have been supplemented by a gradual politicization of the Secretariat, which has become – in particular in the area of foreign policies – an autonomous actor.

As a word of caution it should be noted that Article 7 of the European Community Treaty (TEC) and Article 5 of the Treaty on European Union (TEU) refer to the Council as a whole. This book, however, stresses the powers of the Council Secretariat as a distinct actor which has at least some structural autonomy from other bodies in the Council's wider structure – such as Presidencies, specialized Councils, Working Groups, the Committee of Permanent Representatives (COREPER), the Political Committee, the K.4 Committee and other institutions – which are primarily constituted by national governments. Since the Secretariat is clearly not such a nationally constituted institution, it is reasonable to compare it with the other supranational actors and to ask how the Secretariat was involved in shaping EU foreign and interior policies – while acknowledging that in its day-to-day operations the Council Secretariat is closely linked with other actors in the Council's complex institutional structure.

The usefulness of such a distinction between the Council Secretariat and the other aforementioned actors within the Council structure has been acknowledged by other scholars who have analysed the evolution of the role of the Secretariat, in particular with regard to EU foreign policies (M. E. Smith 2003; Christiansen 2002; Hayward-Renshaw and Wallace 1997). This should, however, not lead to the conclusion that the distinction between the Council Secretariat and other Council institutions is 'clear-cut' (Christiansen 2002: 35). While some actors within the Council structure, such as the Presidency, the Council of Ministers and the Working Groups, are characterized by a 'duality' of being both EU and national actors, the role of the Council Secretariat is less blurred (Christiansen 2002: 35). Thus, as Michael E. Smith has argued concerning EU foreign policies, the establishment in the Maastricht Treaty of the CFSP Secretariat has rendered this institution 'an arm of the Council Secretariat General ... a *Community* institution' (Smith 2003: 188). This delegation of powers to the Council Secretariat must not be mistaken for an abdication of political power by member states. In fact, the delegation of powers to the Council Secretariat has been used by member states in an attempt to avoid delegation to another supranational actor, namely the Commission. The establishment of in the Maastricht and Amsterdam Treaties of the offices of the CFSP Secretariat, the High Representative for the CFSP (who also acts as Secretary-General of the Council), the Policy Planning and Early Warning Unit (PPEWU) and the Special Representatives points to an increasing shift of power *between* supranational actors from the Commission to the Council Secretariat.[4] Thus:

> the Council Secretariat has gained additional powers and responsibilities in recent rounds of treaty revision, in particular with respect to the establishment of the EU's foreign, security and defence institutions – a development that, while reflecting concern among member states that

such powers should not be accrued by the Commission, also underlines the ability of the Council Secretariat to provide institutional solutions in such a context.

(Christiansen 2002: 46)

The inclusion of the Council Secretariat into the analysis of this book does not, therefore, suggest that it is the most powerful actor within the complex institutional structure of the Council (see Hayes-Renshaw and Wallace 1997). Neither does it imply that the distinction between Secretariat and other Council actors is sharp. For example, the Council Secretariat – and also the European Political Co-operation (EPC) Secretariat from 1986 to 1993 – is characterized by a strong institutionalized interrelationship with and dependence on the rotating Presidencies. Thus the

> Secretariat's relationship with the Presidency . . . is a flexible one. Much of . . . the significance of the Council Secretariat's role in drafting agendas and meetings, providing legal and other advice, and fine-tuning the detail of negotiations crucially depends on the permissiveness of the Presidency to provide such opportunities for influence.
>
> (Christiansen 2002: 47–8)

However, this form of intense structural coupling between the Council Secretariat and other Council actors must not only be seen as a limitation to the influence of the Secretariat. In fact, its close institutional relationship with member states in parallel with its overall political responsibility to the EU as such (and not to Presidencies or member states) actually provides the Council Secretariat with a strong institutional backing vis-à-vis both member states and other supranational actors, in particular the Commission. Hence, the observation of a growing importance of the Council Secretariat in policy-making, in particular in the area of foreign policies, must be viewed against the background of both the Secretariat's close linkage with member states and the Presidencies on the one hand, and its role as an executive counter-weight to the Commission on the other.

Having said this, it is essential to note that while being closely linked to other actors within the Council's institutional structure, the Secretariat differs from these other actors in a crucial way, for the Secretariat does not fully or partly represent individual member states' governments but, as Michael E. Smith argues, represents the 'power of the Community's bureaucratic machinery' (2003: 148). This does not neglect the sense of hierarchy ingrained in the Treaties between the Secretariat and other Council institutions, for example in the area of EU foreign policies. Thus Article 18 of the TEU emphasizes that it is the Presidency that represents 'the Union in matters coming within the common foreign and security policy'. In this context, the High Representative 'only' has the task of assisting the Presidency. However, in contrast to the provisions prior to the Maastricht Treaty, in which the EPC Secretariat was directly responsible to the rotating Presidency, the Maastricht and Amsterdam Treaties have fostered the autonomy of the Secretariat – and the High Representative – as supranational actors. Thus the new directive for the CFSP Secretariat (which became part of the Council Secretariat) and, with Amsterdam, the High Representative and the PPEWU, was 'to serve the CFSP (rather than the EU Presidency)', thereby consolidating the status of the Council Secretariat as a supranational actor (Smith 2003: 188).[5]

As this book will argue again and again, member states continue to play the key role in policy-making in the two areas of foreign and interior affairs, thus reflecting the close link of these two areas with traditional national prerogatives. Yet, while there is ample evidence in the literature of the decisive role of national governments and Council institutions in EU foreign and interior policies, the precise role of supranational actors in both policy areas has arguably received much less attention. Thus this book follows the conceptual demand raised by Christiansen who has argued that a 'systematic analysis of the role of supranational institutions ... is not only promising, but indeed necessary' (Christiansen 2002: 34). While not neglecting the central role of national governments in the policy-making process – for example in providing political leadership and continuity of policy-making – the permanent and systematic involvement of supranational actors in foreign and interior policies endows 'the EU bargaining context with a rich normative environment that cannot be explained away as epiphenomenal or a mere lubricant of intergovernmental negotiation' (Lewis 2000: 261). At this point a second clarification must be introduced, namely that there is an important difference with regard to the case studies in this book. While Middle East policies are pursued in all of the various contexts related to EU foreign policies in both the first pillar and the CFSP, migration policies are only one among several issue areas in the interior policy setting of the EU. Thus JHA co-operation also encompasses issues such as drug prevention policies, the combat of fraud, judicial co-operation in both civil and criminal matters, customs co-operation and, in particular, police co-operation.

While, hence, from the outset the 'subject-matter [of JHA] was heterogeneous', there is nevertheless an important linkage between these various JHA issues which justifies the focus of this book on migration policies (W. Wallace 2000: 494). Thus all of these 'law and order' issues were traditionally considered as 'matters of executive control in all states' and, consequently, as central components of national sovereignty (W. Wallace 2000: 501; see Geddes 2000). However, European integration, and in particular the relaxation of border regimes between EU member states, brought to the fore the requirement to co-ordinate policies in law and order issues at the European level and to collectively respond to new cross-border challenges. Notwithstanding their partially different institutional frameworks, this shared cross-border context of law and order issues is relevant for quite different phenomena in the area of interior policies, such as cross-border movements of migrants, cross-border litigation, cross-border marriages, cross-border drug trafficking and cross-border crime. Given the linkage of all these areas with (internal) sovereignty and erstwhile national prerogatives, EU policies in *all* areas of JHA contribute to the construction of an EU 'internal law and order identity' and, consequently, its nascent political sovereignty.

In the light of these substantive similarities between the different subject matters of JHA, migration policies seem to be a particularly useful case for a detailed analysis of cross-pillar politics in interior policies. This is because migration policies – understood as those policies which regulate conditions of entry and sojourn of non-EU citizen – not only establish EU specific law and order practices, but do so in relation to a clearly demarcated 'Other', namely third-country nationals (TCN).[6] Thus migration policies are a particularly visible example of the consolidation of an internal EU identity induced by policy-making in interior policies in general.

Outline of the book

This book is divided into three main parts. Part I elaborates in greater detail the main contours of the sociological institutionalist framework that informs this study. Part II then addresses the gradual centralization of foreign and interior policies at the EU level from Maastricht to Nice by focusing on institutional and substantive cross-pillar linkages. Part III focuses on the dynamics of policy-making in both areas, in particular the remarkable executive dominance therein. Part I (Chapter 2) starts with an overview of the key literature on EU foreign and interior policies and shows that there is a standard view that assumes that the pillar divide is a fundamental institutional barrier that separates these two policy areas into 'supranational' and 'intergovernmental' domains. As already argued above, this assessment can be explicitly found in both general contributions on European integration and the more specialized literature on EU foreign and interior policies.

However, the manifold substantive and institutional overlaps between the three pillars render such 'pillarized' approaches on foreign and interior policies problematic from both an empirical and a theoretical perspective. Thus Chapter 2 sets out a theoretical framework for the study of EU foreign and interior policies, which allows the conceptualizing of these manifold functional, substantive and institutional cross-pillar overlaps of EU foreign (EC/CFSP) and EU interior (EC/JHA) policies. Rather than taking the three-pillar structure as the starting point of analysis, Chapter 2 addresses the specific *function* that EU foreign and interior policies have for the political system of the EU. Building on insights from sociological institutionalism, it shows that policy-making in both areas relates to a shared 'functional frame' of an EU insider/outsider distinction (Fligstein and Mara-Drita 1996). Notwithstanding the often meagre substantive outcomes in both areas and the nascent status of the EU's internal and external identity, the emerging insider/outsider distinction is of huge political significance. Thus the gradual consolidation of this insider/outsider distinction through policy-making in EU foreign and interior policies constructs the EU as a distinct 'Self' vis-à-vis 'Others'. Hence, the insider/outsider distinction functions as a 'focal point' which underpins the social construction of a distinct EU sovereignty dimension, both internally and externally (Garrett and Weingast 1993; Christiansen, Jørgensen and Wiener 2001).

This argument not only brings to the fore the shared function which policy-making in both areas has for the political system of the EU, it also allows the conceptualizing of both areas as constituting a distinct policy type, as has in the past successfully been done with regard to regulatory or redistributive policies in the first pillar (Majone 1996; Hix 1999). As already argued above, since both policy areas across the three pillars are constitutive for the consolidation of the EU as a political system with its own sovereignty dimension, this policy type is building on the work by Theodore Lowi referred to here as the policy type of 'constituent policies' (Lowi 1964). The main hypothesis which stems from this theoretical argument is that the dynamics and limits of integration in these two policy areas must be seen in relation to the manifold institutional and substantive cross-pillar overlaps which result from these *shared functional features* of both policy areas rather than intergovernmental or supranational logics.

Part II (Chapters 3, 4 and 5) shows in an in-depth empirical analysis how these functional cross-pillar dynamics have shaped institutional characteristics and substantive outcomes in both policy areas across the three pillars. In order to trace the institutional cross-pillar linkage Chapters 3 and 4 focus on the delegation of capabilities by member states to supranational actors in both policy areas (Tallberg 2002; Ballmann, Epstein, O'Halloran 2002). Chapter 3 looks at those capabilities which have been delegated to supranational actors in the Treaty reforms of Maastricht, Amsterdam and Nice. Chapter 4 then analyses those capabilities which have been delegated to supranational actors in-between Treaty reforms through decisions of the (European) Council. This analysis shows that notwithstanding the formal persistence of the pillar structure, member states have increasingly delegated powers to supranational agents across the three pillars, thereby blurring the factual relevance of the pillar structure. These delegation dynamics have been the consequence of the functional unity of both EU foreign and interior policies across the three pillars, i.e. the fact that due to the functional cross-pillar dynamics outlined in Chapter 2, the separation between the different pillars can hardly be upheld in day-to-day policy-making. The main argument put forward here is that due to these delegation dynamics, both EU foreign (EC/CFSP) and interior (EC/JHA) policies are indeed characterized by a gradual centralization at the EU level. However, this centralization has not resulted in a supranationalization of foreign and interior policies, as has been the case in many 'classical' first-pillar areas.

Thus, while supranational actors have profited from an increased involvement in EU foreign and interior policies, member states have enacted tight control mechanisms through the Council across the three pillars at all stages of the decision-making process. Moreover, delegation to supranational actors has been uneven. While executive actors, such as the Commission and the Council Secretariat, have profited to a great degree from delegation across the three pillars, the Court of Justice and the European Parliament have been delegated many fewer capabilities. A major insight of this empirical analysis is that delegation dynamics have primarily increased the powers of executive actors within and across the pillars. With regard to inner-executive relations between the Council, the Council Secretariat and the Commission, the Treaties provide for manifold interlocking powers, thereby establishing an institutional impetus for co-operative modes of interaction within the 'triple EU executive'. Yet the aforementioned control mechanisms, in particular committee control procedures, ensure that within this 'triple executive' the Council maintains the main sources of power.

Chapter 3 analyses those capabilities that have been delegated by member states to supranational actors in the areas of foreign and interior policies in the Treaty reforms of Maastricht, Amsterdam and Nice. Due to the origin of these capabilities in primary law, they are defined as 'primary capabilities'. As the in-depth empirical analysis of this chapter shows, each Treaty reform provided for the additional delegation of primary capabilities across the three pillars to supranational actors. This development increased the number of institutional linkages between the three pillars, without the formal abolition of the pillar structure. Consequently, these Treaty changes paved the way for the emergence of a *hybrid institutional setting* at the Treaty level, which today characterizes cross-pillar politics in EU foreign and interior affairs. A detailed look at the provisions of the Treaties on both policy areas across the three pillars shows that they are characterized by a remarkable institutional fragmentation that is more complex than the pillar metaphor suggests.

This chapter analyses in particular the delegation by member states of legislative, executive, budgetary and judicial powers to supranational actors. As far as legislative capabilities are concerned, it offers a detailed elaboration on the powers of the Commission and the European Parliament in the manifold legislative procedures which govern policy-making in foreign and interior affairs. This analysis brings to the fore the fact that both policy areas are characterized by an institutional fragmentation which cuts across the pillar divide. The analysis of executive powers shows that with each Treaty reform the Commission and the Council Secretariat have been delegated new capabilities. However, member states have curtailed these capabilities by establishing tight control mechanisms across the three pillars on the Treaty level. A look at the budgetary dimension as well as judicial remedy in foreign and interior policies shows that the delegation of powers in these two fields has been rather cautious (see also Monar 1997b). Since this has affected the capabilities of the European Parliament and the Court of Justice in EU foreign and interior policies in particular, this development has further exacerbated the executive dominance which characterizes both policy areas.

These primary capabilities must be distinguished from those capabilities that supranational actors derive in-between Treaty reforms as a result of delegation by the (European) Council through day-to-day policy-making. Since these capabilities are based on secondary law, they are referred to here as 'secondary capabilities'. As Chapter 4 shows in a detailed empirical study of Middle East and migration policies, delegation in-between Treaty reforms has been a significant element in the gradual centralization of EU foreign and interior policies. The rationale to distinguish between primary and secondary capabilities is based on the observation that these two kinds of capability differ significantly with regard to the institutional rules from which they originate. This is where, from the perspective of member states, the value added of this form of delegation comes in. Thus day-to-day decision-making in the Council allows member states to delegate capabilities to supranational actors without the formal requirements – and publicity – relating to overall Treaty changes. Chapter 4 analyses all Council decisions in Middle East and migration policies from 1993 until 2003 and focuses on the delegation of capabilities to supranational actors in these decisions.

The main argument put forward in this chapter is that secondary delegation has further exacerbated the manifold institutional cross-pillar overlaps that exist in EU foreign and interior affairs on the Treaty level. Not only did the delegation of secondary capabilities give 'flesh' to the abstract provisions of the Treaties, thereby equipping supranational actors with concrete institutional resources within and across the three pillars, it also led to the delegation of entirely new capabilities that were not foreseen by the Treaties themselves. This insight is a powerful challenge to intergovernmentalist approaches to European integration which view the time in-between Intergovernmental Conferences (IGC) as a mere 'intervening period of consolidation' (Moravcsik 1998). In contrast to such approaches, Chapter 4 shows that these 'intervening periods' are characterized by significant dynamics of integration which are induced by the functional dynamics outlined in Chapter 2. However, the degree to which different supranational actors have profited from this kind of delegation has varied considerably. Thus it was primarily the Commission (scoreboard[7] for the 'area of freedom, security and justice'; role in CFSP instruments) and the Council Secretariat (Special Representative to the Middle East peace process; integration of Schengen Secretariat) that were strengthened through the delegation of these secondary capabilities. While this development further increased the executive bias in both areas it should not be understood as an abrogation by member states. On the contrary, as the empirical analysis of Council decisions in this chapter shows, member states have ensured that the delegation of capabilities to the Commission and the Council Secretariat in Middle East and migration policies does not undermine their powers in either area. Thus secondary capabilities of the Commission and the Council Secretariat are counter-balanced by the establishment of tight committee systems and other control mechanisms of member states in both areas.

Chapter 5 then analyses the substantive developments in EU foreign (EC/ CFSP) and interior (EC/JHA) policies after the Maastricht Treaty. In order to detect how substantive decisions in foreign and interior policies across the three pillars have 'given flesh' to the insider/outsider dimension of the EU and, thereby, consolidated the status of 'constituent policies' at the EU level, it provides for an in-depth empirical analysis of the two case studies, EU Middle East and migration policies. Rather than focusing on the often meagre substantive outcomes (see Aoun 2003; Guiraudon 2003; Musu 2003), this chapter argues that these policies cannot only be measured with regard to their material reach. A proper assessment of the dynamics and limits of integration in EU foreign and interior policies must also take into account how substantive decisions on concrete issues such as Middle East and migration policies contribute to the construction of a distinct insider/outsider dimension at the European level. On this basis, this chapter shows that in parallel with the institutional cross-pillar linkages discussed in Chapters 3 and 4, there has also been a steady increase in *substantive cross-pillar linkages* in both policy areas after the Maastricht Treaty. These substantive cross-pillar linkages have not only fostered the functional unity of EU foreign (EC/CFSP) and interior (EC/JHA) policies from an institutional perspective, they also provide for a concrete underpinning of an EU insider/outsider distinction, thereby consolidating the EU's nascent internal and external sovereignty dimension.

With regard to EU Middle East policies, Chapter 5 looks in particular at EU economic and political policies towards Israel and Palestine in the context of the Euro-Mediterranean Partnership and EU bilateral agreements with Israel and Palestine, as well as EU policies on the Middle East peace process. It also discusses cross-pillar linkages in the European Council's Common Strategy on the Mediterranean (2000) and the Middle East section of the European Security Strategy (2003). It argues that while EU Middle East policies have often been rather declaratory in nature and suffer from considerable implementation problems, the manifold substantive cross-pillar linkages in this area have consolidated an insider/outsider distinction in EU foreign policies, to which EU Middle East policies increasingly relate. A similar picture emerges when looking at EU migration policies. This chapter analyses all major substantive decisions in EU migration policies in the first and third pillars (asylum; external borders; free movement of third-country nationals; visa issues; refugees; immigration) from Maastricht to Nice. It shows that notwithstanding the often limited material reach of these decisions, a holistic perspective brings to the fore a gradual increase in substantive cross-pillar linkages that has consolidated an insider/outsider distinction with regard to the EU's internal identity. As already outlined above, the *passerelle* of migration policies to the first pillar in the Amsterdam Treaty should not be regarded as a supra-nationalization of migration policies, but rather as a further increase of cross-pillar linkages in this area. These substantive cross-pillar linkages can also be traced in the conclusion of the European Council in Tampere (1999) and subsequent documents on the establishment of an 'area of freedom, security and justice'.

Part III (Chapters 6 and 7) then provides for an in-depth empirical study of how these functional, institutional and substantive cross-pillar overlaps affect policy-making processes in EU foreign and interior policies. Chapter 6 analyses the policy agendas of supranational actors in the two case studies of EU Middle East and migration policies. This analysis shows that supranational actors do not have shared preferences in the two policy areas, as assumed by both supra-national and intergovernmental theories. The policy agendas of supranational actors rather resemble their institutional location within the cross-pillar set-ting outlined in Chapters 3 and 4. Chapter 7 then focuses on the dynamics of policy-making in both areas, in particular on how the dominance of the 'triple EU executive' affects policy-making processes across the three pillars. This chapter looks at the manifold co-ordination mechanisms between the Council, the Commission and the Council Secretariat in the two policy areas and outlines the conditions which affect the efficiency (and lack thereof) of inner-executive co-ordination. Moreover, it elaborates on the indirect means through which the European Parliament and the Court of Justice have attempted to circum-vent their formally more limited capabilities in both areas.

The key argument of Chapter 6 is that the preferences of supranational actors in EU foreign and interior policies do not fit into a simple intergovern-mental/supranational dichotomy. As much as supranational actors perform quite different institutional roles, they have also developed quite divergent policy agendas which cannot be subsumed under one integrationist heading. Because of these different institutional roles in the policy-making process it can be shown that the preferences of supranational actors vary considerably, most notably between executive and non-executive actors. This chapter focuses on the policy preferences of supranational actors in foreign and interior policies on three dimensions. First, in an analysis of documents from the three IGCs of Maastricht, Amsterdam and Nice it looks at the general preferences of supra-national actors on the future development of EU foreign and interior policies. Second, it looks at the policy preferences of supranational actors with regard to the two case studies, namely Middle East and migration policies. In a third step, it scrutinizes the internal organizational structures within the Commission, the Council Secretariat and the European Parliament in order to show that these actors have adapted to their respective capabilities in the two areas. What this analysis brings to the fore is that, at the time of the Maastricht Treaty, supranational actors had quite similar policy preferences with regard to both foreign and interior policies in general, and Middle East and migration policies in particular. However, over time these shared preferences have given way to increasingly divergent policy agendas. These divergent agendas closely corre-late with the respective institutional powers of supranational actors in the two areas. Thus the Commission and the Council Secretariat have developed a pragmatic and managerial approach and tend to accept the general political guidance of the (European) Council in both areas. In contrast, the European Parliament and the Court of Justice voice more fundamental criticism of EU policies in the two areas and call for fundamental reforms, which would ensure proper parliamentary and judicial control in both policy areas.

Chapter 7 then shows how the executive dominance in EU foreign and interior policies affects policy-making processes in both areas. By taking a closer look at the two case studies of Middle East and migration policies, it shows that the Council, the Council Secretariat and the Commission jointly hold the key institutional resources in the policy-making process of EU foreign and interior policies across the three pillars. This executive dominance in the two policy areas, which results from the often overlapping capabilities of these three actors in foreign and interior policies, necessitates a co-operative approach to policy-making between executive actors. However, as this chapter argues, inner-executive co-ordination in EU foreign and interior policies is not a smooth and harmonious process. Thus this chapter analyses policy-making processes in the context of the implementation of the scoreboard for an 'area of freedom, security and justice' and of EU developmental assistance to Palestine. It shows that inner-executive co-ordination in both areas is characterized by power struggles and manifold co-ordination problems within the triple executive (see also Stetter 2004, 2003). Moreover, this chapter shows that the capabilities of the European Parliament and the Court of Justice in both policy areas across the three pillars are severely limited. Only in a few instances, such as in the case of the MEDA Democracy funds, did the European Parliament have a significant impact on the policy-making process. Due to its limited capabilities in both foreign and interior policies across the three pillars the impact of the Court of Justice has also been rather marginal. However, as the analysis in Chapter 7 of two important cases (*Visa Lists* of 1997; *Airport Transit Visas* of 1998) shows, the Court of Justice has been quite assertive when offered the rare chance to construct rights across the pillars. The conclusion of this book (Chapter 8) summarizes the main results of this analysis and shortly outlines how the provisions of the Draft Constitutional Treaty – and the crisis following the failed referenda in France and the Netherlands – affect the functional, substantive and institutional cross-pillar linkages which developed between Maastricht and Nice.

Part I

Theoretical framework

Addressing the functional dynamics in the integration of foreign and interior policies at the EU level

2 The construction of an EU insider/outsider distinction

Introduction

The Maastricht Treaty of 1993 fundamentally altered the political system of the EU by integrating two important policies, which hitherto were not part of the formal governance structure, into the Treaties (W. Wallace 2000). These policies became known under the acronyms of CFSP and JHA or – with reference to ancient Greek architecture – as the second and third pillar of the EU.[1] Notwithstanding this significance of the Maastricht Treaty's provisions, the origin of joint policies in both areas dates back to the early 1970s when member states established Europeanized frameworks for co-operation in foreign and home affairs, albeit on a purely intergovernmental basis (Lobkowicz 1994; M. E. Smith 1998; Wallace and Wallace 2000). While these foreign and interior policy settings had already gradually been linked with institutional structures of the EC before the Maastricht Treaty, intergovernmental paths endured and significantly shaped the provisions on CFSP and JHA.[2] This path dependence was also replicated on a linguistic level. Thus most commentators still continue to refer to the 'two intergovernmental pillars' when analysing foreign and interior policies, despite the existence of a European 'single institutional framework' which formally covers policies across the three pillars (Denza 2002; Bieber and Monar 1995; Regelsberger et al. 1997; Wallace and Wallace 2000). This terminology mirrors the 'official' pillar terminology which member states originally agreed upon during the Maastricht IGC (Majer 1999).

Yet, as already indicated, CFSP and JHA were never strictly intergovernmental fora, but were from the outset characterized by an inherent tension between the attempt to continue with established intergovernmental practices on the policy-making level and the integration of both areas into the 'single institutional structure' of the 'new overarching entity – the European Union' (McGoldrick 1997: 13). Thus both areas can best be characterized as institutional hybrids which allowed for collective decision-making under the umbrella of the EU while at the same time keeping policy-making as separate as possible from the classical EC working methods of the supranational first pillar (Moravcsik 1998). On the face of it, the Amsterdam Treaty of 1999 did provide for significant changes to the way in which both policy areas are dealt with at the EU level (Weidenfeld 1998). However, in substance it did not fundamentally change the three-pillar design, since even those policy areas that were transferred to the first pillar were not communitarized in the 'classical' sense (Duff 1997; Moravcsik and Nicolaïdis 1998 and 1999; Stetter 2000).[3]

Thus migration policies shifted from the third pillar to the first pillar; yet with regard to decision-making, implementation and judicial overview, there have been minimal changes to the provisions of the Maastricht Treaty. Only after a five-year period, in May 2004, were member states allowed to decide – unanimously – to regulate this policy area with the 'classical' Community method. At least until the end of this transitory period, migration policies were part of a *semi-communitarized* institutional setting which still contains many features of the third pillar, such as unanimity requirements in the Council, a shared right of initiative for both the Commission and member states, a weak role for Parliament in the legislative process, and restrictions to the jurisdiction of the Court of Justice (den Boer 1997; Stetter 2000). However, it can well be argued that the 'intergovernmental' legacy endured after the May 2004 deadline. Thus it is true that since 1 January 2005 most parts of Title IV TEC have been governed by the co-decision procedure (Council 2004). However, while this decision 'clearly shifts the policy-making framework further from intergovernmentalism and introduces a greater degree of supranational democracy', it still reflects the cautious approach to integration in migration policies, as illustrated by the remaining areas of unanimous decision-making as well as the on-going limitations to the jurisdiction of the ECJ (Maurer and Parkes 2006: 10).

Intergovernmental bargains? Challenging the standard view of pillar politics

This formal separation of both policy areas into three pillars – one supranational and two intergovernmental – has led many scholars to assert that there are indeed 'pillarized' political processes at the EU level, thus assuming a relatively clear-cut separation between the pillars. Notwithstanding some noteworthy exceptions to this rule, this lack of communication between research on the first pillar on the one hand, and the two 'intergovernmental pillars' on the other, has not substantially changed until today (see also Wessel 2004).

The underlying consensus in the literature on a separation of the pillars has even been able to bridge the otherwise deep divide between intergovernmentalist approaches to the study of the EU on the one hand, and those studies which analyse the EU from a neo-functional or comparative politics perspective on the other. Andrew Moravcsik, for example, notes concerning foreign and interior policies that the Maastricht IGC created 'the three-pillar structure, in which these policies remained intergovernmental' (1998: 467). Following this statement, Moravcsik's 'basic explanation of the process and outcome' of IGCs can *mutatis mutandis* be applied to the study of decision-making in CFSP and JHA (Moravcsik and Nicolaïdis 1999: 59). The institutional features of the second and third pillars – such as unanimity requirements between member states and seemingly severely restricted roles for EC institutions – resemble those of IGCs. Therefore, Moravcsik's famous statement that 'the EC has developed through a series of celebrated intergovernmental bargains, each of which set the agenda for an intervening period of consolidation' could be refined as a liberal intergovernmentalist perspective on the second and third pillars (1993: 473). Thus similar institutional rules for IGCs on the one hand, and CFSP and JHA on the other, would result in domestic preference formation on the basis of economic interests, interstate bargaining on the basis of asymmetrical interdependence and institutional choice on the basis of the need to ensure credible commitment between member states, the key variables for explaining outcomes in the intergovernmental pillars (Moravcsik 1998: 24).

From a different theoretical perspective, Geoffrey Garrett and George Tsebelis have made similar predictions with regard to outcomes in the two 'intergovernmental' pillars. They argue that 'the dynamics of decision making in these areas are identical to that in the era of the Luxembourg compromise' (1996: 282). Their institutional critique of intergovernmentalism, therefore, explicitly does not cover CFSP and JHA. In their view, these areas are indeed dominated by the Council and decision-making power rests 'effectively with the government with the least interest in changing the status quo'; while being less sceptical than Moravcsik about the prospect for further integration, they nevertheless conclude that for the areas of CFSP and JHA it is 'reasonable to conceive of decision making in terms of the Luxembourg compromise period and to ignore the roles played by other EU institutions' (1996: 283). In fact, Garrett and Tsebelis echo a widespread scepticism in EU studies about the extent to which insights from the study of policy-making in the first pillar can be applied to the EU at large. Thus Mark Pollack explicitly notes that his hypotheses on supranational influence only apply to the EC pillar and not to the 'two *strictly* intergovernmental pillars' (1997: 99, my emphasis). Also Simon Bulmer points out that the 'diversity of governance between the three pillars of the EU is striking' (1998: 367). He concludes that his findings on governance in the EU cannot, without recalibration, be applied to the second and third pillars of the EU (1998: 382).

Scholars who have focused on the two areas of CFSP and JHA have always been sceptical with regard to such far-reaching conclusions regarding the differences between the pillars (Peers 2000; M. E. Smith 2003). The specialized literature cites many examples which show that the relationship between the pillars on the Treaty level and in day-to-day policy-making since Maastricht is stronger than suggested by the aforementioned body of literature. Yet, while most CFSP and JHA scholars acknowledge that there is some kind of interrelationship between the three pillars, the precise shape of 'interaction and overlap' between the Union's alleged supranational and intergovernmental legal orders remains 'often hotly disputed' (Peers 2000: 1). There is, thus, a widespread assumption even in the CFSP and JHA literature that 'the distinctions between the three pillars are quite substantial' (Peers 2000: 13; see also Wagner 2004). John Peterson, notes that 'the CFSP is distinct from the rest of what constitutes the "European Union"' and emphasizes that the special character of the second pillar stems from the quasi-constitutional character, which even technical decisions in this sensitive policy area have (1998: 15). Reinhardt Rummel and Jörg Wiedemann argue that in CFSP 'any political issue will automatically be viewed as a means for bargaining over institutional arrangements' (1998: 63). For these two authors, the pillar structure is foremost characterized by institutional paradoxes and dichotomies which are 'contradictory rather than complementary' (1998: 53). Thus, despite the provision that all three pillars shall be governed by a single institutional framework, scholars continue to refer to both areas as belonging to 'the sphere of inter-governmental cooperation' (Denza 2002; Hailbronner 1995: 95; Hailbronner 2000: 47–50). This might then also be the deeper reason why research in both areas is 'frequently "content driven"' rather than starting from an institutional analysis of policy-making (Wessel 2000: 1135).

Cross-pillar politics and supranational actors

This chapter challenges these explicit or implicit assumptions of pillarized political processes at the EU level and thereby attempts to foster the linkage between integration studies on the first pillar on the one hand, and research on CFSP and JHA on the other (Peers 2000; Zielonka 1998a; Schimmelfennig and Wagner 2004). It argues that the functional dynamics of EU policy-making in general, and of EU foreign and interior policies in particular, have led to the emergence of a cross-pillar institutional setting in these two areas. Moreover, this cross-pillar setting reflects the gradual erosion of the three-pillar design of the Maastricht Treaty without its formal abolition. This empirical observation has some far-reaching theoretical consequences, for it challenges intergovernmentalist assumptions which hold:

> that European integration was a series of rational adaptations by national leaders to constraints and opportunities stemming from the evolution of an interdependent world economy, the relative power of states in the international system, and the potential for international institutions to bolster the credibility of interstate commitments.
>
> (Moravcsik 1998: 472)

In stark contrast to these arguments, this chapter provides evidence that European integration has led to the emergence of distinct functional dynamics in foreign and interior policies which provide the primary focal point for actors, national governments and European institutions alike. These functional dynamics of EU policies in foreign and interior affairs render policy-making at the European level closely interlinked but structurally independent of the national level as well as of mere interstate bargaining. It must be noted from the outset that such functional dynamics at the EU level in no way means that the process of integration in EU foreign and interior policies is predetermined. What it does mean, however, is that actors operate within a functionally confined policy space and that the specific 'policy logics' of EU foreign and interior policies render, first, certain policy agendas more likely than others; second, structure the way in which institutional provisions work in the political process; and, third, shape the set of policy options available to all actors. More specifically, it is argued here that EU foreign and interior policies are characterized by a *shared* 'functional frame' – i.e. a specific allocation function which both policy areas have for the political system of the EU (see below).

This argument builds upon those analyses in EU studies which have focused on the structural interrelationship between the three pillars. Thus William Wallace has suggested that while CFSP and JHA 'remain distinctive from other fields of EU policy' the main dividing line in EU politics does not derive from the pillar design (W. Wallace 2000: 537). Nevertheless, he emphasizes the special character of CFSP and JHA and notes that both areas share a similar *policy mode* which he identifies as 'transgovernmentalism' (2000: 525). Notwithstanding the importance of national governments, the 'flow of policies' in both areas takes place within a single EU system of collective government, thus weakening the differences between the pillars (2000: 530). Accordingly, Elfriede Regelsberger *et al.* have pointed out that the CFSP is subject to a 'viability of an increased interconnectedness between the second and first pillars' (1997b: 9; see also Schimmelfennig and Wagner 2004: 657–9). Similar observations have been made with regard to the interconnectedness between the third and first pillars, which are characterized by a 'highly heterogeneous field [of] considerable overlap' between the provisions of the TEC and the TEU (den Boer and Wallace 2000: 499).

However, while these studies are helpful in detecting the increasing relevance of cross-pillar linkages from an empirical perspective, they focus less on the underlying driving forces of this institutional cross-pillarization. It is on this basis that this book argues that cross-pillar dynamics on the institutional and substantive levels are triggered by specific functional dynamics related to the two policy areas of foreign and interior affairs. As the systematic analysis of the various substantive, legal and institutional linkages between the three pillars in the subsequent chapters of this book will show, these functional dynamics have underpinned the process of de facto merging of the pillars, despite the on-going *formal* separation between them.

From an actor-related perspective, these functional dynamics of integration in foreign and interior policies become particularly visible when focusing on the way in which over time supranational actors were indeed able to make use of the functional unity of both policy areas despite the on-going institutional fragmentation within the fields of foreign and interior policies. By doing so they were able to establish and to exploit various linkages between the pillars and to shape policies *across* all three pillars, thus at least partially overcoming their formally negligible role in CFSP and JHA on the Treaty level.

Supranational actors were thus able to shape 'intergovernmental' bargains since the functional unity of both policy areas provides a stable EU-specific frame of reference within which the preferences of supranational actors *and* national governments unfold. Turning the spotlight on policy-making processes in the two areas from Maastricht to Nice, this book thus argues that EU foreign and interior policies cannot sufficiently be explained by looking solely at member states' preferences and bargains between them, but are to a significant extent shaped by the inputs of supranational actors as well. This does not imply that supranational actors were able to dominate policy-making. Indeed, member states continue to hold the most powerful institutional resources in both areas (Hill 1996 and 1997; Kuijper 2000). Notwithstanding these limitations to the role of supranational actors, a systematic analysis of the conditions under which they can make use of their formal and informal powers in policy-making, which often stem from first-pillar prerogatives, is well suited both to account for the centralization process in the two areas and to capture the institutional complexities of cross-pillar politics.

The political and legal unity of the EU across the three pillars

The focus on the manifold cross-pillar linkages in EU foreign and interior policies thus brings up the question of the underlying factors which lead to such a cross-pillarization of both areas. Addressing this question, this chapter argues that these linkages have been underpinned by specific political, legal and, in particular, functional dynamics. With regard to the *political dynamics*, the general characteristics of the EU as a political system do not stop at the borders designated by the different pillars and provide a constant institutional environment that pushes the pendulum towards further cross-pillarization (on the EU as a political system see Lindberg 1969; Wallace 1982; Hix 1999).

Broadly speaking, the features of the EU political system relate to four main dimensions: first, the existence of a 'stable and clearly-defined set of institutions for collective decision-making', consisting of the (European) Council, the Commission, the EP and jurisdiction by the ECJ; second, that 'citizens and social groups seek to achieve their political desires through the political system'; third, that 'collective decisions [at the EU level] have a significant impact on the distribution of economic resources and the allocation of social and political values'; and, finally, that 'there is a continuous interaction ("feedback") between these political outputs, new demands on the system, new decisions, and so on' (Hix 1999: 8).

What matters here is that these four dimensions do not only shape first-pillar policies but stretch across the three pillars of the EU, thereby ensuring that EU foreign and interior policies are structurally embedded in the policy environment of the EU political system. First, while the powers of supranational actors are limited in the two 'intergovernmental' pillars, the rules on decision-making procedures in all three pillars refer to the same set of institutional actors, i.e. the Council, the Commission, the European Parliament and the

European Court of Justice. Moreover, in both areas interest groups have mushroomed which scrutinize and influence the policy-making process and provide information and advice to policy-makers and citizens.[4] Second, as far as citizens of the EU are concerned, it is quite remarkable that the areas of external and internal policies consistently receive the highest scores when it comes to the question of which policies EU citizens would like to see regulated at the EU level (Eurobarometer 2003). Third, collective decisions in EU foreign and interior policies do allocate specific and significant political values, as can be seen, inter alia, when looking at the critique that policy-making in both areas helps to erect a fortress Europe, which literally closes its doors to outsiders, be it through 'Othering' processes vis-à-vis certain third countries or through the securitization of migration policies (see below). Finally, as W. Wallace has noted, there is by now a consistent 'flow of policies' (2000: 530) in both areas, which ensures that outputs continuously generate new demands for collective decision-making – independently of whether these decisions are regarded as effective or not. To avoid misunderstandings, it should be stressed that due to the contested dimension of democratic accountability and legitimacy, the EU is still a polity in the making, i.e. a political system but not necessarily a political community (on this distinction see World Society Research Group 2000; see also Weiler 1997; Wallace 1999).

Second, legal scholars have following the Maastricht Treaty and the Amsterdam Treaty, developed a new holistic perspective on the interplay between the various Treaties and thereby addressed the dynamics of cross-pillarization from a different perspective.[5] Thus Armin von Bogdandy argues that the significance of the Maastricht Treaty goes beyond the establishment of three only loosely connected pillars. Challenging mainstream legal perspectives which assume a separation between the pillars, he notes that the establishment of the EU led to the emergence of a 'single organisation ... called the "European Union"' and that, therefore, the 'terms "Communities" and "pillars of the European Union" do not demarcate different organisations but only different capacities with partially specific legal instruments and procedures' (1999: 1). This argument has some far-reaching consequences for policy-making in all three pillars, since 'all the Treaties and secondary law form a single legal order' (1999). Therefore, legal principles developed for the first pillar can, under certain conditions, be equally applied to the second and third pillars.[6] It is worth noting that Bogdandy's analysis reveals the existence of a legal environment at the EU level that was neither planned nor foreseen by member states during the Maastricht IGC. On the contrary, at Maastricht member states agreed upon the pillar design since (some) member states wanted to avoid a 'contamination' of CFSP and JHA with traditional EC practices (Moravcsik 1998: 467). Both the aforementioned political and legal dynamics help to explain why this contamination has actually taken place, thereby undermining the argument that the time between IGCs should be considered as merely an 'intervening period of consolidation', while it is in fact a period characterized by its own political dynamics (Moravcsik 1993: 473).

Notwithstanding this focus on political and legal dynamics which affect policies across the three pillars, it must again be emphasized that it is not claimed here that the cross-pillarization of foreign and interior policies from the first pillar on the one hand, with those from the second and third pillars on the other, is an automatic, predetermined process. The degree to which such a merging between the pillars takes place rather depends upon concrete political decisions in day-to-day policy-making in foreign and interior policies and on the extent to which the merging *potential* offered by the Treaties is actually made use of. Moreover, since this merging of foreign and interior affairs is an unintended consequence of the prior institutional choice to establish a pillarized system for both areas, the occurrence of such processes is likely to provoke conflict between those member states with preferences for a formal separation of the pillars on the one hand, and those member states (and, supposedly, supranational actors) which support such a merging on the other. Against this background it can be explained that also after the Amsterdam Treaty there has been a continuity at the Treaty level with regard to the guiding principles of the original pillar structure, including the semi-communitarization of migration policies. Therefore, in spite of manifold merging dynamics at the policy-making level, the persistence of (some) member states' preferences, as expressed during the Maastricht, Amsterdam and Nice IGCs, has left the pillar structure formally intact. In other words, the formal linkage between sensitive policy areas such as foreign and interior affairs on the one hand, and inter-governmental institutions for co-operation on the other, has not yet been entirely abandoned. Consequently, the legal and political set-up of EU foreign and interior policies continues to reflect the reservations held by some member states with regard to a communitarization of both areas (Hill 1998a; Hix 1995; Hix and Niessen 1995).

The policy frame of an EU insider/outsider distinction

However, the focus on general political and legal dynamics of the EU political system fails to take into account the more specific dynamics of integration which relate to individual policy areas. Based on this observation, this chapter argues, by drawing from sociological institutionalism, that the starting point of analysis should be the specific functional features of both policy areas (Fligstein and Mara-Drita 1996). It thereby takes the observation of a political and legal unity of the EU one step further and addresses the 'functional context' to which both policy areas relate. By analysing the functional features of both policy areas, this approach builds on insights from sociological institutionalism, which – from various perspectives – has dealt with the impact of taken-for-granted concepts in policy-making in the context of the EU and beyond, i.e. the process through which norms 'become so widely accepted that they are internalized by actors and achieve a "taken-for-granted" quality that makes conformance with them almost automatic' (Finnemore and Sikkink 1998: 904). Thus Fligstein and Mara-Drita have focused on the way the European

Commission in the 1980s succeeded in turning the Single Market Programme into a 'general cultural frame' (1996: 25), by arguing that distinct 'cultural practices structure what is possible in any given situation by eliminating certain possibilities and constraining what actions are "reasonable"' (1996: 5). By taking this approach, which was limited to one area of EC policy-making, one step further Fligstein and Stone Sweet have from a similar perspective developed a theory of European integration that builds on shared theoretical perspectives derived from sociological institutionalism (2002; see also March and Olson 1989; DiMaggio and Powell 1991). In a nutshell, they argue that:

> the institutionalization of European arenas of governance has occurred through a self-reinforcing process. As one set of European institutions has grown up, it has induced integration elsewhere. Integration has been a powerful force because it has *served to embed interests and identities* in a dynamic, expansionary way.
>
> (Fligstein and Stone Sweet 2002: 1236, my emphasis)

However, they explicitly exclude the second and third pillars from these 'arenas of European governance', arguing that 'important institutional arrangements that are in place for the first pillar ... are not in place for the other pillars of the European Union' (2002: 1209). Yet, as the focus of this study on manifold cross-pillar linkages on the functional, institutional and substantive levels shows, it might indeed be premature to argue that foreign and interior policies (parts of which are located in the first pillar anyway) do not form a specific policy arena at the European level which is by and large subject to similar policy dynamics to other fields of European governance, for two reasons.

First, on a general level, there is no reason to limit a sociological institutionalist framework to entirely supranational settings. Thus Barnett and Coleman (2005) have applied such a framework to the study of Interpol, a 'classical' international organization (IO). Their findings also show that within such IOs 'the existing cultures and rules will strongly influence how external pressures are interpreted and what sort of response is considered to be appropriate and desirable' (2005: 600). Thus,

> IOs exercise power by virtue of their ability to fix meaning, which is related to classification. Naming or labeling the social context establishes the parameters, the very boundaries, of acceptable action. Because actors are oriented towards objects and objectives on the basis of the meaning that they have for them, being able to invest situations with a particular meaning constitutes an important source of power.
>
> (Barnett and Finnemore 1999: 711)

While it should be emphasized that such dynamics operate in all organizations (i.e. in national governments as well), this argument shows that there is from the outset no reason to restrict the reach of such 'cultural frames' to national or supranational settings. Second, from an empirical perspective the strong delineation between the first pillar on the one hand, and the second and third pillars on the other, seems untenable, for it fails to address the processes of cross-pillarization dealt with at length in this study.

In that context, it must be emphasized that the emergence of such cultural frames is not necessarily an actor-related process in which norm entrepreneurs strategically advance certain rules which sustain the strengths of the specific organization at hand (Finnemore and Sikkink 1998). From this perspective it is particularly useful to focus on the underlying scripts that inform policy-making in specific contexts. Thus Fligstein and Stone Sweet are right in arguing that the institutionalization process in 'classical' first-pillar areas has been subject to its own specific features (2002). However, this does not preclude the operation of other scripts of Europeanization in the second and third pillars (as well as the linkages both pillars have with the first pillar).

Seen from that perspective, EU foreign and interior policies can be conceptualized as distinct organization fields (Mörth and Britz 2004; Mörth 2003). Thus 'organizational fields consist of organizations held together by institutionalized rules. These rules determine how issues are interpreted and categorized (i.e. framed)' (Mörth and Britz 2004: 962). The question then is to which organizational field(s) EU foreign and interior policies belong. The relevance of this question becomes immediately apparent when considering that 'the EU's new phase of positive integration embraces issues that concern the core of state sovereignty, which cannot be decided according to the "Community method" but need more national autonomy and flexibility' (Mörth and Britz 2004: 970). In the literature on both policy areas there are several competing perspectives on the underlying 'frames' which structure policy-making processes. First, in studies on European foreign policies scholars have addressed the underlying functional dynamics which establish 'the broad ideational parameters within which competing policy options are considered' (Hyde-Price 2003: 109; M. Smith 2003). In that context several authors have directed attention to the securitization dynamics related to EU foreign policies. Thus it is argued that the emergence of the EU leads to the establishment of new borders between the EU and the outside world. What matters in that context is that such processes often go hand in hand with processes of 'Othering' in which the EU asserts its identity by way of securitizing its relations with outsiders (Neumann and Welsh 1991). This framework, and in particular the problems related to a 'geopoliticisation of European identity constructions' since the 1990s (Diez 2004: 332) might indeed account for various 'exclusionary' dynamics in EU foreign policies, such as hegemonic projects vis-à-vis outsiders in the context of the EMP (Stetter 2005), the militarization of EU foreign policies or the 'framing' of certain outsiders (or semi-outsiders) as a threat (Diez 2004).

However, as Bahar Rumelili has shown, the EU's mode of differentiation between inside and outside must not necessarily be based on such negative 'Othering' processes (2004). Thus on the other side there are approaches which stress the role of the EU as a force for good in world politics, which acts (or should act) as a 'normative power' (Manners 2002). The focus on the civilian power of the EU thus advances a different understanding of the guiding 'cultural frames', namely the reference to the EU's emphasis in international relations on diplomacy, developmental assistance and multilateralism (see Youngs 2004). From a more general perspective this closely relates to the argument that the EU – and more specifically European integration – will help to 'overcome conflicts and maintain peace and stability' in Europe and beyond Europe's borders (Diez, Stetter and Albert 2006). The purpose of this section is not to embark on the debate about whether the dynamics of securitization or civilization have had the upper hand in the context of EU foreign policies. Rather, what matters is that the evolution of European foreign policy does 'construct important areas of difference, distinguishing the EU and its members from international interlocutors and generating powerful role conceptions that affect individual and collective behaviour' (M. Smith 2003: 569; see also Manners and Whitman 2003). Since these 'modes of differentiation' (Rumelili 2004) are characterized by countervailing securitizing *and* civilizing dynamics of operating in this policy area they deprive the EU of a clear-cut 'cultural frame' (see also Diez 2004).

Arguably, a similar practice can be observed in the field of EU migration policies. Scholars have also addressed the underlying 'cultural frames' with regard to this policy area (Caviedes 2004: 297). In a way similar to the case of EU foreign policies, opinions are split on whether integration in interior policies is characterized by securitization practices or liberalization. Thus, by looking at migration policies, Jef Huysmans has shown how 'the development of security discourses and policies in the area of migration is often presented as an inevitable policy response to the challenges for public order and domestic stability of the increases in the number of (illegal) immigrants and asylum seekers' (2000b: 757). This linkage between internal security and migration is a recurrent theme at the EU level as a result of perceived threats which were, inter alia, related to the consequences of the fall of the Iron Curtain in the late 1980s or increasing migratory movements across the Mediterranean Sea since the late 1990s. Huysmans has pointed out that this securitization of migration policies must be understood in a larger context, namely the securitization of the EU internal market. Thus this securitization follows 'the assumption that, after the abolition of internal border controls, transnational flows of goods, capital, services and people will challenge public order and the rule of law' (Huysmans 2000b: 758). As Virginie Guiraudon (2003) has emphasized, this securitization of migration policies has been facilitated by processes of 'venue shopping'. Thus 'the migration policy domain cannot be understood as the bargaining outcome among states with a coherent or aggregated set of preferences on these issues. Instead, only one "camp" in the national policy field went transnational', namely national immigration officials with their respective rather exclusionary policy agendas (2003: 264). Overall, this combination of securitization processes and specific actor constellations in a policy domain such as migration policies, which is characterized by a history of 'intensive transgovernmentalism' (W. Wallace 2000), has led many observers to argue that policy-making in EU interior policies contributes to the erection of a 'fortress Europe' (see also Geddes 2000).

However, in contrast to these approaches, Alexander Caviedes has pointed out that 'those who argue that EU immigration policy is merely the extension of a protectionist nation-state mentality have not adequately considered the dual aims' of recent policy proposals in this area (2004: 304). Thus Caviedes' empirical data suggests that while EU policies are characterized on several dimensions by a strong 'security component', issues of liberalization and co-ordination are equally present (2004). What matters here is the emphasis that, rather than being characterized by one specific frame (such as securitization), migration policies are a prime example of an area with 'a multitude of divergent policy goals and mechanisms' (2004: 306). From a different theoretical angle, William Walters has made a similar argument when identifying the rather ambiguous frames of governmentality in JHA and has argued that there are 'diverse and heterogeneous practices involved in making Europe governable as an "area of freedom, security and justice"' (Walters 2002: 94).

Thus the oscillation between securitization and liberalization in both policy areas shows that there is no clear 'cultural frame' available to which actors can easily resort. While both policy areas exhibit strong dynamics of securitization and exclusion, as the debates on 'Othering discourses' and 'fortress Europe' illustrate, there are other cultural frames that relate to liberalization and inclusion, such as the 'civilian power' notion or the 'cultural frame' offered by the objective to establish an area of freedom, security and justice. While the pendulum might swing between extremes, it seems fair to say that neither of the two sides has gained a permanent hegemony in EU politics. Seen from that perspective, the question of whether the EU's internal and external identity will be defined in terms of inclusion or exclusion remains a deeply political issue. What is clear, however, is that this struggle for identity already reflects on a much more basic level the emergence of a distinct identity dimension at the European level. In other words, EU foreign and interior policies – across the three pillars – contribute to the emergence of the distinction between the EU as a distinct 'Self' vis-à-vis 'Others'.

Thus, notwithstanding the often meagre substantive outcomes in both areas and the nascent status of the EU's internal and external identity, this insider/outsider distinction is of huge political significance. The gradual consolidation of this distinction through policy-making in EU foreign and interior policies consolidates the internal and external identity of the EU (Cederman 2000) by distinguishing the EU and EU citizens on the one hand, from third countries and third-country nationals on the other. Hence, the insider/outsider distinction functions as the underlying 'focal point' for policy-making in EU foreign and interior affairs and the subsequent gradual construction of a distinct sovereignty dimension at the EU level – independently of whether concrete actors prefer an inclusionary or an exclusionary identity for the EU.

While it is true that from an institutional and substantive perspective the pace of integration in foreign and interior policies has often been rather slow, this sovereignty dimension of both areas on the functional level renders their integration at the EU level nevertheless a highly significant endeavour – which also explains the critique which more exclusionary political practices in both areas have received (Diez 2004; Huysmans 2000b). In these cases, securitization is based on discursive processes that construct antagonistic and binary insider/outsider distinctions and represent the outside as a threat. However, as has been shown above, there is also an alternative view that points to the political significance of the underlying dynamics of inclusion in both areas. This book does not aim to settle this debate, but rather wants to underline that the mere debate on whether EU foreign and interior policies are inclusionary or exclusionary points to the underlying insider/outsider distinction which informs both political practices. It is in that sense that the dynamics of cross-pillarization in both areas, which will be discussed in detail in subsequent chapters, have equipped the EU with its own power. As Nassehi has noted, 'political power must create visibilities' such as 'internal/external borders' (Nassehi 2002: 47). In that context, the increasing visibility of these borders at the EU level between an inside and an outside points to the functional dynamics unleashed by the seemingly innocent decisions of the Maastricht Treat to establish three formally separated pillars, thereby underlining the political significance of integration in both areas for the EU political system at large.

The manifold substantive and institutional overlaps in both policy areas across the three pillars thereby point to the functional unity that characterizes foreign and interior policies at the EU level. Ultimately, this argument not only brings to the fore the 'functional frame' of an EU-specific insider/outsider distinction to which all processes of policy-making in both areas constantly relate. It also allows the conceptualizing of both areas as constituting a distinct policy type, as has successfully been done in the past with regard to regulatory or redistributive policies in the first pillar (Majone 1996; Hix 1999).

The attempt to classify policies into typological categories, although not yet applied to EU foreign and interior affairs, is quite a common exercise for the study of other policy areas at the EU level. The basic idea behind the concept of policy types is to replace 'the descriptive, subject-matter categories' of many case studies with a *functional* approach that identifies arenas comprising different policy areas, with each arena 'developing its own characteristic political structure, political process, elites, and group relations' (Lowi 1964: 689–90). Theodore Lowi demonstrated in his seminal work that shared functional features of different policy areas on the policy dimension lead to similarities in the way in which these areas are dealt with in the political process. Following Lowi's basic typology, scholars of EU politics have most commonly distinguished between regulatory, distributional and redistributional policies. Hix has used another related categorization, namely Musgrave and Musgrave's typology of regulatory, re-distributional and macro-economic stabilization policies, to account for political processes at the EU level (Musgrave and Musgrave 1959; Hix 1999).

Notwithstanding the popularity of policy typologies in EU studies, they have mainly been used in order to account for socio-economic policies and have not yet been extended to cover foreign and interior affairs. Interestingly enough, if they are applied to the EU, Lowi's and Musgrave and Musgrave's typologies relate to first-pillar areas. Policies covered by the second and third pillars do not easily fit into one of these categories, although they might comprise elements of the aforementioned policy types, such as regulatory features of migration policies (Stetter 2000). Thus the gradual consolidation of the aforementioned insider/outsider distinction through policy-making in EU foreign and interior policies across the three pillars allows the construction of the EU vis-à-vis 'Others', either third countries or third-country nationals. As a result, the EU incrementally acquires an external and an internal identity. Due to this constitutive function of both policy areas for the entire political system of the EU, it can be argued, on the basis of Theodore Lowi's classification, that both areas *jointly* constitute a distinct policy type at the EU level, which will be referred to here as 'constituent policies', thereby acknowledging the fundamental impact which the consolidation of an EU-specific insider/outsider distinction has for the political system of the EU at large (Lowi 1964, 1972). This also follows Antje Wiener's observation that 'associative factors' such as constitutional rules and identities contribute to institution-building processes in constitutive policy areas (Wiener 2001: 79; 2003). As the empirical analysis in subsequent chapters shows, it is this functional feature as well as the specific allocation function of both areas – i.e. the value allocation of an insider/outsider distinction – rather than inter-governmental or supranational logics that spurs the dynamics of integration in both areas.

This is also the reason why, as many scholars have noted, the emergence of Europeanized settings in both areas stands in a somewhat ambivalent relationship with traditional notions of national sovereignty. By providing policies which construct new identities for insiders and outsiders, with the EU and EU citizens on the one hand, and third countries and third-country nationals on the other, the EU becomes the bearer of the two main principles of what Max Weber has identified as the central elements of sovereignty and, indeed, of statehood itself. In his famous Munich lecture on *Politik als Beruf*, Weber argued that 'today, however, we have to say that a state is a human community that (successfully) claims the *monopoly of the legitimate use of physical force* within a given territory. Note that "territory" is one of the characteristics of the state' (Weber 1988: 506, my translation). Thus the development of an insider/outsider dimension strengthens the territorial and authoritative significance of the EU, which develops in parallel to the persistence of national prerogatives in foreign and interior policies. However, while acquiring its own sovereignty dimension as a result of the functional dynamics inherent in the integration process in foreign and interior affairs, the EU is not claiming a Weberian monopoly to regulate both areas – but no longer is the (European) nation-state (see also Albert 2005).

To summarize, both EU foreign and EU interior policies serve to construct and maintain an external and an internal identity for the EU. Interestingly enough, such a goal is explicitly recognized by the Treaties – although the political implications of these objectives might often be rather unintended. Thus Article 2 TEU, which refers to the objectives of the EU, states in its second indent that it is one of the objectives of the EU 'to assert its identity on the international scene'. In a similar way, Article 2, fourth indent TEU, formulates the objective of an internal identity for the EU by calling for the development of a border-free 'area of freedom, security and justice' within the EU in parallel to the establishment of rules for 'external border controls, asylum, immigration', and thus draws a distinction between the internal and the external.

Seen from that perspective, the value allocation inherent in foreign and interior policy-making serves the purpose of giving substance to the afore-mentioned 'functional frame' of an EU insider/outsider dimension. In both areas the EU 'allocates' values which construct an inside and an outside, i.e. third countries on the one hand, and TCNs on the other. Being aware of these substantial functional similarities between foreign and interior policies and recalling Lowi's verdict that policies determine politics, it is not surprising that in spite of all the differences between the two areas the institutional provisions, actor constellations and interaction dynamics of 'constituent policies' do indeed share many structural features, which will all be discussed in subsequent chapters. In this context it should finally be noted that what sets apart these two areas from other areas of EU politics is not the institutional provisions as such but rather the particular functional features of constituent policies which provide the frame within which all actors – supranational and national – operate (Lowi 1964).

Conclusion

Foreign and interior policies have often taken a somewhat awkward position in EU studies since the division of the two areas into separate pillars has led many scholars to argue that parts of both areas (i.e. those in the 'intergovernmental' pillars) would operate somewhat beyond the normal logic of EU politics. In contrast, the argument of this chapter has been that by drawing from sociological institutionalism a more comprehensive understanding of the specific dynamics of integration in both areas can be achieved, since this allows the functional frames to which policy-making in both areas relates to be addressed. What is of interest then is the way in which actor preferences relate to the specific 'frames' (i.e. the insider/outsider distinction) and how these frames, in a second step, structure policy-making processes. By drawing a distinction between the inside and the outside of the EU, the political system of the EU has entered new political territories since Maastricht.

What, then, sets apart foreign and interior policies from other (first-pillar) policies at the EU level is not so much institutional provisions, such as specific rules on agenda-setting, voting in the Council or inter-institutional relations, or actor preferences, such as preferences for intergovernmental forms of co-operation on the side of some actors versus preferences for communitarization on the other side. The main differences with regard to politics in foreign and interior affairs primarily relates to the specific functional features of both areas, namely of providing the EU with a distinct sovereignty dimension. It is this functional frame which brings up a particular 'policy logic' and which structures the way in which institutions and actors operate. In other words, the same institutions and actors operate differently, if other functional frames such as, for example, regulatory or redistributional policy types are in place. Having said that, it has to be clearly emphasized that the primacy accorded here to 'functional frames' does not mean that institutional roles or actor preferences do not matter. What it does mean, however, is that institutions and preferences cannot be seen in isolation from the functional context to which they constantly relate and which structures the space within which they operate.

Part II

The institutional and substantive dynamics of cross-pillarization

3 Authority delegation to supranational actors
Primary capabilities

Introduction

This chapter investigates the capabilities of supranational actors in foreign and interior policies as defined by the Treaties, thus turning to the analysis of the institutional factors which relate to the functional features of foreign and interior politics set out in Chapter 2. Since these capabilities have been delegated by member states to supranational actors by primary law, they will be referred to here as 'primary capabilities'. Following the lines of argument outlined in Chapter 2, the main questions which are addressed here are as follows. How do the functional features of constituent policies affect the primary capabilities of supranational actors? Hence, to what extent do the capabilities of supranational actors reflect the 'pillar divide' of both foreign and interior policies? Given the formal endurance of these two basic institutional arenas, what is the actual difference with regard to the powers of supranational actors between those parts of foreign and interior policies which belong to the first pillar on the one hand, and those parts belonging to the second and third pillars on the other? Also, are there differences regarding the capabilities of supranational actors when comparing their *individual* role in foreign and interior policies?

As outlined in Chapter 2, this analysis aims to contribute to a better understanding of the interrelationship between the three pillars and, more precisely, of the interplay between 'supranational' and 'intergovernmental' institutions in foreign and interior policies. In particular, it seeks to shed light on the question of what role member states devised in both areas for collective actors at the EU level – such as the Commission, Parliament, the Council Secretariat, the Court of Justice and the Court of Auditors. As a background to the analysis on the primary capabilities of supranational actors, this and the subsequent chapter draw from the insights of delegation theory (Kiewiet and McCubbins 1991; Pollack 1997). In the context of EU foreign and interior policies, market integration and, subsequently, negative externalities stemming from (market) integration have been a stimulus to initiate co-operation between member states in these two policy areas (see, from a general perspective, Gatsios and Seabright 1989). Building on the arguments of Chapter 2 on the emergence of constituent policies as a new policy type at the EU level, this chapter argues that the particular functional characteristics of foreign and interior policies, namely the linkage between both areas with a distinct sovereignty dimension, explain both the cautious delegation of capabilities to supranational actors and the noteworthy institutional fragmentation of their capabilities in the two areas.

It was by the Treaty of Rome that external economic co-operation and developmental assistance, as well as provisions on the free movement of persons, became part of the EC. In contrast to this communitarization of *economic* foreign and interior policies, co-operation on classical diplomatic relations and security policies, as well as on migration, policing and judicial policies, remained outside the EC context prior to the Maastricht Treaty (Peers 2000: 9–15). However, this merely intergovernmental co-operation in both areas faced, first, serious credibility and co-ordination problems (Majone 1996) and, second, 'the economic logic of market-making had political consequences that drew issues of high politics into the EU's remit' (Geddes 2000: 93). Therefore, member states decided in 1993 to bring the *political* arenas of foreign and interior policies within the 'single institutional setting' of the EU, thus replacing the previous 'working model of intergovernmental cooperation without formal integration' through a model that tried to reconcile intergovernmental co-operation *and* formal integration (Forster and Wallace 2000: 466). By doing so, member states also agreed to delegate within the newly created fields of the Common Foreign and Security Policy on the one hand, and Justice and Home Affairs on the other, certain capabilities to supranational actors (Regelsberger 1993; Monar and Morgan 1994). However, the actual powers of these actors remained small when compared to their entrenched capabilities in economic sectors of foreign and interior policies. 'The reason is that Member States take the view that JHA cooperation, and foreign policy cooperation, are issues so central to their sovereignty that the "supranational" approach of Community law must be set aside' (Peers 2000: 13). And, indeed, this overall 'pillar design' of the EU has not been subject to substantial change either in the Amsterdam or in the Nice Treaty (Denza 2002; den Boer 1997; Monar 1997a).

Notwithstanding this observation, supranational actors have in all three Treaty reforms of the 1990s been delegated new capabilities in all institutional arenas of foreign and interior policies. While national governments maintain the main sources of power and legitimacy in both areas, they have begun to share some of these with supranational actors. Such a delegation of capabilities should not be regarded as a zero-sum game in which delegated capabilities necessarily mean a loss of capabilities on the side of principals. Principals can thus 'use delegation to effectively pursue their policy objectives' (Kiewiet and McCubbins 1991: 234). Hence, this chapter on the capabilities of supranational actors does not argue that there has been a kind of 'abdication' of member states (Kiewiet and McCubbins 1991: 234). Instead, member states share power with supranational actors, notably the Commission and, increasingly, the Council Secretariat. This process has resulted in two main features. First, the dominant institutional divide in EU foreign and interior politics is between executive actors (Council, Council Secretariat, Commission) on the one hand, and legislative and judicial actors (Parliament and the Court of Justice) on the other – with the powers of the latter being considerably less developed when compared with executive actors. Second, inner-executive relations are mainly characterized by co-operative modes of interaction. Open conflicts are rare but do, of course, occur. Chapter 7 will discuss these patterns of interaction in greater detail.

Primary delegation and the role of supranational actors

At the Maastricht Treaty summit member states put in place the three-pillar structure of the EU which is characterized by one 'supranational' and two 'intergovernmental' pillars. This division between a 'classical' communitarized institutional arena on the one hand, and member states' dominated arenas on the other, has subsequently not been subject to radical change.[1] Treaty reforms in Amsterdam and Nice did not lead to a wholesale turn towards one of these two ideal types of EU governance. While the Maastricht Treaty led to the incorporation of two previously strictly intergovernmental policies into the EU system of governance, the type of Europeanization in foreign and interior policies was quite different from in other policy areas. The qualitative gap between the EC on the one hand, and CFSP and JHA on the other, becomes particularly evident when looking at the capabilities of supranational actors within these two different institutional arenas.

Thus, as H. Wallace has noted, 'for the new "high politics" issues of foreign and security policy, and justice and home affairs, the price for their inclusion within the scope of what would thereafter be the Union was that they would be subject to different and weaker institutional regimes' (1996: 55). Along the same lines, Moravcsik has analysed the capabilities of supranational actors in the second and third pillars. He has argued that member states designed 'this three-pillar structure, a metaphor proposed by the French representative Pierre de Boissieu ... to restrict definitively, through qualitative institutional breaks, the Commission and Parliament's prerogatives in foreign and interior policy' (1998: 450).

However, such an exclusive focus on the second and third pillars does distort a policy perspective on foreign and internal affairs. 'The three-pillar institutional structure of the European Union comes under fire ... because it artificially separates external and internal sectors of public life' (Zielonka 1998b: 5). Moreover, a closer look behind this dominant pillar structure reveals, as has already been indicated in the previous chapters, that both the CFSP and the JHA are but some of the various 'institutional regimes' of EU foreign and interior policies and these regimes are spread across all three pillars. Based on this understanding, this chapter investigates the cross-pillar capabilities of supranational actors in these two policy areas. By doing so it does not follow the argument 'that the place to look for "foreign policy" is in the development of external economic policies' (M. Smith 1998: 77). It is rather argued here that in order to comprehensively grasp developments in both policy areas, one must focus on the Treaty provisions in all three pillars equally.

Since the analysis of this chapter is based on the provisions of the Maastricht, Amsterdam and Nice Treaties, the specific kind of capabilities that are investigated here will be understood as 'primary capabilities'. Such a terminology rests on the observation that Treaty provisions are not the only source of the delegation of capabilities.[2] Moreover, a study of the primary capabilities of supranational actors promises to be particularly fruitful for a cross-pillar comparative analysis. Indeed, this section reveals both important differences but also similarities between first-pillar provisions on the one hand, and the more intergovernmental provisions on the other. Thus, while the capabilities of supranational actors in foreign and interior policies are much more pronounced in the first pillar, these actors nevertheless possess capabilities across all types of institutional regimes across the three pillars. The analysis of this chapter proceeds in three steps, thereby focusing on the main domains in which capabilities have been delegated to supranational actors on the Treaty level. First, it considers the *legislative powers* of supranational actors in both areas. Thus it focuses on the powers of the 'legislative triangle' consisting of the Council, the Commission and Parliament, and their respective roles in the various legislative regimes of both areas. Second, the capabilities of the Commission and the Council (Secretariat) as part of the EU executive are analysed. Third, spill-over provisions from the first pillar, these being budgetary authority and judicial remedy, and their effect on the cross-pillar capabilities of supranational actors, such as the Commission, Parliament, the Court of Justice and the Court of Auditors, form the substance of the final section.

Four main insights are the result of this analysis. First, a study on primary capabilities shows that the pillar structure of the EU continues to be highly relevant for a proper understanding of foreign and interior policies at the EU level. Thus there is a clear distinction between the capabilities of supranational actors in the first pillar on the one hand, and their powers in the second and third pillars on the other. Supranational actors are, generally speaking, much more powerful in the former. The Treaty provisions, therefore, seem to support arguments in favour of a 'pillarized perspective' on foreign and interior policies. Even the transfer of migration policies from the third to the first pillar in the Amsterdam Treaty did not result in a communitarization of this area. Rather, migration policies do present a 'new institutional regime' halfway between the two kinds of pillars. As Hailbronner notes, 'the Member States have been anxious to retain a certain *domaine réservé* and an active say on its definition; Title IV was framed on this premise' (2000: 36).

Second, despite this general endurance of two parallel institutional frameworks, each Treaty reform provided for both more delegation of cross-pillar capabilities to supranational actors and an increasing amount of linkages between the three pillars. Therefore, the original quite strict division between these two different institutional arenas is incrementally undermined. Third, these Treaty changes paved the way for the nascent 'hybrid institutional setting' which characterizes both areas. Thus the functional context of constituent policies – i.e. its sovereignty dimension – left its mark on the precise capabilities which supranational actors received through primary delegation. In this context of executive dominance, member states continue to dominate and control developments in foreign and interior policies to a much larger extent than they usually do in classical first-pillar areas. To that extent, the 'EU remains a partial polity, without many of the features which one might expect to find within a fully developed democratic political system' (W. Wallace 2000: 533).

As a result, it can be argued that the 'pillar perspective' tends to underestimate the considerable differences which exist *between* supranational actors with regard to their individual cross-pillar capabilities. Since it is argued here that the integration process in foreign and interior policies has in particular strengthened *executive* supranational actors, it was mainly the Commission and the Council Secretariat which were able to increase their leverage vis-à-vis the member states. The legislative and judicial branches of the EU political system, on the other hand, have not been delegated similar capabilities. While Parliament, the Court of Auditors and the Court of Justice have received some new powers through Treaty reforms, the institutional endowment for these three actors does not put them on a footing equal to the EU executive, including member states.

Legislative powers across the three pillars

The legislative process in the EU is based on three main principles. First, legislative politics in the EU is embedded within a bicameral system in which the Council and Parliament are the key decision makers. However, the legislative system is also characterized by a variety of legislative procedures. While a majority in the Council is required under each of these procedures in order to pass a legislative act, the powers of Parliament vary considerably. Under some of these procedures Parliament acts on an equal footing with the Council, i.e. in the co-decision and the assent procedures a parliamentary majority is required for the adoption of a legislative act. Under the co-operation procedure Parliament can, under certain conditions, amend legislation, while the consultation procedure allows at least for a delay in the adoption of legislative acts. Finally under the 'information procedure', as well as for those cases in which it is not mentioned at all, Parliament does not really act as a legislature but rather as a forum which publicly scrutinizes Council legislation, either before or after its adoption. Table 3.1 presents an overview on the powers of Parliament in each of these six procedures. The ranking in Table 3.1 suggests that the powers of Parliament decrease in descending order. This ranking is based on two observations. First, the greatest weight is given to the question if a parliamentary majority is required for the adoption of a piece of legislation. The second consideration then is whether Parliament can propose changes to such a legislative proposal or not.

Table 3.1 Role of Parliament in the six legislative procedures in foreign and interior policies

Procedure	Role of Parliament
1. Co-decision	• Three-stage procedure (earlier agreement possible); • parliamentary majority required at each stage (absolute majority in plenary, simple majority in Conciliation Committee); • Parliament can propose changes to legislation; • if no agreement in first two readings, Conciliation Committee between Parliament and Council convenes; • procedure introduced with Maastricht Treaty, reformed with Amsterdam Treaty which further strengthened the role of Parliament (Article 251).
2. Co-operation	• Two-stage procedure; • parliamentary majority not required (but easier for Council to accept proposals from Parliament than to reject them); • Parliament can propose changes to legislation (Parliament as 'conditional agenda setter' (see Tsebelis 1994); • introduced with the Single European Act, but for foreign and interior policies abolished with the Amsterdam Treaty.
3. Assent	• Single-stage procedure; • parliamentary majority required; • Parliament cannot propose changes to legislation.
4. Consultation	• Single-stage procedure; • parliamentary majority not required (but following the 1980 Isoglucose case at the Court of Justice Parliament has a de facto power of delay since Council has to await the opinion of Parliament before the adoption of a legislative act); • Parliament can propose changes to legislation.
5. Information	• Council and Commission are asked but not bound to keep Parliament informed; • no powers to prevent, change or delay legislation; • Parliament can publicly scrutinize legislation; • introduced for the second and third pillars with the Maastricht Treaty.
6. No Parliament	• No role for Parliament at all; • note: applies also to certain first pillar areas.

Sources: Hix (1999); Nugent (1999).

A second characteristic of the EU legislative process is that the Commission also participates as an active player by taking on the role of an agenda-setter.[3] Through its right of initiative the Commission holds a powerful resource in shaping future decisions. However, the actual significance of the right of initiative, which the Commission enjoys in all institutional arenas of foreign and interior policies save defence issues, depends on both the exclusivity of this provision and the voting rules in the Council. In some institutional regimes, the Commission is the only institution that can initiate a legislative proposal, whereas in others it has to share this right with the member states. This, of courses, reduces the Commission's capabilities since member states can rely on their own legislative activism (Pierson 1998: 35–38).

As mentioned before, the third important element in the legislative process is the majority requirements within the Council. These rules, for example, determine the actual significance of the Commission's sole right of initiative. Thus, if the Council decides by a qualified majority, the sole right of initiative of the Commission has a greater weight than for cases in which the Council decides by unanimity. This is because, under qualified majority, the Commission can propose legislation that is closer to its 'ideal point' than under unanimity. In the former case, the Commission can 'ignore' those member states that are most distant from its own proposals and which are not required for such a majority. In contrast, under unanimity the Commission has to incorporate even the positions of those member states that are most distant from its own policy positions (Tsebelis 1994). Having this ideal typical model in mind, the actual usage of qualified majority voting in the EU policy-making process should not be overestimated. Empirical studies have shown that the Council often prefers to decide on a consensual basis even in those areas in which the Treaty requires a qualified majority only (Hayes-Renshaw and Wallace 1997). This insight has also been confirmed by research conducted for this book. To give one example: an official from the Council Secretariat, when reflecting about the possible use of majority voting on migration policies, has stated that 'a constant use of QMV against Germany is not possible on this issue'.[4] Table 3.2 presents a list of all the legislative constellations for foreign and interior policy across the three pillars. It incorporates a 'triangular' perspective on the two policy areas, thus taking note of the role of Parliament as defined by the six different legislative procedures, the role of the Commission as exemplified by the rules on its right of initiative and, finally, the voting rules in the Council.[5]

It is, therefore, not surprising that the Commission tends to adopt a cautious approach on whether the right of initiative is sole or shared when initiating legislation independently.[6] It was only in those areas in which the Commission has already enjoyed longstanding Community prerogatives that it was willing to use the right of initiative in a more proactive manner. The economic basket of the EMP, and thus trade issues and developmental assistance, was mentioned as such an example (Licari 1998).[7] However, in these communitarized areas the Commission has also had to keep a watchful eye on the Council. Thus one official lamented that the Commission 'never used its right of initiative to combine trade and politics', since member states continue to regard political relations with third countries as their prerogative.[8]

The Commission's legislative powers in foreign policies remained largely unchanged between the Maastricht and the Nice Treaties. Thus no major changes occurred with regard to those institutional regimes in which the Commission has the sole right of initiative and those in which this right is shared with the member states. The sole right of initiative covers the first-pillar foreign policy areas, these being external economic relations and developmental assistance, while in the second pillar the Commission shares this right with the member states.[9] When looking at the voting rules in the Council,

Table 3.2 Institutional fragmentation in foreign and interior policies: legislative regimes from Maastricht to Nice

Parliament: legislative procedure	Commission: Right of initiative/voting requirements in the Council			
	Sole/qualified majority	Shared/qualified majority	Sole/unanimity	Shared/unanimity
Co-decision	• All development assistance • * Most free movement, except services *Parts of visa policies after 2004 (automatically)*	*All/some Title IV TEC after 2004/ after prior Council decision (unanimity required)*		
Co-operation	All development assistance			
Assent			• * Most Association Agreements	
Consultation	• All visa policies	All visa policies after 1995	• Some Common Commercial Policy: Article 133(5) TEC	• Most Title IV *(voluntarily shared right of initiative after 2004)* All visa policies before 1995
Information		• Some CFSP: prior Common Strategy, implementation of Joint Action or Common Position (simple majority for procedure) Some CFSP: procedure/prior Joint Action Some JHA: implementation of Joint Action, Conventions (2/3 majority)		• * Most CFSP Most JHA
No Parliament	• * Most Common Commercial Policy: Articles 132(1) 133(2) TEC • * Some Association Agreements: Article 301 TEC • Some free movement: providing services: Article 49 TEC • * Internal borders: Article 14 TEC Some free movement: Social security			

Source: Own compilation; parts of this table are presented in Stetter (2004).

Note: **Bold** /bullet points refers to Amsterdam Treaty; normal type refers to Maastricht Treaty; *italic* refers to Nice Treaty and automatic/possible changes to Amsterdam Treaty; asterisk refers to those provisions of Amsterdam Treaty which already existed in the Maastricht version.

however, the picture becomes more complex. While in developmental assistance the Council votes with a qualified majority, the bulk of the decisions in external economic relations and the CFSP are decided by unanimity. Parliament, finally, has its strongest role in the area of developmental assistance, where it is a co-legislator in the framework of the co-decision procedure. Whereas for some international agreements Parliament's assent is required, it is a peripheral actor in the common commercial policy and the CFSP. Thus, when comparing the powers of the Commission and Parliament in the legislative domain of external economic relations, the former has been delegated the greater number of primary capabilities. However, due to the predominance of unanimity voting in the Council in this area, member states hold the key to effective control over the way in which the Commission uses the right of initiative.

The economic dimension of EU foreign policies has two Treaty bases, these being the Common Commercial Policy on the one hand, and the provisions on Mixed Agreement on the other. With regard to the Common Commercial Policy, Articles 132(1) and 133(2) TEC delegated to the Commission the sole right of initiative on all legislative measures in this field. Moreover, in the Amsterdam Treaty, this right was extended by Article 133(5) TEC to cover the issues of services and intellectual property, which were previously not part of the Common Commercial Policy. The actual political weight of the sole right of initiative in this field is strengthened by the provisions on the powers of the Council and Parliament. Thus on all issues related to the Common Commercial Policy the Treaty stipulates that the Council decides with a qualified majority. Parliament, surprisingly for such a 'classical' first-pillar arena, is virtually excluded from the legislative process. Thus the Maastricht Treaty does not mention Parliament at all in its provisions on the Common Commercial Policy. It was only with the Amsterdam Treaty that a minor change in favour of Parliament was introduced. Since then, Article 133(5) TEC allows Parliament, on the basis of the consultation procedure, to scrutinize legislation on the issues of intellectual property and services in international agreements.

Notwithstanding these provisions, the main Treaty base for economic relations with third countries in general, and Middle Eastern countries in particular, is not the Common Commercial Policy, but the provisions on 'Mixed Agreements' and 'Association Agreements' pursuant to Articles 300 and 310 TEC. On Association Agreements, which are the kind of agreement the EU has concluded with both Israel and Palestine, the Commission's legislative role is more restricted and Parliament's powers are significantly enhanced when compared with their respective capabilities under the Common Commercial Policy. While the Commission also has the sole right of initiative for Association Agreements, its actual significance is circumscribed by the unanimity requirement in the Council. Article 300 TEC stipulates that unanimity is required for all Association Agreements and for all those agreements which cover 'a field for which unanimity is required for the adoption of internal rules'. Indeed, both the Association Agreements and all other bilateral agreements with Israel and Palestine in the 1990s did actually cover areas in which the internal rules of the EU required unanimity.[10] Qualified majority voting only comes into play in the case of sanctions against countries with which the EU has concluded an Association Agreement. Following Article 301 TEC, the Commission has in this case the sole right of initiative, while the Council decides – without any parliamentary involvement – by qualified majority.[11] Notwithstanding this limitation to Parliament's role, its rights in the legislative process in this institutional regime are greater than in the Common Commercial Policy.

Association Agreements require the assent of Parliament. Parliament has occasionally used its rights under the assent procedure to link its vote with political demands towards third countries. Since a parliamentary majority is required for the conclusion of Article 300 agreements, such a linkage is quite a 'credible threat'. In Middle East policies such a linkage was successfully made in 1988 when Parliament blocked the conclusion of three trade agreements with Israel. As Hollis notes, 'the hold-up was temporary, but the point was made' (1994: 129).[12] Finally, in order to speed up the decision-making process – and to prevent Parliament from delaying decisions – Article 300 TEC allows that Council and Parliament can jointly determine a time limit for the assent prior to any decision.

It has been argued that the exclusion of Parliament from Article 133 Agreements can be explained by the need to have a fast-track procedure for international agreements between the EU and third parties alongside Association Agreements which, in addition to parliamentary involvement, also require unanimity in the Council. This constellation brings to the fore an interesting alliance between those member states seeking to limit the Commission's influence under Article 133 TEC on the one hand, and Parliament trying to push for international agreements to be concluded pursuant to Article 300 TEC on the other (McGoldrick 1997: 92–3).

Compared to this wide range of institutional regimes in external economic relations, the delegation of legislative capabilities to the Commission and Parliament on developmental assistance has been quite straightforward and establishes one standard procedure only. Thus, since the Maastricht Treaty, the Commission has had the sole right of initiative in this area, whereas the Council decides across the board with a qualified majority. It was only with regard to Parliament's powers that the Treaty provisions have undergone some changes. While the Maastricht Treaty delegated to Parliament a legislative role in the framework of the co-operation procedure, the Amsterdam Treaty introduced the co-decision procedure for all developmental assistance decisions, thus rendering Parliament a powerful co-legislator alongside the Council.

The roles of the Commission and Parliament remain much more restricted in the area of the CFSP. While there were some changes between Maastricht and Nice with regard to the legislative process in the second pillar, these changes only related to the voting provisions in the Council. The rules on the legislative capabilities of the Commission and Parliament have remained completely unchanged since Maastricht. With regard to the Commission's right of initiative, Article 22(1) TEU stipulates that the Commission, but also any member state, 'may refer to the Council any question relating to the common foreign and security policy and may submit proposals to the Council'. However, more legislative proposals in this field are tabled by the member states, while the Commission remains cautious in making use of the right of initiative.[13] According to Article 23 TEU, unanimity is required for the adoption of legislative acts in the Council. There are, however, some exceptions to this rule. Thus, whereas the Maastricht Treaty provided for qualified majority voting only on procedural issues and on those joint actions where the Council decided beforehand to do so, Article 23(2) TEU of the Amsterdam Treaty foresaw qualified majority voting for all legislative acts that are either based on a common strategy or are for implementing decisions for joint action or a common position. Moreover, the rules on procedural questions were further relaxed and the Amsterdam Treaty asked for a simple majority in the Council only.

In contrast to the role of the Council and also the Commission, Parliament's capabilities regarding its impact on decisions in the CFSP are severely restricted (Grunert 1997). Article 21 TEU provides for a 'consultation' and an 'information' of Parliament in this area. However, since these institutional rights are not enforceable, Parliament cannot use the second-pillar consultation mechanism in the same way as it can for consultation in the first pillar.[14] Therefore, Parliament's involvement in the decision-making process of the second pillar depends upon the goodwill of the member states and the Commission to keep it informed about decisions which are awaiting adoption in the Council.[15] However, members of the European Parliament (MEPs) are usually lacking in such goodwill and one parliamentarian complained 'that the Council always informed us after taking decisions', thus undermining the already weak control function of Parliament in the second pillar.[16]

Turning now to the legislative capabilities of supranational actors in interior policies, a similar distribution of powers can be observed. While the Commission has been delegated the right of initiative within all institutional arenas, this right has to be shared with the member states in the third pillar as well as for most migration policy issues in Title IV TEC of the Amsterdam Treaty. While the Council decides by qualified majority in those institutional regimes which have been communitarized with the Maastricht Treaty, most decisions in migration policies do still require unanimous consent. Parliament, finally, is a weak actor on the legislative dimension in interior policies in most institutional regimes. Even the transfer of migration policies from the third pillar to the TEC has changed little with regard to Parliament's legislative powers. On most issues Parliament can neither amend nor prevent legislation.

Both the Commission and Parliament have been delegated considerable capabilities in the 'classical' first-pillar fields of interior policies, such as free movement and the issuing of visas. However, when comparing the capabilities of these two actors, Parliament has profited less from primary delegation. Thus the Commission enjoys the sole right of initiative in all these policy fields, whereas Parliament's powers are somewhat more restricted. In fact, the capabilities of Parliament range from institutional regimes in which it does not take any part in the legislative process to regimes in which it acts as a powerful co-legislator in the framework of the co-decision procedure. With one exception the Council always decides by qualified majority.

Co-decision was the standard operating procedure for legislative acts related to the free movement of workers, save social security issues, before the Amsterdam Treaty. Thus on freedom of movement issues the Commission has the sole right of initiative and a parliamentary majority is required for every legislative act, while the Council decides by qualified majority.[17] In the Maastricht Treaty social security decisions related to freedom of movement already required a qualified majority in the Council on the basis of a Commission proposal. However, prior to the Amsterdam Treaty, which also introduced the co-decision procedure on these issues, Parliament was excluded from the decision-making process. In the field of freedom to provide services, which has often been linked with migration policy issues, Article 49 TEC defines the decision-making procedure. Thus the Council acts by a qualified majority on the basis of a Commission proposal, while Parliament has not been delegated any legislative capabilities.

With regard to those interior policy issues that have been part of the first pillar since the Maastricht Treaty, and which are directly linked to migration policies, the powers of both Commission and Parliament are more limited. Thus, in the field of visa policies, ex-Article 100c TEC delegated to the Commission the sole right of initiative. On the other hand, however, this clause was somewhat ambiguously curtailed by ex-Article 100c (4) TEC, which introduced a kind of 'voluntarily shared right of initiative', and which stated that 'the Commission shall examine any request made by a member state that it submit a proposal to the Council'. This provision reflects the caution of member states to communitarize interior policies even when they are legally part of the first pillar. This reluctance is also visible in the Maastricht Treaty's two-stage model for Council decisions on visa policies. During the first stage, until the end of 1995, the Council thus decided by unanimity in the framework of the consultation procedure, in which Parliament only has a power of delay. It was only in the second stage, i.e. three years after the Maastricht Treaty had finally come into force, that qualified majority had automatically been introduced. No changes, however, were made regarding the involvement of Parliament. Finally, the reluctance of some member states to delegate capabilities to supranational actors in interior policies can be observed when looking at the provisions of Article 14 TEC, which deals with the abolition of internal border controls, in which there is no parliamentary involvement. In spite of this exclusion of Parliament, the Commission has the sole right of initiative, while the Council acts with a qualified majority.

Notwithstanding certain limitations to the powers of the Commission and Parliament in the 'classical' first-pillar fields of interior policies, a look at their capabilities in both the third pillar and the migration policy chapter of the Amsterdam Treaty reveals much greater constraints upon their legislative roles. In fact, the provisions of the Maastricht Treaty on JHA closely resembled those on the CFSP. According to ex-Articles K.2 and K.9 TEU, the Commission shared the right of initiative with the member states on both migration policy issues and a possible *passerelle* of migration policies to the TEC. Moreover, following ex-Article K.4(3) TEU, unanimity was required for all decisions, except for implementation measures for joint actions and conventions. In the former case a qualified majority was required, while in the latter case the Treaty demanded a two-thirds majority. The provisions on the rights of Parliament, which were set out by ex-Article K.6 TEU, mirrored exactly the wording on Parliament's powers in the second pillar. Consequently, Parliament had a right of 'information' and 'consultation', but was not able to force the Council or the Commission to inform or consult. Thus Parliament had to rely on good personal contacts with the executive. As one official from Parliament explained, 'we receive a lot of documents informally through good contacts with colleagues in the Commission and Council. Officially, we receive them only after their adoption.'[18] These limitations on the role of Parliament can be interpreted as the result of a strategic alliance of national and European administrations, namely the Commission, being part of the same transgovernmental network in this area, at the expense of both Parliament and non-governmental organizations (Guiraudon 2000: 268).

Thus the transfer of migration policies to the first pillar in the Amsterdam Treaty did not result in a communitarization of this policy area. It is, therefore, not surprising that the provisions of Title IV TEC on the legislative powers of Parliament and the Commission introduce only minor changes when compared to the institutional regime of the Maastricht Treaty. It was only at the end of the transitional period in May 2004 that a complete communitarization was possible, although the Council made only partial use of this (Maurer and Parkes 2006). The legislative procedure in migration policies is set out by Article 67 TEC. It stipulates that during the transitional period the right of initiative is shared between member states and the Commission, while the Council continues to decide on most issues by unanimity. Parliament has only been delegated powers under the consultation procedure.[19] It was only after this transitional period that the Commission was delegated the sole right of initiative, with similar limitations to those outlined above in the case of ex-Article 100c TEC. Thus, even with the sole right of initiative, the Commission 'shall examine any request made by a member state that it submit a proposal to the Council'.[20] While this 'voluntarily shared right of initiative' will be introduced automatically, a complete shift towards a communitarized regime requires the consent of all member states. Consequently, Article 67 TEC introduced a 'new *passerelle*' which envisages a unanimous decision by the Council in order to bring about the co-decision procedure – thus greater parliamentary involvement as well as qualified majority voting – on all migration policy issues.

The only exceptions to these provisions of Title IV TEC are visa policies, an issue which had to a large extent already been part of the first pillar since the Maastricht Treaty. The Amsterdam Treaty thus established a specific regime for those visa issues which were dealt with by ex-Article 100c, these being the positive and negative visa lists on the one hand, and the uniform format for visas on the other. On these two issues the Commission has the sole right of initiative, while the Council acts with a qualified majority. Parliament had been delegated the power of delay under the consultation procedure. The remaining parts of visa policies, namely 'procedures and conditions for issuing visas' and 'rules on uniform format', which became part of the first pillar with the Amsterdam Treaty, are subject to yet another legislative procedure. While these two issues will also be initially governed by the consultation procedure, the co-decision procedure will be introduced automatically after the end of the transitional period. It is striking that this automatic *passerelle* does not cover the 'Article 100' visa issues which seem to be dealt with under the consultation procedure even after the May 2004 deadline, although they had been part of the first pillar since the Maastricht Treaty.

Some minor modifications towards increased communitarization of legislative decisions have, finally, been introduced by the Nice Treaty. Thus the new Article 67(5) TEC stipulates that if the Council has already agreed – by unanimity – on 'common rules' and 'basic principles' in the areas of 'asylum policies' and 'minimum standards for temporary protection of refugees and displaced persons', that all further decisions will be taken on the basis of the co-decision procedure.

The results of this analysis on the legislative capabilities of the Council, Commission and Parliament are summarized in Table 3.2. It identifies in particular the powers of Parliament and the Commission in legislative politics in foreign and interior affairs. Note that the Council is pivotal in every single legislative regime. The table shows the four different institutional constellations under which the Commission participates in the legislative process (horizontal column headings), as well as the six different legislative procedures which relate to Parliament's involvement (vertical rows). The table, therefore, includes all three dimensions on which the analysis of this chapter has been based. Thus it incorporates the voting rules in the Council, the design of the right of initiative and the six legislative procedures. The table does also suggest that there is a qualitative difference with regard to the role of Parliament and the Commission under the various legislative regimes. Thus in the vertical rows Parliament's impact decreases in descending order, whereas the Commission's powers, which are represented in the horizontal column headings, decrease from left to right.[21] A combination of these three dimensions brings up 24 possible legislative regimes, out of which ten directly relate to foreign and interior policies between Maastricht and Nice. The table, moreover, reveals that there has been a minor simplification of legislative provisions with the Amsterdam Treaty. The total number of legislative regimes in both areas has been reduced from eight in Maastricht to seven in the Amsterdam version.

Table 3.2 illustrates further that when comparing the capabilities of the Commission and Parliament, the former has been delegated greater powers in both policy areas. Most institutional regimes are thus located on left-hand side of the horizontal column headings where the Commission can make greater use of its role as an agenda setter due to the predominance of qualified majority voting in the Council.[22] Parliament, in contrast, acts mainly in institutional arenas that appear on the lower side of the vertical rows, in the framework of those procedures in which its role as a co-legislator is severely curtailed.

In Table 3.3 this observation is taken a step further. It provides data on the way in which the capabilities of the Commission and Parliament in foreign and interior policies have developed since the Maastricht Treaty and proposes a quantification of their respective powers.[23] Consider, for example, the 12 different bullet point entries in Table 3.2 which represent each legislative regime in the foreign and interior policies of the Amsterdam Treaty. The 'capability index' presented in Table 3.3 shows that the Commission has profited to a greater extent from the delegation of legislative capabilities compared with Parliament. In fact, when looking at the Amsterdam Treaty, the 'capability index' of the Commission is 77.1 per cent of its maximum score, whereas Parliament only has 35.0 per cent of its maximum powers. Both actors, however,

Table 3.3 Capability indices of the Commission and Parliament in foreign and interior policies: Maastricht and Amsterdam compared

Legislative procedure	Parliament		Commission		Right of initiative/ voting in Council
	Maastricht Treaty	*Amsterdam Treaty*	*Maastricht Treaty*	*Amsterdam Treaty*	
Co-decision	1	2	6	7	Sole/qualified
Co-operation	1	0	3	1	Shared/qualified
Assent	1	1			
Consultation	2	3	2	2	Sole/unanimity
Information	4	2	3	2	Shared/unanimity
No Parliament	5	4	–	–	No involvement
Total number of legislative domains	14	12	14	12	Total number of legislative domains
Capability index Parliament	**28.6**	**35.0**	**76.9**	**77.1**	**Capability index Commission**

Source: Own calculation; parts of this table are presented in Stetter (2004).

Note

This is based on Table 3.2. The indices have been calculated as follows: for Parliament the number of entries in each legislative domain has been multiplied with a 'legislative procedure score' (co-decision = 5; co-operation = 4; assent = 3; consultation = 2; information = 1; no Parliament = 0); for the Commission each entry has been multiplied with a 'right of initiative/voting in Council score' (sole/qualified = 4; shared/qualified = 3; sole/unanimity = 2; shared/unanimity = 1). The 'capability index' is the total sum of these scores divided by the maximum score possible (if all domains were co-decision for Parliament or sole right of initiative/qualified majority for the Commission). In other words, the index is 100 if Parliament had been delegated co-decision in all legislative domains, or if the Commission could act with a sole right of initiative and qualified majority voting rules in the Council in all legislative domains.

have profited from the reform of the Maastricht Treaty and have been delegated more capabilities by the Treaty reforms in Amsterdam. Yet there is only a minimal increase in the Commission's capabilities of 0.2 per cent. The increase in the powers of Parliament has been greater from Maastricht to Amsterdam, but it has to be considered that Parliament is still a far cry from its maximum 'score'.[24] Notwithstanding this remark, Parliament had been delegated new powers in the Amsterdam Treaty that have significantly increased its 'capability index' from 28.6 per cent to 35.0 per cent, an increase of 6.4 per cent.[25]

Moreover, what has to be considered when analysing the results in Table 3.3 is how the powers of the Commission relate to specific legislative procedures. This applies in particular to those parts of foreign and interior policies governed by the co-decision procedure. Here the powers of the Commission are somewhat weaker than under the other types of procedure, since the Commission 'is structurally unable to affect the decisions of Parliament' and the Council, due to the ability of these two actors to come up with their own legislative amendments within the Conciliation Committee, which do not need to take account of the original preferences of the Commission (Garrett 1995: 303). Thus the right of initiative of the Commission under the co-decision procedure is considerably weaker compared with other legislative procedures. However, turning to Table 3.3, these remarks apply to only a small number of legislative domains. Under the Maastricht Treaty only one legislative domain, namely parts of the free movement of persons provisions, was governed by the co-decision procedure. This changed only slightly with the Amsterdam Treaty which extended the application of the co-decision procedure to cover developmental assistance policies as well. However, this is a policy area in which the Commission traditionally holds important executive powers. Therefore, the minor increase of the Commission's capability index must be read in conjunction with the relative weakening of its sole right of initiative in developmental assistance policies since the Amsterdam Treaty following the introduction of the co-decision procedure.

Two main conclusions can be drawn from this analysis of the primary capabilities of supranational actors in foreign and interior policies. First, there are three actors at the EU level that participate in the legislative process and their powers vary considerably. Thus the Council is the only institution that has a strong position in each of the various institutional regimes. There is no piece of legislation in EU foreign and interior policies which does not require a majority of votes in the Council. The Council's role in both areas is, moreover, characterized by the prevalence of the unanimous majorities required to pass a piece of legislation. Notwithstanding this general pattern of Council dominance in many institutional regimes, the Council has to co-operate closely with the Commission and Parliament. Moreover, in all legislative regimes the Commission has a right of initiative. Nevertheless, it often has to share this with the member states. Parliament participates in the legislative process as the second chamber. Its powers, however, are still weak when compared to the capabilities of both the Council and the Commission.[26]

Second, the distribution of powers between these three actors still reflects the logic of the pillar division. Thus, as a general picture, Parliament and the Commission are stronger in the first pillar, whereas their capabilities in the second and third pillars, as well as in the post-Amsterdam migration policy regime, remain more limited. Moreover, the Council often decides by qualified majority in the first pillar, whereas unanimity predominates in all other institutional arenas and also in some first-pillar fields. Thus the pillar division still underlies the legislative dimension in foreign and interior policies. As a rule, primary delegation to the Commission and Parliament has been less pronounced in the sovereignty-related regimes of foreign diplomatic relations and migration policies than in those regimes which are directly related to economic issues. Notwithstanding this general pattern, the capabilities of Parliament and the Commission have overall been strengthened from Maastricht to Nice thus pointing to an increasing centralization of foreign and interior policies at the EU level.

Executive powers of the Commission and the Council Secretariat

When looking at the Treaty provisions on the executive dimension of EU foreign and interior policies, similar conclusions as those on legislative issues come to the fore. Thus supranational actors have been delegated executive capabilities in both areas across all three pillars. On the executive dimension, it was the Commission and the Council Secretariat that were the recipients of this delegation. However, in spite of various cross-pillar linkages, the dividing line between the two types of pillars is also characteristic of the institutional structure of EU executive politics in foreign and interior affairs.

Member states have delegated executive powers in foreign and interior policies across the three pillars to both the Commission and the Council Secretariat. When compared with legislative politics, the institutional structure of executive relations is less complex. Thus, in all regimes that are part of the TEC, the Commission acts as the main executive, whereas in the second pillar, as well as in interior policies before the Amsterdam Treaty, the 'executive core' at the EU level was located in the Council and its Secretariat. Notwithstanding this division of executive powers, both the Commission and the Council Secretariat have been delegated additional powers that allow them to encroach into institutional regimes beyond the narrow pillar confines. Thus, despite these divided executive capabilities, neither the Commission nor the Council can act independently of each other in foreign and interior policies. Under the surface loom various bonds between these two actors, which have installed a system of power sharing between the Council and the Commission within all institutional arenas of foreign and interior policies. Due to the functional indivisibility of both policy areas this 'tandem' relationship between the Commission and the Council shapes foreign and interior policies across the institutional pillar divide (Hayes-Renshaw and Wallace 1997: 179).

In a sense, the EU executive system in the two areas functions like two aeroplanes whose movements have to be co-ordinated. Based on the afore-mentioned pillar division, executive capabilities have been delegated to one of the two actors – either the Commission or the Council – which then steers the 'EU aircraft'. At the same time, however, the second actor sits right next to the captain, thus sharing overall responsibility for the manoeuvres of the aircraft. While in 'classical' first-pillar arenas there is only one plane in the skies, the two-pillar dimension of both foreign and interior policies leads to rather heavy air traffic. There are two planes whose flights have to be co-ordinated above the EU airspace. In one plane, the Commission is the captain while the Council acts as its deputy. The powers of the Council, then, stem from the comitology system which establishes a control system over the Commission's decisions on direction and speed (Wessels 1998). The second plane, which was initially constructed for the second and third pillars, is – following the Amsterdam Treaty – limited to the area of the CFSP and non-migration-related areas of interior policies in the remaining third pillar. Here, the Council is the captain, with the Commission acting as a deputy who might not control direction and speed but who is permanently informed about the course of the aircraft. 'As for the two new pillars of the TEU, here the Council Secretariat and the Council presidency have functions that, under the Community pillar, are the respon-sibility of the Commission' (Hayes-Renshaw and Wallace 1997: 185). As a result of these linkages between the Council and the Commission, the cross-pillar design of foreign and interior policies binds both actors to co-ordinate actions within their respective executive prerogatives if they do not want to risk the two planes crashing. Thus a need for close executive co-operation between the Council and the Commission is an inherent characteristic of the EU's foreign and interior policy system, notwithstanding the more limited 'deputy function' of the Commission in the second and third pillars, when compared with the role of member states in the first pillar.

The primary delegation of executive capabilities in foreign and interior policies has thus led to a system in which the capabilities of supranational actors must be viewed against the background of 'the interface of the EU dual-executive' (Hix 1999: 41). While some parts of this interface are regulated by secondary decisions, which are analysed in the following chapter, important provisions have also been made directly by the Treaties. The interface consists of two elements, which are a complex committee system on the one hand, and a joint responsibility of both actors vis-à-vis other EU institutions and states outside the EU on the other. Comitology is an institutional mechanism that allows both the Commission and the member states to be involved in all stages of policy-making at the EU level (Ballmann, Epstein and O'Halloran 2002; Franchino 2000).[27] However, it is important to stress that comitology functions in a different way when looking at the two types of pillars. Thus in the first pillar the Commission is the main actor for the execution of policies, while the member states are involved at all stages of policy-making via specialized committees. In the second and third pillars, however, the main responsibility for executive policy-making lies with the Council, while the Commission participates within the various committees as a an additional member, albeit without any voting rights and much more reduced powers than member states have in first-pillar committees. Consequently, the structure of executive relations between the Commission and the Council in foreign and interior policies can be described by an X-structure, as exemplified by Figure 3.1. It is important to note again that the member states possess greater capabilities than the Commission across the pillars. Thus member states have a veto power on decisions by the Commission in many first-pillar committees, while the Commission has no such powers vis-à-vis the Council in the second and third pillars (Hayes-Renshaw and Wallace 1997).

However, empirical evidence in foreign and interior policies supports the notion of such an X-structure of executive relations despite the obviously more circumscribed powers of the Commission in the second and the remaining third pillars. For example, in foreign policies the second pillar includes a joint responsibility for the Council (and the Presidency) and the Commission in the external representation of the EU in third countries. Indeed, as far as Middle East policies are concerned, such a joint approach to external representation has been developed between the Presidencies, the Special Representative and the Commission Delegations in the region.[28] This corresponds with the observation that it is 'on a day-to-day basis [that] the Commission and the Council have to find operating procedures to handle external representation' (Hayes-Renshaw and Wallace 1997: 191). Moreover, despite its formally more reduced role in second-pillar decision-making, the Common Strategy on the Mediterranean Region of July 2000 was jointly drawn up by Council and member state officials, together with officials from DG RELEX, thus pointing to the considerable overlap of powers between these two institutions.[29] Thus the need for co-ordination does not primarily stem from formal Treaty provisions, but rather from the requirements of the functional unity of foreign policies.

In interior policies a similar structure of first- and third-pillar executive relations can be observed, although the substantive overlaps between interior policy issues across the pillars is not as firm as in foreign affairs. However, what matters here is that due to an increase of institutional capabilities in the various Treaty reforms, and a parallel increase in personnel resources, the Commission

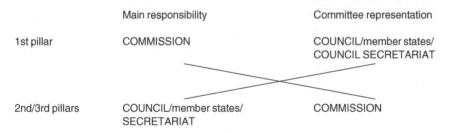

Figure 3.1 X-structure of executive relations in foreign and interior policies.

Source: Own compilation.

has consolidated its representational role in interior policies across the pillar divide (Peers 2000: 43). This has been the case with the Amsterdam Treaty reforms for the remaining third pillar but, of course, also for the shift of migration policies to their current semi-communitarized framework. Given these clarifying remarks on the formally weaker role of the Commission in committee representation in the second and third pillars when compared with the role of member states in first-pillar committees, the X-structure neverthe-less describes well the day-to-day operation of cross-pillar co-operation within the executive in the areas of foreign and interior affairs. From an institutional perspective constant co-operation – rather than competitive battling over formal powers – between the two institutions is required for effective policy-making. Thus, despite an obvious imbalance in the cross-pillar distribution of executive powers, the Commission and the Council

> need to be peddling in the same direction for movement to be sustained. If either brakes hard, movement is virtually impossible. There is a kind of division of labour between the two institutions, but there is also an interweaving and overlapping of functions, not least in the areas of foreign and interior policies.
>
> (Hayes-Renshaw and Wallace 1997: 179)

The Treaties do not specify the comitology relations between the Council and the Commission with regard to every single institutional regime in foreign and interior policies. Hence, in first-pillar arenas of foreign policy, comitology provisions are explicitly outlined only with regard to external economic relations. In the field of developmental assistance secondary provisions on comitology apply.[30] The executive relations between the Commission and the Council in external economic relations are identical for both the Common Commercial Policy and for Association Agreements. In both cases it is the Commission that makes recommendations to the Council on the opening of negotiations with third countries and which then negotiates these agreements. These rules are laid down in Articles 133 and 300 TEC. Both articles refer to a 'Special Committee' which consists of representatives of the Commission and the member states. This committee has to be consulted by the Commission when negotiating international agreements. The Nice Treaty has added two new elements to Article 133 TEC. First, as a result of previous tensions between the Commission and the Council over the interpretation of the relationship between certain provisions of international agreements on the one hand, and internal EC rules on the other, the Treaty now stipulates that compatibility with the Community must be ensured by the Commission and the Council.[31] Second, this consolidation of Community prerogatives in trade policies has been accompanied by a tightening of the control exercised by the member states over the Commission's actions in the negotiating process on international agreements. Consequently, the Treaty now requires the Commission to 'report regularly to the special committee on the progress of negotiations'.

The aforementioned relationship between the executive powers of the Commission and the Council is reversed in the second pillar. The CFSP is characterized by the executive dominance of member states in general, and the Presidency and the Council Secretariat in particular. It is Article 18 TEU that sets out the powers of the Presidency as the key institution in the framework of the CFSP. Thus the Presidency represents the EU on the international stage and is responsible for the implementation of decisions in the framework of the second pillar. It was the Amsterdam Treaty that provided for the strengthened capabilities of supranational actors in that arena. Delegation, nevertheless, only led to a reshaping of capabilities within the Council and it was, subsequently, the Council Secretariat and not the Commission that was delegated a considerable number of new powers. Accordingly, Article 18(3) TEU delegated executive functions to the Secretary-General of the Council, who acts as a High Representative for the CFSP. The specific tasks of the High Representative were further specified by Article 26 TEU which states that the High Representative

> shall assist the Council in matters coming within the scope of the common foreign and security policy, in particular through contributing to the formulation, preparation and implementation of policy decisions, and, when appropriate and acting on behalf of the Council at the request of the Presidency, through conducting political dialogue with third parties.

It should be kept in mind that prior to the Amsterdam Treaty the Council Secretariat, under the guidance of its Secretary-General, has been a central yet mainly administrative body (Hayes-Renshaw and Wallace 1997: 105–9).

The differentiation of an autonomous Secretariat alongside member-state-based Council structures in the area of foreign policies can be dated back to the SEA of 1986 and the subsequent establishment of the EPC Secretariat. As M. E. Smith has pointed out, discussions on a strictly administrative Secretariat emerged in the early 1970s and were mainly led by the German and Italian governments, and later the British government. Thus it was the London report of 1981 that called for the establishment of a small, permanent administrative EPC Secretariat. However, due to French resistance, mainly about the location of this Secretariat, its establishment was deferred until the SEA, when France ultimately accepted that the EPC Secretariat was to be based in Brussels rather than Paris. However, there was no autonomous role for the EPC Secretariat, from an administrative let alone a political perspective. The main task of the EPC Secretariat was to assist the rotating Presidencies and, consequently, its political responsibility was directed towards the Presidencies. The EPC Secretariat also remained small in terms of staff numbers and its personnel was seconded from national ministries. Moreover, member states were careful to separate the tasks of the EPC Secretariat from EC activities in which the Council Secretariat was involved, thereby attempting to prevent any spill-over from EC practices into the operation of EPC (see M. E. Smith 2003: 166–70).

This situation changed with the Maastricht Treaty which can, therefore, be rightfully regarded 'as a critical juncture' for the EU's foreign policy (Lewis 2000: 275). Thus the EPC Secretariat was transformed into the CFSP Secretariat which was now formally integrated into the infrastructure of the Council Secretariat. While the strong linkage between the Council Secretariat in the area of CFSP with the rotating Presidencies was upheld, the Maastricht Treaty nevertheless provided for some incremental, yet highly significant changes towards a greater autonomy of the Council Secretariat in foreign policies. Thus the formal responsibility of the CFSP Secretariat was no longer primarily directed towards the Presidency (a member state) but towards the CFSP as a whole (thus a policy area of the EU). Moreover, the staff of the CFSP Secretariat was almost double that of the EPC Secretariat and officials from the Council Secretariat were added to officials seconded from national ministries. Hence, the provisions of the Maastricht Treaty on the primary capabilities of the Council Secretariat provided for limited, yet significant provisions which fostered the autonomous role of the Council Secretariat as a supranational actor rather than an intergovernmental body of member states. Notwithstanding the significance of this development, the linkages of the Secretariat with member states and other actors within the Council's operating structures remain much stronger than those of other supranational actors. However, 'the new CFSP Secretariat was an improvement over the previous EPC unit' and by delegating primary capabilities to the Secretariat, member states fostered the centralization of EU foreign policies without delegating considerable powers in the CFSP to the Commission (M. E. Smith 2003: 188).

It was, then, the merging of the two offices of the Secretary-General and the High Representative in the Amsterdam Treaty that provided the Secretariat for the first time with a Treaty base that established an explicit political function within the EU system. An official from the Council Secretariat has confirmed such a conclusion when suggesting that, when compared with his 'invisible' predecessor, 'Solana [the High Representative] is something completely new.'[32] This is further exemplified by the establishment of a nucleus of political staff, comparable to the cabinets of individual Commissioners, at the disposal of the High Representative. Thus, the PPEWU, which was established through a Declaration attached to the Amsterdam Treaty, has – in contrast to the Council Secretariat's traditional mainly administrative focus – 'clear policy responsibilities (monitoring, assessments, early warning, and policy options)' (M. E. Smith 2003: 229). Comprising around 20 officials (thus more than the initially 17 officials who worked for the EPC Secretariat in 1986), it was 'expected that this Unit ... would establish greater cooperation among the Commission and EU member states to help ensure the coherence of the EU's external policy', as well as to support the High Representative in building up a political capacity in foreign policies separate from the Commission, which could make use both of its several DGs dealing with foreign policies and of its web of delegations in third countries (M. E. Smith 2003). Indeed, the PPEWU played an important role in strengthening the position of the High Representative in EU foreign policies vis-à-vis the Commission, and it was staff from the Unit who, jointly with the Commission (and member states' officials), drafted the Common Strategy for the Mediterranean Region which was then presented to the European Council in Feira (see Heusgen 2003).[33]

This trend towards both delegation of foreign policy capabilities in the second pillar to supranational actors, and a simultaneous limitation of the Commission's say in this arena, is also exemplified by Article 18(5) TEU which provides the Council with a Treaty base on the appointment of a special representative 'with a mandate in relation to particular policy issues'.[34]

While the Commission is participating alongside the Council on the operative dimension of the CFSP, it does not yield comparable powers as, for example, member states do in the first pillar. The executive powers of the Commission at the EU level, which were originally set out by the Maastricht Treaty, are mentioned in Articles 18 and 27 TEU. Both articles provide for a 'full association' of the Commission in this field. Article 18 TEU additionally provides for a strengthened role of the Commission when compared to the Maastricht Treaty. Thus it not only associated the Commission with the Presidency, but also rendered the Commission part of the EU Troika.[35] Article 27 TEU, then, associated the Commission with all 'work carried out in the common foreign and security policy field', and thus, for example, the work in the second-pillar committees. It is, finally, Article 25 TEU that established such a special committee, the so-called 'Political Committee' (Kiso 1997).[36]

As mentioned above, the role of the Commission in these second-pillar committees is weaker than the role of member states in the first pillar. In addition to this general pattern of member states' dominance, the Amsterdam Treaty added the conclusion of international agreements, which previously were only mentioned in the TEC, to the second pillar. It is interesting to note that Article 24 TEU, which sets out the rules on these second-pillar agreements, duplicates the provisions of Articles 133 and 300 TEC but with reversed competencies. Thus, in contrast to the first pillar, the central role in the second pillar has been delegated to the Presidency. 'Article 24 agreements' can be initiated by the Council and they do not require a prior recommendation by the Commission. It is also the Presidency and not the Commission that initiates and negotiates these agreements with third countries. The Commission can only assist 'as appropriate' the Presidency in this task.

To conclude, the role of the Commission in the comitology system of the common foreign and security policy is largely limited, as the Treaty repeatedly reiterates, to a 'full association', and the Commission lacks any direct influence over the decisions taken within committees or the Council. There is, however, one issue in the second pillar on which the Commission had been delegated stronger capabilities, i.e. the EU's role abroad. In this field, the Treaty establishes a system of co-operation between the executive branches which fosters the X-structure of executive relations in foreign policies depicted in Figure 3.1. It is Article 20 TEU that deals with the relationship between member states' embassies and Commission delegations in third countries, and which stipulates that they jointly ensure the implementation of second-pillar decisions on the ground, as well as exchange 'information, carrying out joint assessments'. It is noteworthy that Commission delegations are not mentioned in the TEC. Their role has until now only been specified within the framework of the second pillar. Since the actual capabilities of Commission delegations relate mainly to trade matters, developmental co-operation and other first-pillar issues, Article 20 TEU is not only an interesting example for the actual legal linkages between the pillars but also of the delegation of capabilities to supranational actors, such as the Commission, beyond the classical Community sphere.[37] As Allen notes on the role of the Commission and the Council in foreign policies, 'the TEU allowed both institutions legitimately to claim a certain competence over *all* aspects of the Union's external activities' (Allen 1998: 51).

The executive relations between Commission and Council in interior policies follow similar patterns as regards foreign policies. In those arenas that are part of the TEC, the Commission is the actor with the main executive capabilities. This is the case, for example, in the field of free movement of persons. As in foreign policies, however, the autonomy of the Commission is constrained by comitology provisions in secondary legislation. This relationship within the EU executive is reversed when looking at the provisions of the third pillar. Within this institutional regime, which came to an end for the area of migration policies with the Amsterdam Treaty, member states bore the main responsibility for executive politics while the Commission was linked to the activities of the Council. In Amsterdam the role of the Commission was strengthened. While the Maastricht Treaty still referred to the Presidency as the main actor for executive politics in the third pillar, the Amsterdam Treaty provided for an increased delegation of powers to the Commission. Due to the shift of migration policies to the first pillar, the Commission was the main recipient of primary capabilities in executive politics in interior affairs. Notwithstanding this development, the institutional rules on migration policies continue to embody key elements of the decision-making structure of the third pillar. Thus, while the Commission has been strengthened as the core executive of the EU migration policy regime, its powers are not comparable to 'classical' first-pillar areas.

The only interior policy committee referred to in the Treaties was the 'Co-ordinating Committee' for third pillar issues according to ex-Article K.4 TEU (Niemeier 1995). This so-called 'K.4 Committee' is comparable in its tasks to the Political Committee of the second pillar. As regards the role of supranational actors, ex-Article K.4(2) TEU stipulated, thus reiterating the wording of the parallel provisions in the second pillar, that 'the Commission shall be fully associated with the work in the areas referred to in this Title'.

The distinction between the executive powers of supranational actors in the first and third pillars has, however, never been categorical. As was the case with foreign policies, from the Maastricht Treaty onwards interior policy provisions also contained rules on the overlapping capabilities of supranational actors. It is thus noteworthy that the Maastricht Treaty defined the powers of the Co-ordinating Committee beyond the confines of the third pillar. This linkage between the pillars was based on ex-Article 100d TEC which extended the powers of the committee to cover those parts of visa policies that were already incorporated into the first pillar. This cross-pillar extension of the K.4 Committee's mandate has been an encroachment on to the capabilities of the Commission – and also COREPER – which, for policies referred to in the TEC, usually deals with member states in first-pillar committees (Lewis 2000).

An important change with regard to the capabilities of supranational actors in interior policies has been the abolition of the K.4 Committee's responsibility for those parts of interior policies that were transferred to the first pillar in the Amsterdam Treaty. Due to this reform, executive policy-making in the area of migration has become one of the Commission's executive competencies comparable to those in other fields, such as free movement, external economic relations or developmental assistance. There is, however, a reservation within the migration policy chapter regarding this transfer of executive capabilities to the Commission which is otherwise atypical of the first pillar. Recalling to a certain extent the provisions on the relations of member states' embassies and Commission delegations in foreign policies, Article 66 TEC calls for a joint executive approach in the migration policies of member states on the one hand, and the Commission on the other. Thus the national ministries responsible for migration policies, as well the Commission, should 'take measures to ensure co-operation' between them in this area. This provision is a reminder that member states continue to keep a watchful eye on how the Commission makes use of its new executive powers on migration policies.

In sum, the Treaties established a cross-pillar system of executive relations in foreign and interior policies. The two bodies that manage the executive dimension are the Commission on the one hand, and the Council and its Secretariat on the other. Unlike in 'classical' first-pillar areas, executive actors operate on the basis of pillarized capabilities. In the first pillar the Commission has the main executive capabilities, while in the second and third pillars the Presidency or the Council Secretariat bear the main role. Both sides are linked in their executive tasks, namely the implementation of policies, through the comitology system. However, while the Council occupies a central space in those first-pillar committees mentioned in the Treaties, the Commission only has a weak role in both the Political Committee and the former K.4 Committee. Thus the pillar division still underlies the institutional structure of executive relations in foreign and interior policies. However, the two Treaty reforms in Amsterdam and Nice have led to a further centralization process on the executive dimension of both areas, thus adapting to the functional cross-pillar dynamics of constituent policies outlined in the previous chapter. While member states maintain the key role, supranational actors, such as the Council Secretariat in foreign policies and the Commission in migration policies, have been delegated considerable capabilities in both areas.

Limited authority delegation to 'control actors'

In both foreign and interior policies supranational actors have been delegated additional capabilities that add to their executive and legislative powers. These additional capabilities are judicial remedy on the one hand, and powers in the budgetary process on the other. In a similar way, as regards executive and legislative politics, it is also in these two domains that the Treaties establish a pillarized distribution of capabilities. Thus, in classical first-pillar arenas, supranational actors have the full right of judicial remedy, thus rendering the Court of Justice a key actor in these parts of foreign and interior policies. In contrast, the provisions on the second and third pillars, as well as those on migration policies following the Amsterdam Treaty, exclude or severely restrict the ability of supranational actors to seek judicial remedy. It is only with regard to the budgetary dimension of EU politics that the pillarized division of capabilities between member states on the one hand, and supranational actors on the other, is less pronounced. Here the usual first-pillar interplay between the Commission, the Council and Parliament extends to almost all institutional arenas of foreign and interior policies. This renders the budgetary dimension the only playing field on which classical communitarized rules apply almost exclusively in both areas. Furthermore, the budgetary provisions equip Parliament in particular with additional capabilities, thus, at least to some extent, balancing the overall marginalization of Parliament in both the second and third pillars as well as the Amsterdam migration policy regime.[38]

In foreign economic relations and developmental assistance, the Commission and Parliament enjoy the complete range of judicial remedy according to Articles 226 and 230 TEC. The former article allows the Commission to start an infringement procedure against a member state at the Court of Justice, to 'ensure that they comply with their obligations under the EU Treaties and under EU legislation' (Hix 1999: 106). The latter article endows the Commission and Parliament with the right to seek a judgement from the Court of Justice on the legality of legislative acts. While the Commission can bring all cases to the Court, Parliament – and also the Court of Auditors – can only bring those cases forward in which they want to protect their own institutional prerogatives. The third procedure is laid down by Article 234 TEC which enables national courts to ask for a preliminary ruling from the Court of Justice.

In contrast to the powers of Parliament, the Commission and the Court of Justice in first-pillar foreign policy regimes, the provisions on the CFSP exclude the Court of Justice from making any judgements in this institutional arena.[39] Neither Parliament nor the Commission nor national courts can seek judicial remedy on second-pillar issues. Until the Nice Treaty came into force, however, there was one important exception to this pillarized structure of judicial remedy. Thus Article 300 TEC, on the basis of which the EU concluded its Association Agreements with the Mediterranean countries, stipulates that 'the

Council, the Commission or a Member State may obtain the opinion of the Court of Justice as to whether an agreement envisaged is compatible with the provisions of this Treaty'. Parliament was thus excluded from judicial remedy in a key first-pillar field of EU foreign policies. It is only with the Nice Treaty that this 'executive bias' has been rectified.[40] The new Article 300 TEC of the Nice Treaty states that Parliament, along with the aforementioned actors, can also make recourse to the Court of Justice on legal issues related to Association Agreements.[41]

The cross-pillar 'judicialization' of interior policies has always been a main demand from both Parliament and the Commission (Stetter 2000). They have based this claim on the strong relationship between interior policy issues on the one hand, and individual rights of EU citizens and third-country nationals on the other. Notwithstanding this demand, the Treaties have until now reflected a pillarized division of capabilities with regard to judicial remedy. Only in those interior policy fields that were already part of the first pillar in the Maastricht Treaty do all supranational actors enjoy judicial remedy without any reservations.[42]

There was, however, no judicial remedy whatsoever for supranational actors in the third pillar, save ex-Article K.2(3) TEU (Drüke 1995; Neuwahl 1995). This article allowed member states to include, by a two-thirds majority in the Council, jurisdiction of the Court of Justice in the provisions of third-pillar conventions. Note that this jurisdiction of the Court of Justice on third-pillar conventions was not mandatory. Also the scope of the Court of Justice's possible jurisdiction should not be equated with its first-pillar prerogatives. In fact, ex-Article K.2(3) TEU stipulated that the Court of Justice has jurisdiction only 'in accordance with such arrangements as they [i.e. the member states] may lay down'.

The reform of judicial remedy in interior policies was a key issue during the 1996 IGC. Notwithstanding the subsequent transfer of migration policies into the TEC, the provisions on the role of the Court of Justice in the Amsterdam Treaty still reveal a significant difference between Title IV TEC on the one hand, and classical first-pillar areas on the other. Thus Article 68 TEC lays down the rules on judicial remedy in migration policies, thereby limiting the role of supranational actors on that issue. First, while Article 68(1) TEC allows preliminary rulings according to Article 234 TEC on migration policy disputes for the first time, this right is severely curtailed. Thus it is only national courts of last resort that can request a preliminary ruling of the Court of Justice on the application of Title IV TEC. Therefore, contrary to all other first-pillar areas, the well-documented 'alliance' between the Court of Justice on the one hand, and lower national courts on the other, cannot materialize with regard to migration policies (Alter 1998). Second, Article 68(2) TEC rules out any jurisdiction of the Court of Justice on issues related to Article 14 TEC, which deals with the abolition of internal border controls.[43] Finally, Article 68(3) TEC limits the capabilities of supranational actors as they are usually provided for by the aforementioned Article 230 TEC. Thus, similar to the pre-Nice

Treaty provisions on Article 300 TEC, only the Commission and not Parliament can request a judgement from the Court of Justice on the legality of acts in migration policies.[44] It is quite interesting to note that the provisions of Title IV TEC even revoke some of the rights of supranational actors for judicial remedy which existed prior to the Amsterdam Treaty. Thus the provisions of Article 68 TEC apply to all parts of migration policies including visa issues. In this field the Maastricht Treaty originally provided for the complete applicability of Articles 226, 230 and 234 TEC. Therefore, the provisions on judicial remedy on visa policies has shifted from a system of complete communitarization towards the more limited system which is now characteristic of Title IV TEC.

Another domain in which supranational actors have been the recipients of primary capabilities in foreign and interior policies are the rules on the adoption of the EU budget. Indeed, budgetary powers are an important institutional resource for supranational actors in both areas. As Laffan explains, 'historically, budgets have been of immense importance in the evolution of the modern state and they remain fundamental to contemporary government' (Laffan 1996: 71). The same conclusions can be reached when analysing the budgetary provisions on foreign and interior policies, although the overall limited size of the budget of constituent policies, which will also be analysed in Chapter 5, should be kept in mind. In fact, it was after the Maastricht Treaty that the three pillars were interlinked by the budgetary provisions in the Treaties and supranational actors were delegated capabilities in that domain.

The budgetary procedure of Articles 268 to 280 TEC is the only direct reference to the first pillar that appears in the provisions on both CFSP and JHA. Thus ex-Articles J.11(2) (now Article 28(4) TEU) and K.8(2) TEU defined the conditions under which the regular budgetary procedure of the EU applies to the second and third pillars. The wording of these articles was identical for both arenas. In the Maastricht version, the Treaty stipulates that all administrative expenditure is charged to the EC budget. Moreover, for each operational expenditure the Council can decide by unanimity that these expenses are charged to the EC budget as well. Without such a decision, operational expenditure would have to be charged to the budgets of the member states.

Due to the transfer of migration policies to the first pillar in the Amsterdam Treaty, all kinds of expenditure in this field now fall under the EC budget. It was, however, also in the second pillar that some reforms on the budgetary provisions were decided, thereby also bringing operational expenditure into the realm of the EC budget. As opposed to the aforementioned provisions of the Maastricht Treaty, the Amsterdam Treaty now makes the EC budget the automatic budgetary basis for all kinds of expenditure. The only exceptions are military expenditure and those cases in which the Council decides by unanimity not to do so. Moreover, Article 28(4) TEU states *expressis verbis* that for all expenditure charged to the EC budget, the first-pillar provisions of Articles 268 to 280 TEC apply. This provision irons out some of the confusion about the unclear wording of the Maastricht Treaty on this issue, where the direct reference to the EU budgetary procedure was only made with regard to operational expenditure, not administrative expenses. The rules on the budgetary process for expenditure on foreign and interior policies are, thus, a prime example of the 'explicit interconnectedness' of the pillars (Regelsberger 1997: 81). From that perspective, it is also interesting to note that Article 268(1) TEC on the budgetary provisions is the only direct reference in the TEC to the second and third pillars.

It is not necessary to embark upon the precise capabilities of supranational actors in the budgetary process which would require a detailed analysis on its own.[45] What matters here is that, due to their capabilities in the budgetary process, supranational actors have indirectly been delegated additional capabilities in foreign and interior policies. This empowerment through the budgetary process strengthens the role of Parliament and the Commission on the legislative, executive and judicial dimensions of foreign and interior policies. Thus, first, with regard to the legislative dimension, the applicability of the budgetary procedure for parts of the expenditure in all three pillars fosters the standing of Parliament as the second chamber in the bicameral EU system. This allows Parliament to encroach into those institutional arenas of both areas in which it has otherwise, due to the provisions of the second and third pillars, been marginalized. The importance of the budget for Parliament's role in all three pillars is thus regularly emphasized by parliamentarians and acknowledged by representatives of other EU institutions.[46]

Second, the budgetary provisions have fostered the role of the Commission. Due to the Commission's overall responsibility for the implementation of the EU budget, this cross-pillar design of the EU budget provides the Commission with a significant leverage vis-à-vis the Council in the framework of the EU executive.[47] Finally, the general applicability of these first-pillar provisions allows for greater control of the acts of EU institutions in all institutional arenas of foreign and interior policies. Thus both the Court of Justice and the Court of Auditors can make use of their powers under the first pillar when dealing with second- and third-pillar issues which directly relate to Articles 268 to 280 TEC. As has been seen, the budgetary provisions provide the means for both a centralization of foreign and interior policies at the EU level and a stronger involvement of supranational actors than originally provided for by the executive, legislative and judicial provisions of the second and third pillars.

Conclusion

The pillarized design of the Treaties with regard to foreign and interior policies is an indication of the reluctance of some member states to delegate capabilities in these two areas to supranational actors. On the one hand, it was the intention of some member states, when drafting the Maastricht Treaty, to establish a pillarized system of governance in which the regulation of both policy areas was split into two distinct institutional arenas. While existing Community powers in both policy areas remained within the already established communitarized framework, these member states attempted to retain tight control over those parts of foreign and interior policies that they regarded as intrinsically linked with national sovereignty and which became part of the Treaty structure at Maastricht. Indeed, this pillarized structure of the Treaties is still central to a proper understanding of EU foreign and interior policies. As a consequence, this pillarization of both areas has also affected the primary capabilities of supranational actors whose role outside the first pillar remains limited. The centralization of foreign and interior policies at the EU level was, therefore, accompanied by the attempt by member states 'to expand and strengthen the Brussels-based machinery ... but to try to contain this expansion and strengthening within the Council structure' (Allen 1998: 55).

On the other hand, however, a more detailed glance at foreign and interior policies reveals that behind this pillar structure looms a complex system which is characterized by multiple linkages between the pillars. The analysis of this chapter on primary capabilities provides evidence for this observation by exposing the degree of delegation to supranational actors across the pillars. Thus it is argued that the role of Parliament, the Commission, the Council Secretariat and the Court of Justice can best be understood when looking at the manifold institutional regimes which come to the surface when looking beyond the pillar structure. Within these institutional regimes, the capabilities of supranational actors can then be differentiated according to the domains of legislative, executive, judicial and budgetary politics. Such an excursion into the labyrinth of supranational actors' capabilities in foreign and interior policies does not only disclose the existence of many cross-pillar linkages but also casts more general doubts over the allegedly sharp demarcation brought about by the pillar structure in both areas.

Along these lines, this chapter suggests that the main differentiation in EU foreign and interior affairs is not along the 'pillar dimension' – the often assumed supranational/intergovernmental divide – but rather on an actor dimension that cuts across the supranational/intergovernmentalist divide (Branch and Øhrgaard 1999; Sandholtz and Stone Sweet 1999). It is argued that the functional cross-pillar dynamics of foreign and interior policies analysed in the previous chapter, namely the linkage of both policy areas with sovereignty, have fostered the role of executive actors at the expense of the legislative and judicial branches. Consequently, the Commission and also the Council Secretariat have emerged as central actors in all institutional regimes of both policy areas alongside member states which continue to hold the key political resources within the EU executive. On the other hand, Parliament and the Court of Justice have not been delegated capabilities which are comparable to their role in those policy areas that are entirely rooted in the first pillar.

Developments in EU foreign and interior policies from Maastricht to Nice, as exemplified in this chapter by an analysis of the primary capabilities of supranational actors, reveal the emergence of a new 'hybrid institutional setting'. Within this member states have attempted to accommodate the requirements stemming from the functional unity of constituent policies at the EU level, as outlined in Chapter 2. Torn between the need to have a joint European approach on foreign and interior affairs and the unwillingness of some member states to give up their traditional national prerogatives in these two areas, this process has led to the emergence of an institutional regime that for the time being remains open to both communitarization and on-going national predominance.[48] While the developments since the Maastricht Treaty in both areas point in the direction of a more centralized approach to EU foreign and interior policies, the way is long and cumbersome. Incremental reforms are also likely to dominate the regulation of both areas in the future. An official from the Council Secretariat has, therefore, asked for patience and stated that 'the Community method is the only way to get somewhere ... But let us not build Rome in one decade. This is too much.'[49]

4 Authority delegation in between treaty reforms

The secondary capabilities of supranational actors

Introduction

Secondary capabilities are defined here as those capabilities which supranational actors derive from secondary legislative acts of the Council in between Treaty reforms. This chapter analyses the secondary capabilities of the Commission, the Council Secretariat, Parliament, the Court of Justice and the Court of Auditors in foreign and interior affairs by looking in greater detail at the two case studies of Middle East and migration policies. The rationale for distinguishing between the primary and secondary capabilities of supranational actors is based on the observation that these two kinds of capabilities differ significantly with regard to the institutional rules from which they originate. This is based on the observation that a mere analysis of the powers of supranational actors, as set out by the Treaties, does not provide the full picture of their institutional cross-pillar capabilities in both areas. While the delegation of primary capabilities requires the unanimous consent of the governments and parliaments of all member states, and even, for some member states, of a popular majority in national referenda, the delegation of secondary capabilities faces many fewer institutional hurdles. Thus secondary delegation does not depend upon recourse to the national level but solely on the adoption of legislation, either by unanimity or by qualified majority, at the EU level, namely within the Council.

This chapter seeks to provide answers to the following questions. How do the provisions of the Treaties on the capabilities of supranational actors in foreign and interior policies relate to the secondary capabilities these actors have over time been delegated in the narrower fields of Middle East and migration policies? What precise capabilities do supranational actors have in the two areas and are there differences between them? And how do these secondary capabilities actually affect the overall pillar design of the Treaties? Finally, how do secondary capabilities relate to the functional dynamics of constituent policies as outlined in Chapter 2?

In an attempt to provide answers to these questions, this chapter argues that the relationship between the primary and secondary capabilities of supranational actors in foreign and interior policies has two dimensions. On the one hand, secondary legislation has 'given flesh' to the provisions of the Treaties, thereby equipping supranational actors with concrete institutional resources across the three pillars on the basis of prior Treaty provisions. On the other hand, secondary legislation has also brought to the fore new capabilities that do not explicitly appear in the Treaties. This is where, from the perspective of the Council, the value added of secondary delegation comes in, since day-to-day decision-making allows member states to delegate authority without the formal requirements relating to overall Treaty changes. In the cases of Middle East and migration policies, secondary capabilities do, thus, both *sustain and enhance* the general dynamics of integration in foreign and interior policies. Seen from that perspective, the delegation of capabilities to supranational actors through secondary legislation allows some of the mismatches between the formally pillarized institutional provisions at the Treaty level on the one hand, and the functional unity of both policy areas on the other, to be 'repaired'. Moreover, secondary capabilities also serve the purpose, on a practical level, of establishing bridges between the pillars. In conjunction with the insights of the previous chapter, it can thus be argued that the delegation of authority has been a key response of the Council to meet the dilemma inherent in any (international) community that aims to undertake collective action (Kiewiet and McCubbins 1991). However, the need for delegation also has a more EU-specific background. Thus the delegation of capabilities to supranational agents across the three pillars can be understood as part of a process of 'institutional gaming' in order to accommodate the need to shift between 'a maze of multiple institutions serving separate and perhaps incompatible purposes' (Goodin 2000: 531). As the previous chapter has shown, while the primary capabilities of supranational agents are strongly affected by the pillar structure of the Treaties in foreign and interior policies, secondary capabilities allow these quite strict demarcation lines between the pillars to be bridged. Secondary decisions, thus, often provided for 'procedural, institutional and functional connections' between the two sides of the 'unbalanced and lopsided' structure of foreign and interior policies (Geddes 2000: 92–3). Somewhat ironically, these bridges stabilize the current institutional equilibrium in EU foreign and interior policies since they allow easier communication across the pillars, while this very pillar structure continues at the same time to be formally characterized by two 'different internal "logics of appropriateness"' (Goodin 2000: 530).

But why is the Council interested in equipping *specific* supranational actors such as the Commission, the Council Secretariat, Parliament, the Court of Justice and the Court of Auditors with certain capabilities in the two areas? It is argued here that the reason for this particular kind of delegation is that the second and third pillars were not created within an institutional void. They are, as has been shown in the previous chapter, due to the functional indivisibility of foreign and interior policies subject to multiple linkages with an entrenched institutionalized structure, namely the EC. Most importantly, this linkage exists on an organizational level and, therefore, delegation to already 'established actors' is less costly than the creation of an entirely new institutional regime with new collective actors (Bogdandy 1999). Moreover, this 'competition' between those parts of foreign and interior policies belonging to the first pillar with those parts related to the second and third pillars often led to a greater emphasis on day-to-day policy-making by the former. This is due to the simple explanation that deciding and implementing concrete policies – in particular those based on expenses from the EU budget – is much easier in the institutional setting of the first pillar when compared to the rules governing the adoption of policies in the two 'intergovernmental' pillars (Monar 1997b). This also had the result that supranational actors were able to make use of their capabilities in the first pillar within the wider cross-pillar foreign and interior policy setting.

This chapter thus provides further evidence for the argument that EU foreign and interior policies are characterized by the emergence of a hybrid cross-pillar institutional regime, which responds to the general functional dynamics related to constituent policies at the EU level. However, while this hybrid institutional regime facilitates a moderate yet significant delegation of capabilities to supranational actors through secondary legislation, it provides at the same time for an exceptionally strong control and guidance function of member states, acting as a *collective* unit in the Council, in the policy-making process and, in particular, regarding the implementation of policies (W. Wallace 2000).

This chapter analyses all secondary decisions in Middle East and migration policies between 1993 and 2003 with regard to the way in which they equipped supranational actors with new capabilities. In migration policies a total of 132 secondary acts were concluded in the Council, whereas in Middle East policies 29 such decisions were made.[1] The main argument put forward here is that secondary decisions have both further strengthened the primary capabilities of supranational actors and enhanced the cross-pillar characteristics of foreign and interior policies.

The structure of this chapter closely follows the design of the previous chapter, thus focusing upon the different institutional domains in which supranational actors have received secondary capabilities. Consequently, the first section analyses the capabilities of the Commission within the executive domain of Middle East and migration policies. The second part then takes a closer look at the capabilities of the Council Secretariat and also analyses the committee control mechanisms deployed by member states to control executive policy-making by the Commission. The third part then looks at the powers of Parliament, the Court of Justice or the Court of Auditors.

The main arguments put forward here are threefold. First, the delegation of capabilities has been a significant element of secondary decisions in EU foreign and interior policies. Moreover, the specific design of these capabilities adds up to and often extends the powers which supranational actors have already received through prior Treaty reforms. This insight spurs further scepticism regarding the argument for intergovernmentalist approaches to European integration which view the time in between IGCs as a mere 'intervening period of consolidation' (Moravcsik 1993: 473). In contrast, this chapter provides evidence that these 'intervening periods' are characterized by the need to accommodate the functional requirements on the policy dimension with the (imperfect) institutional provisions of prior Treaty reforms, inter alia through additional, albeit cautious delegation of capabilities to supranational actors. Second, however, the degree to which supranational actors profit from their secondary capabilities varies considerably *between* them. Thus the Commission and the Council Secretariat in particular have received a wide array of new powers. When compared with the Treaties' provisions, this development has even widened the power gap between the executive centre of foreign and interior policies on the one hand, and the legislative and judicial branches of government on the other. Moreover, the legislative acts, which are analysed in this chapter, do also show that the specific shape of secondary capabilities has fostered the linkages between the Commission and the Council in both areas. As opposed to these two actors, the capabilities of Parliament are more limited and mainly indirect, such as those resulting from the moderate increase of budgetary resources in the two areas. This process allows Parliament to make use of its capabilities as one of the budgetary authorities of the EU. The Court of Auditors has also profited from this 'budgetization' of EU foreign and interior policies and financial auditing has over time become an integral part of all secondary acts which set up projects financed from the EU budget.

Third, differences do also exist between the two policy areas. For example, secondary capabilities in Middle East policies have since the Maastricht Treaty been delegated to supranational actors within both the first and the second pillar, whereas in the Amsterdam Treaty migration policies are characterized by the wholesale transfer of this issue to the first pillar. This relates to the observation that the *two-pillar* structure in foreign policies is part of an institutional equilibrium, whereas the original cross-pillar design in interior policies of the Maastricht Treaty had to be replaced by a structure that integrates strong cross-pillar features into a *single* institutional structure, somewhere halfway between the classical Community model and the previous JHA approach.

Notwithstanding the different institutional designs of the two areas, both are today regulated by hybrid institutional regimes which contain both strong Community and strong member state components (W. Wallace 2000). In the case of Middle East policies this hybrid institutional regime is part of an explicit cross-pillar institutional design, whereas in migration policies the cross-pillar logic is still implicitly embedded within the institutional provisions of Title IV TEC of the Amsterdam Treaty.

The role of the Commission in the EU executive

Secondary capabilities in Middle East and migration policies have been delegated to executive supranational actors in particular. Thus both the Commission and the Council Secretariat have received powers that additionally strengthen their capabilities stemming from the Treaties' provisions. Paying tribute to the integration process of both areas, member states devised a central management and co-ordination role for each of these two actors across the three pillars. This process, combined with the establishment of a complex 'comitology system', has also reinforced the X-structure of executive relations in foreign and interior policies (see Figure 3.1), thus putting in place a system of checks and balances between these two executive agents on the one hand, and between the Commission and the member states on the other (Holland 1999; Uçarer 1999).

While in first-pillar areas the Commission has been the main recipient of secondary capabilities, the Council Secretariat's capabilities can be found in the second and third pillars as well as in those parts of migration policies which originally belonged to the Schengen regime. Due to the transfer of migration policies, including previous Schengen provisions, to the first pillar in the Amsterdam Treaty, the Commission has emerged in that policy area as the main executive actor in the implementation of policies, although it is tightly controlled by member states through the committee system and other control provisions contained in secondary legislation. Middle East policies, on the other hand, are characterized by a rivalry between the Commission and the Council Secretariat with regard to the execution of policies, since both actors have considerable secondary capabilities without a clear distinction between their respective spheres of competence. However, the politicization of the Council Secretariat in foreign policies, highlighted by the establishment of the offices of the Special Representative for the Middle East peace process and the High Representative for the CFSP, not only has potential for competition over scarce executive resources between the Secretariat and the Commission but also for tensions between the Secretariat and the member states (Behrendt and Hanelt 2000).[2] In other words, capability delegation to the High Representative and the Special Representative cannot be understood as a continuation of the previously intergovernmental approach to second-pillar policies but as part of the overall centralization process in EU foreign affairs. It reveals the inherent dilemma of this policy area in which member states try to establish a balance between the functional process of centralizing constituent policies on the one hand, and the legacy of the intergovernmental foundations of the EU's external relations on the other.

The secondary capabilities of the Commission in Middle East and migration policies can be distinguished along four main dimensions. First, in an early period secondary capabilities comprised only certain administrative tasks in the second and third pillars, such as the collection of information, the writing of evaluation reports or the organization of administrative contacts with the member states' ministries and embassies. These *administrative* capabilities had the task of giving meaning to the 'full association' concept of the second and third pillars. Second, in all secondary acts in Middle East and migration policies in which a major new budget line has been created, the Commission has become responsible for the organization and implementation of these measures. These *budgetary capabilities* represent the main new area in which the Commission has received capabilities which was not explicitly foreseen by the Treaties. Third, *legislative capabilities* are a recurrent theme of secondary decisions. Thus on several occasions Council decisions have demanded that the Commission propose new legislation even in those areas in which, according to the Treaties, its right of initiative should be shared with the member states. Finally, *organizational capabilities* have appeared in those cases in which new databases or organizational units were located within the Commission.

It was prior to the Amsterdam Treaty that the capabilities of the Commission were strengthened through secondary decisions. On the one hand, the Commission's right of full association in JHA, yet without voting rights, was reconfirmed by various legislative acts right after the Maastricht Treaty (Myers 1995). On the other hand, the Commission has also acquired capabilities that were not explicitly outlined by the Treaties. Most importantly, since the Maastricht Treaty came into force, the Commission has had the main role in the management of the financial basket of EU migration policies. Thus, prior to the Amsterdam Treaty, seven individual measures with an overall budget of €62.5 million came into force and although all of these measures were third-pillar decisions the Commission had the main administrative role of dealing with these funds (Peers 2000).

When on 20 June 1994 the Justice and Home Affairs Council took its first three decisions on migration policies in the framework of the third pillar, two of these measures directly referred to prior reports from the Commission, thus emphasizing the attention which the Council was willing to give to the Commission's activities in this policy area. First, in its conclusions on the Commission's communication on immigration and asylum policies, the Council publicly signalled that it was willing to accept the Commission's involvement in all institutional arenas of migration policies (Council 1994d). This contrasts with the way in which the Council dealt with attempts by the Commission to be heard on migration policy issues prior to the Maastricht Treaty. Thus the 1991 communications of the Commission on migration were never discussed in the Council.[3] Nevertheless, the welcoming of the Commission as a 'somewhat awkward junior partner ... envisioned as one of 16 actors in the third pillar to take initiative in JHA matters' contained some implicit warnings (Uçarer 1999: 251). While the Council accepted that the cross-pillar approach suggested by the Commission for migration policies 'has the great merit of encompassing the various aspects of these policies', it did not make any suggestions of how to translate the Commission's proposals into law but rather proposed to concentrate on those issues which were outlined by the Council itself as the work programme in this area and to focus upon action in the third pillar only, rather than adopting a cross-pillar approach as suggested by the Commission (Council 1994d).[4] Second, the Council supported the suggestions made in a report by the Commission in which the possible transfer of asylum policies to the first pillar according to the *passerelle* provision of ex-Article K.9 TEU, heavily advocated by Parliament, was rejected (Council 1994c). While the Commission would also have profited from a transfer of asylum policies to the TEC, several member states signalled that they were not at this stage willing to consider this issue, only half a year after the Maastricht Treaty came into force. Due to the unanimity requirements in the Council, the Commission therefore chose to adopt a cautious approach and to refrain from proposing any institutional innovation (Fortescue 1995).

Both measures showed that, on the one hand, the Commission's policy perspectives on migration policies were taken into consideration by the Council but that, on the other hand, the Commission had to be careful when making concrete suggestions, thereby taking into account the reluctance among some member states to go beyond the institutional and policy design of the Maastricht Treaty. Against this background it is not surprising that only one legal measure directly referred to the aforementioned communication from the Commission as a stimulus for a subsequent legislative act, namely a Council decision of 1997 on voluntary repatriation (Council 1997c).

Prior to the Amsterdam Treaty secondary decisions on migration policies did not increase the Commission's capabilities as a strong actor alongside the Council, but rather provided for a stepwise integration of the Commission into the Council's operations on a working level, thereby giving a more bureaucratic and less political role to the Commission (den Boer 1996). Consequently, explicit cross-pillar links with Commission prerogatives in the first pillar remained the exception, and only appeared in two legal measures during that period.[5] Most measures between 1993 and 1999 which entailed provisions on the secondary capabilities of the Commission consequently resulted in giving substance to the 'full association' provision of the Maastricht Treaty, thereby showing that this term had more than a mere rhetorical meaning. The concept of 'full association' comprised mainly administrative tasks which, nevertheless, for the first time involved the Commission in an active way with regard to policy-making in the third pillar. These provisions provided the Commission with the administrative role to gather information relating to migration policies at the EU level. Thus, first, the Commission had the task of collecting information on the implementation of migration policies at the national level. It is not surprising that this role was delegated to the Commission with regard to first-pillar issues such as visa policies (Council 1999a). However, the collection and co-ordination of information was not only taking place in the framework of the TEC but comprised third-pillar issues such as residence permits, voluntary repatriation and asylum policies as well (Council 1996a; 1997b and 1997c).

Second, the Commission had the role of overseeing the implementation of legislative acts and of publishing, either solely or jointly with the Presidency, reports on the implementation of these policies on the ground (see Franchino 2000: 68). Such a role appeared in the aforementioned Council Regulation on a common visa list of 1999, and also in all third-pillar acts relating to asylum policies as well as in provisions on burden-sharing for displaced persons and on unaccompanied minors (Council 1995b; 1996f; 1997c and 1997d). Third, the 'full association' of the Commission also covered some new institutional arenas. This was the case after the entry into force of the Dublin Convention, which provides for rules on determining which member state is responsible for dealing with asylum requests (Convention 1997). Article 14 of the Declaration states that the Commission receives from the Council Secretariat statistical data on national asylum figures. Moreover, Article 18 provides for an integration of the Commission into the work of the committee and the working parties which have been set up under the framework of the Dublin Convention. While all these decisions document the stepwise integration of the Commission into the Council's working structure in migration policies in the framework of the third pillar, they can nevertheless all be interpreted as a logical consequence of the 'full association' foreseen in ex-Article K.4(2) TEU.[6]

However, there have also been two areas in which the capabilities of the Commission have exceeded its pre-existing rights under ex-Title VI TEU. First, the aforementioned decision on burden-sharing for displaced persons equipped the Commission with a shared right of initiative to call for an 'urgent meeting' of the K.4 Committee, which then would have to decide on 'whether a situation exists which requires concerted action by the European Union for the admission and residence of displaced persons on a temporary basis' (Council 1996f). No such right was originally included in the Maastricht Treaty. It is, however, quite striking that there has been a similar provision relating to the primary capabilities of the Commission in the second pillar since the Maastricht Treaty. Thus, ex-Article J.4 TEU established such a shared right of initiative with regard to extraordinary meetings of the Foreign Affairs Council, in particular in emergency situations.

Moreover, the greatest number of the Commission's secondary capabilities in migration policies prior to the Amsterdam Treaty can be found in the aforementioned seven decisions which set up a financial framework for EU migration policies. It can be argued that this development is comparable with an observation made by Kiewiet and McCubbins with regard to the delegation phenomenon in US politics. They have argued that 'nowhere is the logic of delegation more compelling than in the appropriation of funds for the myriad programs and activities of the federal government' (1991: 12). This seems to be equally true for EU politics, although on a much smaller scale.

Thus in 1997 the Council set up two one-year programmes to support displaced persons seeking temporary protection, as well as a programme on behalf of asylum seekers and refugees (Koser and Black 1999). The former programme had a budget of €10 million, the latter of €3.75 million (Council 1997f; 1997g). These programmes were renewed one year later with a budget of €13 million and €3.75 million respectively (Council 1998b; 1998c). The other three programmes are multi-annual programmes (programmes lasting several years) addressing the exchange of officials dealing with the issue of identity documents ('Sherlock'), the issues of asylum, immigration and external borders ('Odysseus') and, finally, support for the reception and voluntary repatriation of refugees from Kosovo (Council 1996c; 1998a and 1999b).

These three programmes, which add up to a tiny amount within the EU budget, comprised funds of €5 million, €2 million and €15 million respectively.

The main role of the Commission in the management of these programmes has been to administer the funds, evaluate and choose project proposals, monitor the implementation of these projects and inform the Council of the results. However, on none of these measures is the Commission entirely free to decide how the budget is allocated. Its autonomy is limited by the establishment of member states' committees which scrutinize the action of the Commission in the management of these funds.[7] It is only below a financial ceiling of either €50,000 or €200,000 that the Commission has been delegated the right to administer these funds autonomously, whereas for all measures above that ceiling the Commission has to seek the support of a majority of member states in the committee. The three measures which set up multi-annual programmes have more detailed provisions on financial management. Thus before the start of each financial year the Commission is asked to write a draft annual plan for the Sherlock and Odysseus programmes which has to be submitted to the committee and be accepted unanimously. Only after receiving this consensual mandate can the Commission proceed to allocate the funds and manage their implementation. Moreover, each year the Commission is required to write an evaluation report on these two programmes, together with the Kosovo fund, which then has to be submitted to the Council and Parliament. It must be noted that the legislative proposals for the three multi-annual programmes have been made by the Commission itself, making use of its right of initiative in the third pillar. In fact, the only Commission proposals which led to secondary legislative acts in this area were those on funding programmes and not on 'normative third-pillar rules' (Peers 2000: 21). This supports the view that member states have accepted the participation of the Commission in migration policies on an administrative level, but also have also shown reluctance to allow the Commission to have a more political or agenda-setting role in this area.

Following the entry into force of the Amsterdam Treaty, this reluctance to accept the more active involvement of the Commission changed, and subsequently, as a result of the transfer of migration policies to the first pillar, more provisions on the Commission's capabilities in migration policies appear in secondary legislation. This new approach became visible during the European Council's special meeting in Tampere on 15 and 16 October 1999. This meeting dealt with the future objectives of the newly established 'area of freedom, security and justice' (European Council 1999b). The conclusions of the Tampere Summit entailed, inter alia, a detailed report on the precise measures to be taken to develop EU migration policies. The secondary capabilities of the Commission appear as a recurrent theme in the Presidency's conclusions, which, for example, provide the Commission with the sole right of initiative with regard to various migration policy decisions. Note that the Amsterdam Treaty foresaw only a shared right of initiative for most of these issues. Table 4.1 compares the suggestions made in the Tampere Conclusions on the

Table 4.1 The Commission's right of initiative: primary and secondary capabilities compared

Issue	Title IV TEC	Tampere conclusions
Developing a scoreboard	–	Sole right of initiative
Asylum applications and subsidiary protection	Shared right of initiative	Sole right of initiative
Common asylum procedure and uniform status	Shared right of initiative	Sole right of initiative
Admission and residence of third-country nationals	Shared right of initiative	Sole right of initiative
Fight against illegal immigration	Shared right of initiative	Sole right of initiative

Source: Own compilation.

Commission's right of initiative with the original provisions of Title IV TEC which, of course, from a legal perspective, enjoyed supremacy over the Tampere provisions.

Thus, following the Tampere meeting, the capabilities of the Commission with regard to its role in the legislative process were increased compared with its shared right of initiative as it appeared in the Amsterdam Treaty. Note that on the issue of visa policies the Amsterdam Treaty did already delegate to the Commission the sole right of initiative. Another important institutional innovation, which resulted from the Tampere Summit, has been the decision to delegate to the Commission the task of proposing a 'scoreboard' on measures to be taken inter alia in migration policies in the years ahead.[8] This entrusted the Commission – in co-operation with the Council and on basis of the Vienna Action Plan and the Tampere Conclusions – with the right to come up with a timetable and a set of issues with which the EU would develop its asylum policy *acquis* (European Council 1998; van Krieken 2000). In addition to these explicitly mentioned new capabilities, the Tampere Conclusions also note some other areas in which the Commission is mentioned as a central actor in EU migration policies. Thus point 12 of the Conclusions entrusts both the Council and the Commission with reporting to the European Council of December 2000 on the work in the High Level Working Group on Asylum and Migration.[9] Also, point 16 asks the Commission to explore the possibility of establishing a system of burden-sharing for displaced persons 'on the basis of solidarity between Member States'.

The Tampere Conclusions, in conjunction with the provisions of the Amsterdam Treaty, pointed to a qualitative shift in the way migration policies were dealt with at the EU level. The Commission profited from this change and fostered its role on both the administrative and the political dimension of this policy area. Out of the ten legislative acts concluded in migration policies between May 1999 and July 2002, eight were based on Commission initiatives, while two measures were based on proposals from France and Germany. Out of the Commission's eight proposals, only two related to visa policies, for which the Commission enjoyed the sole right of initiative anyway. In all these legislative acts new capabilities appeared which further strengthened the Commission's role as a key actor in EU migration policies alongside the member states.

Thus, first, the Commission consolidated its administrative role and was delegated the task of collecting statistical information from member states on their visa policies and on the temporary protection of displaced persons (Council 2000a; 2001a). However, stretching beyond this role of information collector, which was already a characteristic capability prior to the Amsterdam Treaty, the aforementioned legislative acts provide for some steps towards an administrative Europeanization at the national level. In that process several measures render the Commission responsible for managing new EU units, together with national interior ministries (Wessels and Rometsch 1996). Thus, the Joint Supervisory Authority of national ministries deals jointly with the Commission on the implementation of the EURODAC Regulation (Council 2000f). The directive on minimum standards for giving temporary protection stipulates that 'for the purposes of administrative cooperation required to implement temporary protection, the Member States shall each appoint a national contact point' (Council 2001a). The Commission and the member states are responsible for ensuring the co-ordination of their respective activities. Most importantly, in order to give substance to Article 66 TEC, which calls for intense administrative co-operation between the Commission and member states, in June 2002 the Council adopted a decision on a co-operation programme for all Title IV TEC activities, the so-called ARGO programme. ARGO, which is managed by the Commission, should, inter alia, explore whether it is useful to found 'a common training institution' for national civil servants working on EU migration policies, thus further institutionalizing the co-operation within the epistemic community of European and national migration policy experts (Council 2002c). The decision on the European Refugee Fund (ERF) even establishes a hierarchical relationship between the Commission and national administrations by allowing the Commission to pursue on-the-spot checks on the implementation of ERF programmes at the national level (Council 2000d).[10]

Second, the Commission is responsible for the implementation of all major decisions in migration policies after the Amsterdam Treaty that had a budgetary effect. The budget, which the Commission has to administer, comprises, for ERF and ARGO alone, €241 million, thus four times more than all funds administered by the Commission in the years between 1993 and 1999 combined. In the case of the ERF the Commission decides, after proposals from member states, which projects at the national level will be supported by the fund.[11] Five per cent, i.e. €10.8 million, can be allocated by the Commission to projects which are of 'common interest' to all member states. The EURODAC Regulation sets up a Central Unit which is responsible for collecting and managing the fingerprints of those third-country nationals whose data can be stored for that purpose. The Central Unit has been established within the Commission, thereby providing it with another administrative unit within the emerging EU migration policy space (Guiraudon 2000). A similar case of access to expert information has been regulated in the provisions on the uniform format for residence permits for third-country nationals. The secret specifications are known only to the Commission and the responsible member states' institutions (Council 2002b).

Third, the secondary capabilities of the Commission following the Amsterdam Treaty also comprise the task of evaluating the implementation of these various legislative measures and of coming up with regular reports which are then passed on to both the Council and Parliament. Such provisions can be found with regard to the ERF, EURODAC, the common visa list, minimum standards for temporary protection and the ARGO programme. Fourth, three of the aforementioned measures provide for further legislative action and in all of these cases the Commission has received the sole right of initiative. This is the case with regard to the ERF decision, which allows for the allocation of additional funds in emergency situations, following a Commission proposal with a qualified majority in the Council. As far as measures on the common visa list and minimum standards for temporary protection are concerned, only the Commission can initiate new legislation, i.e. adding or removing countries from the visa list or subsidiary legislation on specific temporary protection schemes. However, in both cases the legislative acts stipulate that member states can request the Commission to consider a legislative proposal, thus providing for a form of a 'voluntarily shared right of initiative' similar to the provisions of Title IV TEC, referred to in the previous chapter.

In addition to these provisions in the third and first pillars, an important element of EU migration policies has been those decisions which form part of the Schengen *acquis* and which were integrated into the EU framework following the Amsterdam Treaty. The Commission has some capabilities in this institutional setting too. Thus the Commission was guaranteed in a Council resolution a third-pillar-style 'full association' with the Presidency in the process of integrating the Schengen *acquis* into the EU framework (Council 1997h). This full association certainly had a practical necessity given the overlap between Schengen provisions, for example in the fields of administrative co-operation, visa policies or carrier sanctions, and Title IV TEC provisions on similar issues on which the Commission already had quite considerable capabilities (Collinson 1996). For that reason the Commission was also granted the status of an observer in the Schengen Standing Committee, the Schengen Central Group and the various working groups responsible for the implementation of the Schengen *acquis* (Schengen Executive Committee 1998).

However, it has to be noted that the Commission was quite anxious to avoid a 'Schengenization' of its newly acquired primary capabilities in migration policies after the Amsterdam Treaty came into force, to avoid a penetration of the intergovernmental set-up of Schengen co-operation upon the EU migration policy regime (den Boer and Wallace 2000). Thus, as part of a Council decision on the rules for the allocation of the entire Schengen *acquis* to the first or the third pillar, the Commission issued a statement in which it stipulated that the provisions on the integration of Schengen rules into the EU framework do not encroach upon its traditional executive prerogatives or its role as the guardian of the Treaties. Against this background, it is interesting to note that in two important fields regarding the implementation of the Schengen *acquis* the Commission has received secondary capabilities. First, the Commission has taken the lead in negotiating with Iceland and Norway the rules on the participation of these two states in the Schengen co-operation and it is also the Commission that represents the EU in the Joint Committee set up to discuss bilateral issues between Iceland or Norway on the one hand, and the Union on the other (Agreement 2001).[12] Second, the Commission has the task of developing the second generation of the Schengen Information System (SIS) and, once it becomes operative, to manage SIS II. Management of this database within the Commission thus goes hand in hand with the placement – in the framework of Title IV TEC – of other databases, such as EURODAC, within the Commission.

When compared with migration issues, the secondary capabilities of the Commission in Middle East policies exhibit the greater emphasis on the pillar division in EU foreign affairs. Consequently, in those areas of EU foreign policies that belong to the first pillar, such as trade and developmental issues, the Commission appears to be the actor with the main executive capabilities. Executive capabilities in the framework of the second pillar have, in turn, primarily been delegated to the Council Secretariat, namely the Special Representative and the High Representative. Therefore, with regard to the Commission's powers, secondary capabilities reinforced existing powers rather than adding new ones. Notwithstanding this general division between the pillars, the capabilities of the Commission are not entirely limited to classical first-pillar arenas. In fact, out of the 14 Joint Actions on the Middle East between 1993 and 2002, 13 made direct reference to the Commission and its executive role in the context of these decisions. While these functions do not go far beyond the primary capabilities of the Commission, namely its 'full association' in the CFSP, their purpose is to define more precisely what the Treaty concept of 'full association' actually entails. Some of these Joint Actions do, in addition, directly refer to the first pillar and require the Commission to make use of its foreign policy capabilities in these areas, thus establishing additional cross-pillar linkages to those already foreseen by the Treaties.

The pillarized division of EU foreign policies has to some extent been modified by the EMP, which is also the wider institutional framework for the EU's relations with Israel and Palestine. The objective of the EMP is to establish a 'comprehensive' EU policy towards the region, i.e. a policy that aims to combine all areas of EU foreign policy under one strategic umbrella. Secondary decisions on the EMP, such as the Common Strategy on the Mediterranean Region, consequently require the Commission to make use of its first-pillar capabilities in the framework of the CFSP. While the Common Strategy itself is a second-pillar instrument based on Article 13(2) TEU, most policy measures which the Common Strategy proposes actually belong to the first pillar.[13] This development can be studied with regard to EU relations with Middle Eastern countries. Relations between the EU and Israel have traditionally been based on trade co-operation, given Israel's economic outlook (Ahiram and Tovias 1995). Relations with Palestine, on the other hand, have mainly been based on significant financial assistance, in an attempt to sustain and stabilize the weak economic and political structures in Palestine (Stetter 2003; Jamal 2001).

In both areas, namely trade co-operation and financial assistance, the Commission has had since the 1970s the main responsibility at the European level for the implementation of policies. Thus the EMP allows the Commission to combine these entrenched economic powers with the political objectives of the EU's second pillar. The strong preferences of the Commission in sustaining the institutional framework of the EMP, which will be further discussed in Chapter 6, thus become obvious. First, the EMP has strengthened the first-pillar policies towards Middle Eastern countries, since both trade and developmental assistance policies have been widened in scope compared with the protocol period which pre-dated the EMP. Since in both areas it is the Commission that is responsible for executive policy-making, the EMP has also increased the Commission's capabilities in Middle East policies. Second, since the EMP is a second-pillar instrument, and given the heavy reliance of the EMP on first-pillar policies, the Commission has also fostered its role as a key actor in the EU's overall foreign policy. Seen from that perspective, the debate over who was responsible for the actual establishment of the EMP becomes somewhat subordinate. While some authors argue that the EMP originates from within the Commission (Rhein 1999), some suggest that the actual driving force has been the governments of Spain and France (Barbé 1998), while others see the Commission and southern EU member states as equally responsible in a process of broad interest convergence (Gomez 1998).[14] Yet another question seems to be at least equally important, namely how supranational actors perceive their own role within the EMP. The strong support that the EMP receives from within the Commission, which is discussed in greater detail in Chapter 6, seems to support the argument that the institutional design of the EMP is particularly well suited to fit the Commission's policy preferences.

Notwithstanding the predominance of the Commission's capabilities in first-pillar areas, some of its capabilities do also derive from second-pillar legal measures. As has been mentioned before, out of the 14 second-pillar acts that dealt with the Middle East, only one did not refer to the Commission at all.[15] Although it has to be noted that most of these Joint Actions do not establish a direct transfer of authority to the Commission, but rather delegate authority to the Council Secretariat, the question remains why the Council regularly pointed to the Commission in its second-pillar decisions. It is argued here that, similar to migration policies prior to the Amsterdam Treaty, provisions on the

Commission's secondary capabilities had the purpose of giving substance to an unspecified provision of the EU Treaty, namely the concept of 'full association'. Moreover, the inclusion of the Commission into these Joint Actions has resulted in the establishment of cross-pillar linkages in the EU's foreign policy, thereby facilitating the combination of first- and second-pillar instruments in day-to-day policy-making (M. Smith 1998).

It was the first Joint Action on the Middle East that contained a reference to the role of the Commission in the framework of the CFSP. Thus Article 2 of the Joint Action 'in support of the Middle East peace process' encouraged the Commission to submit first-pillar legislative proposals to the Council on the 'rapid implementation of programmes of assistance' for the newly established Palestinian Authority (PA), as well as 'to provide aid in the framework of existing guidelines' to other Middle Eastern countries which are party to the peace process (Council 1994a). The Joint Action also set up support measures for the creation of a Palestinian Police Force. While the main responsibility for implementing this policy has been delegated to the Presidency, the Joint Action demands 'close coordination' between the Presidency and the Commission, in order to ensure that European and member states' financial assistance to the Palestinians on this issue is co-ordinated.

These two kinds of references to the Commission in second-pillar instruments, namely linkages to its first-pillar capabilities and its responsibility for co-ordination of aid with member states, also form the backbone of the provisions on the Commission's role in other Joint Actions. There are four main dimensions in the Commission's capabilities in these second-pillar acts and it is interesting to note that most of them are similar to the Commission's capabilities in the third pillar prior to the Amsterdam Treaty. First, the Commission's secondary capabilities comprise the task of submitting proposals for further legislation or executive measures to the Council. This was the case in the aforementioned Joint Action in support for the peace process. Moreover, the two Joint Actions which lay down the rules for the EU's observer role in the Palestinian elections of 1996 also provide for such an initiative role for the Commission (Council 1995a; 1995c). Thus the Council Decision in support of the Palestinian Elections asks the Commission to draw up a list of observers for participation in the European Electoral Unit and submit this list to the Presidency which has the main role in deciding on the final composition of the Electoral Unit.

The main feature of the role of the Commission in the various Joint Actions is the establishment of parameters for what the concept of 'full association' entails, and therefore specifying the precise role of the Commission in the execution of policies. Thus full association comprises the right of the Commission to be involved alongside the Presidency in the implementation of concrete second-pillar policies such as the creation of a Palestinian Police Force (Council 1994a). This involvement in the Presidency's activities also related to the decision on the final composition of the Electoral Unit and the guidelines determining its operational capacities (Council 1995c). The various Joint

Actions on the mandate of the Special Representative and the EU Adviser to the Palestinian Authority on security issues also demand such a co-ordination with the Commission (Council 1996d; 1997a; 1997e; 1998d; 1999c; 1999e; 1999g; 2000c; 2000g; 2001b). Full association, finally, also entails the right of the Commission to participate in the second-pillar 'Anti-terrorism Committee' (Council 2000c).

Third, all the Joint Actions that relate to the Special Representative and the EU Adviser, together with the decisions on the Palestinian elections, mention the role of the Commission delegations in the region. Their task is to provide 'logistical support' for the activities of the European Electoral Unit, the Special Representative and the EU Adviser.[16] Fourth, following the coming into force of the Amsterdam Treaty, the two Joint Actions on the Special Representative's mandate also contain more detailed provisions on the financing of his/her activities. It is stipulated in these documents that the budget of the Special Representative is subject to a 'contract' between the Commission and the Council Secretariat. As an emphasis of the linkage between the Council Secretariat and the Commission in Middle East policies – and fostering the twin representative functions of the Secretary-General of the Council and the External Relations Commissioner – the two Joint Actions since the Amsterdam Treaty also state that reports by the Special Representative are to be submitted both to the High Representative and the Commission.

To summarize, the Commission's secondary capabilities in EU Middle East policies that are based on second-pillar instruments have brought more clarity to the question of what 'full association' actually entails, but, on the other hand, have not led to a major increase of the overall executive capabilities of the Commission. The bulk of executive capabilities, as the following section will elaborate in greater detail, has been delegated to the Council Secretariat. However, almost all Joint Actions make direct reference to the Commission and set out the requirement for either the Presidency, the Special Representative or the EU Adviser to include the Commission in executive policy-making, and also require the Commission to make use of its first-pillar powers. Moreover, as already emphasized in the previous chapter, the Commission profits from its diplomatic presence in the region, where it is represented by delegations in Tel Aviv and East Jerusalem. On various issues, such as the Palestinian elections, the mandate of the Special Representative or the activities of the EU Adviser, Joint Actions particularly refer to the need for the Presidency or Council actors to co-ordinate their work with the delegations in the region.

Among second-pillar instruments it was the 'Common Strategy on the Mediterranean Region' of June 2000 that set out the largest number of the Commission's secondary capabilities (European Council 2000). In particular, the Common Strategy documents the interrelationship of and overlap between the first and second pillars and, thereby, the need to link the capabilities of the Commission, on the one hand, with those of other executive actors, on the other. Thus, in the section of the Common Strategy on 'Instruments and Means' the Commission is called upon to make use of its first-pillar powers in the framework of the CFSP, while Article 25 of the Common Strategy reiterates that the Commission will 'be fully associated in accordance with Articles 18 and 27 of the EU Treaty' for all second-pillar acts decided on the basis of the Common Strategy. In the policy-related sections, the Common Strategy no longer differentiates between first- and second-pillar areas, but treats them as functionally indivisible. Accordingly, all executive actors, the Commission, the Secretariat, the Council and the member states are referred to in the Common Strategy as responsible for implementing these policies. The Commission is called upon to actively engage according to its 'competencies and capacities' in the implementation of EU Mediterranean and Middle East policies. Article 34 requires the Commission to submit its proposals for priority action for each incoming Presidency, to contribute to the evaluation of progress, to evaluate the contribution of the Mediterranean partner countries, and if need be to submit proposals for changes to this Common Strategy to the European Council. In none of these tasks does the Common Strategy differentiate between the first and the second pillars. Moreover, the agenda-setting role of the Commission is also strengthened by the decision-making rules in the Council, since subsequent second-pillar decisions pursuant to the Common Strategy are decided by qualified majority. Finally, along similar lines as the aforementioned Joint Actions, Article 31 of the Common Strategy calls for co-ordination between member states' embassies and Commission delegations on the ground.

The strong emphasis that the Common Strategy makes with regard to the role of the Commission must be seen against the background of its executive capabilities in trade and developmental policies in the Mediterranean in general, and Israel and Palestine in particular (Asseburg 2001). In both policy areas the EMP has led to an increase in the powers of the Commission, since bilateral relations between the EU on the one hand, and Israel and Palestine on the other, have been intensified since the inception of the EMP. Thus, following the Barcelona Conference of 1995, the Commission negotiated and implemented the new generation of Association Agreements with both the Palestinian Authority and Israel (Agreement 1997a and 2000; Zaim 1999). In addition, the Commission also negotiated a set of other bilateral agreements with Israel in the areas of government procurement, telecommunications, good laboratory practice and scientific co-operation (Agreement 1997b; 1997c; 1999a; 1999b). With regard to relations with Palestine and Israeli–Palestinian peace projects, the Commission also has the main responsibility for implementing the EU's enhanced bilateral and regional assistance programmes in the framework of the MEDA programme (Beck 1997; Veit and Münster 2002).

The EU trade agreements with Israel and Palestine are mainly technical in nature and, with some exceptions, do not contain detailed provisions on the involvement of particular actors, such as the Commission. With regard to questions pertaining to implementation, the agreements refer to specific bilateral committees in which these issues are discussed. However, these agreements refer to the role of the Commission in ensuring that EC trade rules are adhered to. In other words, the agreements form the legal basis that provides the Commission with the means of making use of its executive capabilities in trade-related matters, as far as this can be done unilaterally. The 1997 'orange juice affair' between Israel and the EU has shown that the Commission can use its first-pillar trade competencies in order to pursue more political objectives.[17]

All bilateral issues between the EU and the two Middle Eastern countries are dealt with in specialized committees which are referred to within the Association Agreements. Until 2000 Israeli–EU relations were institutionally embedded within the Co-operation Council, which was originally established by the EC–Israel Free Trade Agreement of 1975 (Giersch 1980). In this Co-operation Council only trade-related matters were discussed, since its scope only covered EC competencies. However, after the Association Agreement came into force in June 2000, a two-layered structure of bilateral relations was put in place which consists of an Association Council and an Association Committee. The Association Council meets yearly at the ministerial level and comprises the members of the Council, the Commission and the government of Israel. The Association Council decides on the long-term objectives relating to the implementation of the Agreement. It is then the role of the Association Committee to deal with the implementation of the decisions of the Association Council or the problems arising from the implementation of the agreement (Association Council 2001).

With regard to the bilateral relations between the EU and Palestine on trade-related matters a Joint Committee oversees implementation, which was established by the Interim Association Agreement of 1997. In relations with Palestine, the agreement only established a one-layer institutional structure, since the agreement with Palestine was concluded on the basis of Article 133 TEC and only covers EC policies. The cross-pillar approach of the EMP Association Agreements, which are Mixed Agreements on the basis of Article 300 TEC, has only been applied to agreements between the EU and recognized states in the Mediterranean (Paasivirta 1999). The Joint Committee comprises members of the Commission on the one hand, and members of the Palestinian Authority on the other.

These new agreements are an example of the hybrid institutional framework of EU foreign policies as it has been fostered in Middle East policies since the establishment of the EMP. While the Commission was able to consolidate its role in the second pillar, it had to relinquish its erstwhile exclusive executive competencies with regard to the implementation of bilateral agreements (Meunier and Nicolaïdis 1999). The EU–Israel Association Agreement delegates both political and economic capabilities to the EU centre, however, not exclusively to the Commission. Thus it was the Council Secretariat that profited most from this new type of agreement. For example, it is an official of the Council Secretariat and not a Commission representative that acts as the secretary of the bilateral Association Council. Moreover, the Association Council is presided over alternately by the Presidency or by Israel, and the same rules apply to the Association Committee. It is only within this Council-dominated institutional framework that the Commission continues to be responsible for the implementation of bilateral relations on first-pillar issues and, for example, chairs committees related to the first pillar.[18] A different institutional structure applies to those fields of bilateral co-operation that are not covered by the Association Agreement. With regard to these agreements, bilateral issues are discussed by the Commission on the one hand, and members of the Israeli government on the other. This applies, for example, to the role of the Commission in the EC–Israel Research Committee established to oversee the participation of Israel as the only non-European country in the framework programmes for research and development (Agreement 1999a).

The Commission's main executive capabilities, finally, relate to developmental assistance. This area constitutes, moreover, alongside economic relations, the main element of EU bilateral relations with the Mediterranean region. As one official from the Commission stated, 'we have projects and budgets and that is why everybody looks at the Commission'.[19] As part of the EMP, aid to the region has increased compared with the protocol period. As has been mentioned before, Israel does not receive funds from the MEDA budget, except for some joint Israeli–Palestinian projects. Palestine, however, is a major recipient of EU aid. Indeed, there is no other country in the world that has received a similar amount of assistance from the EU as Palestine (Stetter 2003). From 1994 to 1998 the EU committed €653 million in grants from the EU budget and Investment Bank loans to Palestine. In 1999 the assistance amounted to €93 million. The Palestinians receive a per capita support of €258.7 compared to €11.2 for the entire Mediterranean region (West Bank and Gaza 2000).

The Commission is, according to the 1996 MEDA I Regulation, responsible for the implementation of these assistance measures (Council 1996b). Moreover, Article 6 of the regulation stipulates that 'supervision and financial control' can be exercised by the Commission on the spot. The regulation also states that the Commission has the sole right of initiative to submit to the Council, voting by a qualified majority, National and Regional Indicative Programmes, i.e. those programmes that outline the precise scope of assistance measures for Palestine and for joint Israeli–Palestinian projects. The Commission has been delegated the task of writing these national and regional indicative programmes, thereby taking the Council guidelines on these programmes into consideration. Yet these guidelines give the Commission considerable scope since they do not specify in great detail precisely how the programmes should be designed (Council 1996e).

The specialized committee of member states, the so-called MED Committee, must be involved in all financing decisions exceeding €2 million. Increases of less than 20 per cent more that the original commitment can be made by the Commission without re-consulting the committee. Implementation by the Commission includes tasks such as the issuing of tenders for specific projects and the conclusion of project contracts with partners in the region. Moreover, the Commission is also responsible for co-ordinating the allocation of MEDA funds with loans from the European Investment Bank (EIB) to the region. According to Article 12 of the regulation, the Commission advises the Bank in its decisions. With regard to risk capital operations, the Commission is responsible for taking the financing decisions on the implementation of projects suggested by the Bank.[20] Finally, the regulation requires the Commission to submit a yearly report to Parliament and the Council on the operation of MEDA and to produce an 'overall assessment report' every three years. An evaluation of each concrete project must be submitted by the Commission every two years to the MED Committee. The MEDA II Regulation of the year 2000 did not add major new elements to these implementing powers but did emphasize on several occasions the need for better co-ordination between the Commission and member states and quicker disbursement of funds in the region (Council 2000e).[21] Following criticism with regard to the goal attainment of implementation, the major innovation of MEDA II is that the Commission's capabilities now include the task of writing country strategy papers which will form the basis for the allocation of funds.[22]

Gaining autonomy: the powers of the Council Secretariat

The secondary capabilities of the Council Secretariat are greater in the area of Middle East policies than in migration policies. The reason for the uneven distribution of capabilities to the Council Secretariat relates to the differences in the structure of the hybrid institutional setting in the two areas. Thus the two-pillar design of foreign policies has supported the division of executive capabilities at the EU level – on both an administrative and a political dimension – between the two supranational actors, thus inter alia putting in place a system of checks and balances between them. In migration policies, on the other hand, the formal two-pillar approach ceased to exist with the Amsterdam Treaty. As a result of the transfer of the entire policy area to the first pillar, the main executive capacities at the EU level have also been transferred to the Commission. The following section will look both at the role of the Council Secretariat and at the committee control systems established in both areas by member states in an attempt to control executive policy-making by the Commission.

The capabilities of the Council Secretariat in migration policies, which derive from secondary legislation, are significantly smaller than those of the Commission. Moreover, the few references made to the Council Secretariat mainly stem from the period prior to the Amsterdam Treaty coming into force. However, it has to be emphasized that a major institutional resource of the Council Secretariat does not relate to capabilities enlisted in secondary legislation, but rather relate to the day-to-day operations of the Council. Thus the Council Secretariat has, in both areas, a central role, due to its task as a 'provider of agenda and drafts' in this area (den Boer and Wallace 2000: 504). This role also correlates with the perception of officials from the Secretariat on their role in EU policy-making. Thus officials from DG H on Justice and Home Affairs have underlined this perspective and an official from DG E on foreign policies has described the Secretariat's role as an institutional memory of the CFSP as the main source of influence. The tasks of the Secretariat thus comprise the writing of Presidency conclusions, the co-chairing of working group meetings and the writing of agenda notes, i.e. the policy history related to a specific issue. Moreover, the tasks of the Council Secretariat comprise the writing of drafts for Joint Actions and the tabling of informal recommendations to the Presidency on compromise proposals. In the words of one official from the Secretariat, 'we ensure consistence between Presidencies'.[23]

The secondary capabilities of the Secretariat in migration policies are mainly its role as an information provider and a collector of statistics. On this dimension an inverse relationship between the capabilities of the Secretariat and the Commission can be observed. In an initial period, which lasted from 1993 until the Amsterdam Summit of May 1997, it was the Secretariat and not the Commission that on several occasions received the right to collect information on member states' policies and to write reports on specific issues. After May 1997 the Secretariat was no longer responsible for providing this kind of information, and consequently the task was taken over by the Commission. A similar development can be observed with regard to the role of the Secretariat as a management office for databases. The two main databases prior to the Amsterdam Treaty, namely CIREA and CIREFI, were managed by the Secretariat (Council 1994e).[24] Due to its intergovernmental nature, the Secretariat of the Article 18 Committee of the Dublin Convention was also located in the Council Secretariat (Convention 1997).

This development has also affected the role of the Secretariat with regard to Schengen co-operation. While before the Amsterdam Treaty came into force the capabilities of the Secretariat, as defined by secondary decisions, included the collection of information, this came to a sudden end in 1999.[25] As the previous section has shown, it was also in this area that the Commission took over an information-gathering role. A noteworthy case is the SIS. As mentioned before, the second-generation SIS is managed by the Commission. However, the initial decision of the Schengen Executive Committee to award contracts to study the establishment of SIS II stems from April 1997, and thus from a period prior to the Amsterdam Treaty coming into force. At this time, it was the Council Secretariat that administered the implementation of SIS II (Schengen Executive Committee 1997). After the Amsterdam Treaty it was only with regard to the SIRENE network, which sets up the communication infrastructure between national governments in the Schengen framework, that secondary decisions provided for the explicit capabilities of the Secretariat. In two Council decisions of December 1999 and March 2000, the Deputy Secretary-General of the Council was appointed on behalf of the Schengen states to negotiate the contracts leading to a second-generation SIRENE network and to administer the financial aspects of the tender procedures (Council 1999f; 2000b).

In the area of Middle East policies, the secondary capabilities of the Council

Secretariat have played a greater role than in migration policies. This is due to the explicit 'two-pillar structure' that characterizes EU foreign policies. Examples for these capabilities are the establishment of three foreign policy units within the Secretariat. First, in 1996 the office of the EU Special Envoy to the Middle East peace process was created; second, an EU Adviser for security issues was appointed in 1997; and, third, in the Amsterdam Treaty of 1999 the office of the High Representative for the CFSP was created.

It is noteworthy that secondary legislation in Middle East policies has mainly had the purpose of providing for such new capabilities for the Secretariat. Thus all Joint Actions on the Middle East between 1995 and 2001 dealt exclusively with this issue. As a result, there has been a further institutionalization of policy-making capacities at the EU level beyond the first-pillar Community sphere and the establishment of two parallel executive centres for EU foreign policies in Brussels, one being located in the Commission and the other in the Council Secretariat (Forster and Wallace 2000). The rationale behind this approach to strengthen the executive capabilities of the Secretariat in the second pillar can be understood when it is contrasted with the capabilities of the Commission in Middle East policies. Thus the Commission is a collective actor separate from the Council and is equipped with a mandate to operate as the 'guardian of the Treaties'. The Commission enjoys more autonomy than other agents, such as the Special Representative and the High Representative, who are politically responsible to the Presidency and institutionally located within the Council. Moreover, the yearly mandates of the Special Representative provide for much closer control of his activities than the alternative of having the Special Representative's office attached to the Commission.

The first Joint Action which provided for the creation of capabilities at the EU level dealt with the creation of the European Electoral Unit which had the task of observing the first Palestinian elections in January 1996. Notwithstanding the significance of this decision, the Electoral Unit was a 'single issue agent' only and its mandate expired after the elections. In an attempt to permanently strengthen the political weight of the second pillar as a counterweight to the Commission's executive powers under the TEC, the Council then decided in November 1996 upon the creation of the office of an EU Special Envoy to the Middle East peace process. His mandate was limited to one year and until 2003 it had been prolonged five times, the last time in that period being 2001.[26] From an institutional perspective, the mandate of the Special Representative is interesting for two reasons. First, it underlines the importance of secondary delegation in EU policy-making. Consider that no such office was foreseen by the Maastricht Treaty, which in fact was very cautious with regard to the centralization of the CFSP. The creation of the office of the Special Representative was, in comparison with the creation of a Treaty base, less costly. As mentioned before, the institutional requirements for a Joint Action are significantly fewer than those for Treaty changes. As a result, Joint Actions are also under less public scrutiny, and member states, which at Maastricht might have resisted such a move, can enter more easily into institutional experiments. If need be, the mandate could also more easily be revoked than a much more solid Treaty base. Overall, the experiment seems to have worked satisfactorily from the perspective of member states since it was, finally, the Amsterdam Treaty that provided for an explicit Treaty base for the appointment of Special Representatives (Peters 2000).

The capabilities of the Special Representative have gradually increased. Initially, he had a mandate to establish links with the various 'parties to the peace process' in the region and at the international level.[27] His mandate also comprised the task of directly reporting to 'Council's bodies' on his activities and the results of his work. This close linkage with the Council is also highlighted by the institutional anchoring of his office, which since 1996 has been permanently located within the Council Secretariat, although this was not explicitly outlined in the various Joint Actions. Moreover, the Special Representative is politically responsible to the Presidency. While the mandate remained unchanged in 1997, a Joint Action of October 1998 provided for some widening in the scope of his responsibilities. Thus the Special Representative should now also participate in the 'EU–Palestinian Security Committee', which was created in early 1998. Following the coming into force of the Amsterdam Treaty, the mandate of the Special Representative underwent a reorientation with regard to political responsibility. While Article 3 of the Joint Action of December 1999 still renders the Special Representative responsible to the Presidency, it also establishes an indirect responsibility to the High Representative via the latter's role in assisting the Presidency. This new hierarchy within the Secretariat is further highlighted by Article 5 of the Joint Action which stipulates that reports by the Special Representative will only be distributed to the Presidency or the Commission after they have been channelled through the office of the High Representative. Finally, the Joint Actions on the Special Representative's mandate also provide for institutionalized linkages with the Commission, thus documenting the close co-operation between both actors on the ground. Thus since 2000 all Joint Actions on the mandate state that 'the management of the operational expenditure shall be subject to a contract between the Special Representative and the Commission', thereby formalising the practice between both institutions which has existed since 1996.

The second agent that has been equipped with executive capabilities is the EU Adviser on counter-terrorism in the Palestinian Territories, whose mandate dates back to a Joint Action of April 1997, which was regularly renewed until 2003 when the activities of the EU Adviser came to an end. The EU Adviser is politically responsible to the Presidency and his main task has been to advise the Palestinian Police Force on counter-terrorist measures and, since 1998, to participate in the EU–Palestinian Security Committee. Since the coming into force of the Amsterdam Treaty, the EU Adviser had, moreover, the chance to make recourse to an increased budget since an EU multi-annual assistance programme for counter-terrorist measures had been introduced with a total of €10 million. The mandate of the EU Adviser furthermore called for a co-ordination of his activities with the Special Representative as well as with the High Representative.

The High Representative has not been subject to an individual Middle East Joint Action, but has been mentioned, as has been shown, in the various Joint Actions since 1999 as hierarchically superior to the Special Representative and the EU Adviser, thus providing for new communication channels within the Secretariat. This new relationship is well documented by the Common Strategy on the Mediterranean Region in which the role of the High Representative in the second pillar is referred to on equal terms with the Commission's role in the first pillar. However, the Common Strategy does also document the somewhat experimental structure of the Secretariat. Thus Article 25 of the Common Strategy does not – as opposed to the wording of the Joint Actions – render the Special Representative politically responsible to the Council or the Presidency, but rather gives political responsibility to the High Representative. Consider the different wording of both second-pillar instruments. The Common Strategy states that 'for the aspects of this Common Strategy falling within the CFSP ... the High Representative for the CFSP, supported by the Special Envoy ... shall assist the Council and the Presidency'. In contrast, the Joint Actions on the mandate of the Special Representative usually have the following provision: 'The Special Representative shall be responsible for implementing his mandate ... in consultation with the Presidency, assisted by the ... High Representative'. Thus both documents state that the High Representative 'assists' the Presidency, yet there is a somewhat blurred institutional anchoring of the Special Representative. According to the Common Strategy his role is to support the High Representative, whereas according to the Joint Action his political responsibility is primarily directed towards the Presidency which he has to 'consult'.

Provisions on committee control in secondary legislation

After the Amsterdam Treaty, all secondary decisions which provide for the Commission's executive capabilities with regard to the implementation of migration policies contain provisions on committees which oversee the implementation. Given the reluctance of some member states to fully communitarize migration policies, this seems to support Franchino's argument that 'the establishment of control procedures is also the result of substantive issue-specific conflict' (2000: 66). Therefore, he concludes, 'more conflictual policy issues are invariably linked to their [i.e. control committees] establishment' (2000: 86).

Before the Amsterdam Treaty came into force, such committees were only put in place for those seven third-pillar decisions for which the Commission managed the budget for specific programmes in migration policies. Two kinds of committee procedures were set out for these financial decisions. In both cases the Commission had responsibility for minor expenses, whereas above a certain ceiling the committee had a veto power on Commission proposals. Thus, in those programmes that established administrative co-operation between the

Commission and national ministries, namely the Sherlock and Odysseus programmes, the Commission needed to submit a draft annual programme to the committee which had to adopt this programme unanimously. In case the committee rejected the draft annual programme the Commission had either to withdraw it or to present it to the Council where, however, unanimity was required for its adoption. In the Sherlock and Odysseus programmes, as well as for those funds earmarked for the repatriation of refugees, two committee procedures applied. On the one hand, for projects of less than €50,000 the Commission only had to take 'full account' of the committee's decision taken by qualified majority, i.e. the Commission was not bound by the vote. On the other hand, projects above that sum required a positive vote by the committee by qualified majority. Otherwise the project either had to be withdrawn or presented to the Council which then decided by qualified majority.

With regard to the four other programmes, which established EU funds for displaced persons, asylum seekers and refugees for the years 1997 to 1999, as well as the Kosovo emergency funds, three committee procedures were set out. For programmes that comprised expenses of less than €200,000 the Commission did not need to submit proposals to the committee and could implement the measures immediately. For those programmes that required a budget of between €200,000 and €1 million the committee voted with qualified majority on the Commission's proposal. Nevertheless, the vote of the committee did not have any binding effect upon the Commission's decisions and the Commission only needed to take 'full account' of the committee's vote. Last, for projects which required a budget of more than €1 million, the Commission needed the support of a qualified majority of the committee. If it failed to gain that support, the Commission either had to withdraw its proposal or submit it to the Council which then decided by qualified majority. As opposed to first-pillar comitology provisions, these decisions did not specify what would happen if the Council failed to take a decision within the time limits set out by the secondary acts. In the first pillar, however, it was the practice that the Commission could then start to implement the measure in question.

Since the Amsterdam Treaty came into force, migration policy has shifted to the first pillar, and the five decisions which have been adopted since 1 May 1999 and which refer to committee procedures all make direct reference to the Comitology Regulation of June 1999 (Council 1999d). Table 4.2 summarizes those comitology procedures which have since been applied to the areas of migration and Middle East policies. There is a significant variation with regard to the 'degree of freedom' the Commission enjoys under these three procedures (Hix 1999: 42). Thus under the advisory procedure the Commission is not bound by the opinion of the committee. In the management procedure member states' representatives have greater influence on the activities of the Commission but they need to gather a qualified majority in order to reject Commission proposals, i.e. a *negative majority* has to be formed. Member states have the greatest say over the Commission's proposals in the case of the regulatory committee. Here Commission projects need the support of a

Table 4.2 Committee procedures on migration policies after the Amsterdam Treaty

Procedure	Decision-making process
Advisory (Article 3)	1. Commission submits draft measures to committee;
	2. Committee gives opinion (within time limit) to Commission, formal vote not necessarily required;
	3. Member states can ask to have their opinion recorded in the minutes;
	4. Commission should take 'utmost account' of the decision. It should inform committee on how it has taken the opinion into account.
Management (Article 4)	1. Commission submits draft measures to committee;
	2. Committee gives opinion (within time limit) to Commission by a qualified majority;
	3. Commission can implement immediately if committee supports the measure *or fails to adopt an opinion*;
	4. Commission has to defer the measure for a maximum of three months if the committee does not support the measure and in that case submits the measure to the Council;
	5. Council can take a different decision within this three-month period. If there is no decision the Commission can implement the measure.
Regulatory (Article 5)	1. Commission submits draft measures to committee;
	2. committee gives opinion (within time limit) to Commission by a qualified majority;
	3. Commission can implement immediately if committee supports the measure;
	4. Commission must submit measure to the Council (and inform Parliament) if the committee does not support the measure *or fails to adopt an opinion*;
	5. Council can reject the proposal within three months. Then Commission has to present new proposal. If there is no decision the Commission can implement the measure.

Source: Council (1999d); own compilation.

qualified majority in the committee in order for the Commission to proceed with implementation. If there is no such *positive majority* in the committee, the Commission can only hope that the Council fails to form a qualified majority against the project. In that case the Commission can implement the project. Note that with regard to the aforementioned financing decisions prior to the Amsterdam Treaty, the committee procedures closely resembled the provisions of the advisory committee for minor expenses and the regulatory committee for all expenditure above a certain ceiling, which gives a tighter form of committee control (Ballmann, Epstein and O'Halloran 2002).

For first-pillar decisions in migration policies, the advisory committee has been put in place for both the ERF and those decisions of the ARGO programme on which there has been prior agreement between the Commission and the committee. However, these decisions are overseen by a management committee, and this can thus be described as the dominant committee procedure for issues relating to the ARGO programme. The regulatory procedure applies to EURODAC decisions and the execution of policies by the Commission with regard to the uniform format for visas on the one hand, and residence permits on the other.

Finally, in the context of the Schengen co-operation, comitology procedures have been used to define the relationship between the Commission and the member states in the execution of policies. This has been the case with regard to the SIS II which is developed by the Commission. Article 4 of the Council Regulation contains a detailed list of issues on whose implementation the member states have reserved an oversight role in the framework of the regulatory committee. For all those decisions taken by the Commission that do not appear on that list, the management procedure will apply (Council 2001c).

The establishment of a committee control mechanism also characterizes secondary decisions in Middle East policies across the pillars. With regard to the second pillar, the aforementioned Joint Actions on the establishment of an EU assistance programme on counter-terrorism in Palestine provided for the establishment of a specialized committee of member states' anti-terrorism experts – and Commission representatives – which has the task of advising the Presidency. The Presidency, however, according to Article 3 of the Joint Action, has the final say over 'specific implementing decisions'. This procedure could thus be described as a 'light advisory committee', since the Presidency must consult the committee but is not bound by the vote, nor does it have to take 'utmost account' of the opinion of the committee, as is the case for the Commission in regular first-pillar advisory committees.

The major area in the framework of the first pillar in which committee control applies is the area of developmental assistance. When implementing MEDA, the Commission has to consult a specialized committee of member states' experts. The MEDA I Regulation of 1996 establishes such a committee, the so-called MED Committee. The regulation provides for a regulatory committee-type procedure (ex-procedure IIIa): thus a relatively tight control system. Accordingly, the MED Committee decides by qualified majority on proposals by the Commission. If the committee supports the measure, the Commission can implement it. However, if there is no qualified majority or if the committee fails to vote, then the measure has to be submitted to the Council, which must decide by qualified majority in order to allow for implementation. The Commission can implement the measure, if the Council supports it or has not acted within a period of three months. As is discussed at length in Chapter 7, this tight control has led to various problems with regard to the implementation of MEDA funds. Against this background, the MEDA II Regulation of 2000 provides for the replacement of the regulatory committee by a management committee, in which the Commission's degrees of freedom are higher. However, this relaxation of committee provisions must also be seen against the background of the intensity by which the MED Committee must be involved by the Commission in the implementation of MEDA assistance. Thus, the so-called 'project circle' comprises six institutional layers, of which the MED Committee is directly involved in five, thus ensuring that member states keep track of executive policy-making by the Commission at all stages of the implementation process.[28]

On the sidelines: the role of Parliament, the Court of Justice and the Court of Auditors

The executive bias, which was already quite pronounced with regard to the primary capabilities of supranational actors, is even stronger when secondary capabilities are considered. Provisions on the secondary capabilities of Parliament and the Court of Justice are rare, and consequently most of these two actors' capabilities stem from the provisions of the Treaties. With regard to secondary decisions on Middle East and migration policies it should, however, be noted that secondary decisions on several occasions provide for an oversight and control function of the Court of Auditors for those decisions in which the Commission has to operate with the EU budget.

Parliament has not received any new capabilities as a result of secondary decisions on migration policies.[29] References to Parliament in the various measures only emphasize its 'right of information'. Thus, prior to the coming into force of the Amsterdam Treaty, three out of the seven financial measures, namely the Sherlock, Odysseus and Kosovo programmes, stated that the Commission must forward its yearly evaluation of these programmes to both the Council and Parliament. In addition, the Odysseus programme goes one step further than Sherlock and also requires the Commission to inform Parliament about the decisions taken within the committee that oversees the functioning of Odysseus and to report back to the Council on Parliament's view. Since the Amsterdam Treaty came into force the right of information appears on a regular basis in most secondary decisions with regard to both migration policies and Schengen co-operation. Thus, mid-term reports or evaluation reports by the Commission are forwarded to the Council and Parliament with regard to the ERF, EURODAC, minimum guarantees for temporary protection, the ARGO interministerial co-operation programme, and the development of SIS II. Moreover, with regard to the activities of the Central Unit of EURODAC, Parliament is also kept informed about the way in which the Commission aims to ensure data protection with regard to the information stored in the Unit.

In Middle East policies Parliament has some minor secondary capabilities both in the first and second pillars. There were references to Parliament in the first two Joint Actions on Middle East policies. In 1994, the Joint Action in support of the peace process announced that if there were to be Palestinian elections, as foreseen by the Declaration of Principles between Israel and the PLO, 'Parliament will be invited to participate in those arrangements'. This was the case one year later when the Council decided in a Joint Action that out of the 300 members of the European Electoral Unit 30 would be members of the European Parliament. With regard to the first pillar, it has been one of the side-effects of the new generation of Association Agreements that Parliament has been acknowledged as an institutionalized actor in bilateral relations. Thus Article 74 of the EU–Israel Association Agreement requires the Association Council to facilitate 'cooperation and contact between the European Parliament and the Knesset'. This interparliamentary dialogue also exists at the multilateral level of the EMP, and four interparliamentary forums were held in which representatives of all 27 national parliaments and the European Parliament participated. In 2004 the Forum was 'updated' into an interparliamentary Assembly, which met in Athens in 2004 and in Cairo in 2005. Against the background of this institutional arrangement it is quite telling that inter-parliamentary co-operation in the framework of the EMP has not been mentioned at all in secondary Council acts but only in the conclusions of the various Barcelona follow-up conferences. For example, the Common Strategy on the Mediterranean Region does not contain a single reference to the European Parliament or to interparliamentary co-operation.

Finally, secondary decisions on Middle East policies provide for the right of Parliament to be informed about the Commission implementing decisions on developmental assistance measures. Thus the MEDA Regulations stipulate that Parliament must be regularly informed by the Commission about the implementation of assistance and that Parliament, together with the Council, should also receive the Commission's yearly implementation reports.

References to the Court of Justice are even more meagre. As Guiraudon has argued, this 'circumscribed role of the ECJ is testament to its influence in other areas of European integration and its expansive jurisprudence on the free movement of workers' (2000: 262). In the entire migration policy *acquis* since the Maastricht Treaty, with regard to both EU and Schengen co-operation, there is not a single reference to the Court of Justice, save the Association Agreement for Iceland and Norway to the Schengen *acquis*. Articles 9 and 10 of this agreement lay down the rules for the involvement of the Court of Justice. Thus, if a request for a preliminary ruling reaches the Court of Justice regarding the application of the Schengen *acquis* in the member states, the governments of Iceland and Norway are allowed to submit written opinions to the Court of Justice on the pending issue. In secondary acts of the Council in Middle East policies there is no reference to the Court of Justice.

Thus, while Parliament and the Court of Justice did not gain much from secondary decisions, this is not true for the Court of Auditors. While there is no direct reference to the Court of Auditors in the Treaties' provisions on foreign and interior policies, several secondary decisions provide for specific capabilities for the Court of Auditors. Thus the Court of Auditors is entitled to implement audits on the management of the EU budget by the Commission in the case of the Sherlock and Odysseus programmes, the Kosovo emergency funds and the ARGO programme. Also with regard to the Schengen co-operation, financial audits have been established with regard to the management by the Deputy-General of the Council Secretariat of the SISNET project. Articles 47 and 48 of the Council Regulation provide for the auditing of the account, which is managed by the Secretariat, by the Court of Auditors.

The Court of Auditors also has capabilities in foreign policies. Consequently, it was referred to in the Joint Action on support for the Palestinian elections, where it was given the right to control the expenditure of the European Electoral Unit. Also, in the framework of Israeli–EU scientific and technical co-operation, the Court of Auditors was given the right to pursue financial audits in Israeli research organizations that participate in the framework programmes. Finally, the MEDA Regulations provide for the auditing of the aid projects implemented by the Commission and also encourage the Commission to take the findings of reports by the Court of Auditors into consideration when implementing its policies.

Conclusion

The insights of this chapter on the secondary capabilities of supranational actors build upon the prior analysis on their primary capabilities. Responding to the functional cross-pillar dynamics related to constituent policies, both foreign and interior policies are subject to a 'partial Communitarization' on the institutional dimension as well; the former policy area with an explicit emphasis on the pillar structure, the latter, since the Amsterdam Treaty, with a mixture of first- and third-pillar rules under one institutional umbrella (Kostakopoulou 2000). This hybrid institutional design of both areas has also affected the secondary capabilities of supranational actors. On the basis of this observation, the leading questions, which were introduced at the beginning of this chapter, can now be readdressed.

Secondary decisions on Middle East and migration policies have, as a general rule, contributed to fostering and, on some occasions, even increasing those capabilities of supranational actors in both areas that stem from primary delegation. Applying a demand-and-supply perspective can only partially help in understanding why this has been the case (Pollack 1997). This is because the question arises why member states have not already delegated these additional capabilities to supranational actors in the Treaties. It is argued here that the different majority requirements relating to Treaty reforms on the one hand, and secondary Council acts – irrespective of whether they are made by unanimity or by qualified majority – on the other, account for this variation. A second reason for the delegation of secondary capabilities to supranational actors, however, pertains to the manifold linkages between the pillars in the implementation of concrete legislative acts in Middle East and migration policies. Due to these overlaps and due to the emphasis on first-pillar policies and instruments in both areas, the capabilities of supranational actors within the two hybrid institutional regimes were fostered by secondary decisions.

Second, a pattern, which has already been observed in the previous chapter, again becomes visible. Thus, when looking at secondary capabilities of supranational actors, the power gap between the EU executive and the other branches of government becomes even more obvious. An interesting exception to this rule, however, concerns the references to the Court of Auditors in secondary decisions. In a sense, this follows Pollack's verdict that 'almost every EC institution besides the Commission plays a role in monitoring and checking the Commission's behaviour' (1997: 116). The advantage, from the perspective of the executive, of a delegation of capabilities to the Court of

Auditors and not to Parliament or the Court of Justice is that the Court of Auditors is much less subject to 'shirking' than the two other institutions. Nevertheless, the bulk of secondary capabilities which have been delegated in both areas were directed towards the Commission and the Council Secretariat. The Commission is tightly controlled by member states' committees in those areas in which it has taken over the main role with regard to the implementation of policies. Yet it has to be noted that in both Middle East and migration policies committee control has slightly decreased over time, with greater emphasis on management committees, whereas prior to the Amsterdam Treaty regulatory committees prevailed.

All this suggests, third, that the pillar structure continues to shape the overall capabilities of supranational actors in both areas but it is doing so under the pressure emanating from the functional dynamics to which both policy areas relate. This is the background against which the approach by member states of using secondary legislation in an attempt to iron out the major problems stemming from the two-pillar structure of foreign and interior policies can be understood. Thus the secondary decisions analysed in this chapter indicate that the distinction between the pillars has decreased in between Treaty reforms as a result of secondary legislative acts, thereby challenging intergovernmentalist approaches on these 'intervening periods' in between IGCs. Notwithstanding this development, the nature of change in EU foreign and interior policies continues to be incremental.

This chapter has also shown that in both areas there has been a huge number of secondary decisions. Ten years after the integration of foreign and interior policies into the EU framework, these two areas have become an integral part of the EU political system, and legislation has given substance to the functional frame that structures policy-making in the two areas.[30] The following chapter will embark on this substantive dimension in greater detail. However, this should not avert attention from the shortcomings relating to both policy areas. Decision-making still suffers from a lack of political leadership and a subsequently strong emphasis on first-pillar areas in the case of foreign policies and on budgetary programmes and projects in both areas. Overall, this lack of leadership has until now prevented the emergence of comprehensive foreign and interior policies at the EU level that would set out a strategic direction, comparable to a governmental programme. As W. Wallace notes, 'incremental policy-making, learning by doing rather than strategic choice, marks both these major policy domains' (2000: 535). The primary and secondary capabilities of supranational actors appear in a different light when confronted with this lack of strategic underpinning. Indeed, as this chapter has shown, supranational (executive) actors certainly do have capabilities, but the question remains, what for? 'Given the fact that there is no common vision, civil servants are deprived of clear direction' (Niessen 1996: 62).

To conclude, for the time being a key characteristic of EU foreign and interior policies is that the institutional equilibrium in both areas has somewhat stabilized in relation to the functional indivisibility of constituent policies and that the system is flexible enough to accommodate gradual reforms through day-to-day legislation. With the integration of foreign and interior policies into its political system the EU has nevertheless entered into new territory. For Europhiles, the good news ten years after the Maastricht Treaty is that the costs of reversal have become very high (Pierson 2000a). This is, however, also true with regard to radical changes in the other direction, which might calm those who prefer both areas to be tightly linked to national institutions. However, the precedent has been set: the EU has its own foreign and interior policies and supranational actors have taken over considerable capabilities with regard to policy-making in these two areas. By drawing from examples from US politics, Kiewiet and McCubbins have shown what unforeseeable consequences the delegation to new actors of seemingly piecemeal powers might entail. Thus events which 'present no serious problems ... until long after the precedent had been set' have finally unfolded when 'times changed' (1991: 10). We do not know when times will change, and certainly the future shape of EU foreign and interior policies remains open. But the analysis of the primary and secondary capabilities of supranational actors provides some indication that the process of the centralization of constituent policies is already well under way, albeit slowly.

5 Substantive cross-pillar linkages in foreign and interior affairs

The cases of EU Middle East and migration policies

Introduction

The analysis of this chapter aims to elucidate the ways in which the substantive decisions in EU Middle East and migration policies across the three pillars relate to the functional unity of the policy areas of EU foreign and interior policies at large. The chapter focuses in particular on the question of how substantive decisions in both areas relate to an EU-specific insider/outsider distinction and how this relationship has underpinned the manifold substantive cross-pillar linkages that characterize day-to-day decision-making in both areas, thereby consolidating not only the pervasiveness of the institutional cross-pillar linkages, which have been analysed in the two previous chapters, but also fostering the actual significance of constituent policies for the EU political system. On this basis, this chapter relates to the integration of EU foreign and interior policies. How is integration of both areas at the EU level proceeding and what is the precise relationship between substantive decisions in the field of constituent policies and the pillar design of foreign and interior affairs? Moreover, what kind of policies in foreign and interior policies does the EU actually provide for? What are, from a substantive perspective, the dynamics of integration in constituent policies in contrast to other policy types?

A mere institutional analysis of decision-making rules in both areas would hardly suffice to explain the fundamental process of integration in two areas so closely linked with a traditional understanding of national sovereignty. As Vivienne Jabri has argued, such a traditional perspective regards the nation as the primary 'location for discursive and institutionalised practices, which at the same time lead to the emergence of both legitimacy and exclusion' (cited in Diez 2002: 191). Integration in foreign and interior policies is challenging these practices and necessitates focusing on the ways in which new, sovereignty-related discursive practices consolidate as a result of day-to-day decision-making in both areas. As already argued in Chapter 2, centralizing constituent policies at the EU level establish entirely new patterns of inclusion and exclusion. Accordingly, this new location for discursive and institutionalized practices differentiates between the EU and EU citizens on the one hand, and third countries and third-country nationals on the other (Morris 1997b; Mitchell and Russell 1996). Antje Wiener has demonstrated how the incorporation into the Treaties of such 'constituent policies' opens up new and often unintended pathways on the dimension of the 'social construction of Europe' (Wiener 2001; Christiansen, Jørgensen and Wiener 2001). Hence, when analysing the integration of constituent policies, not only should the function of communication as a provider of meaning regarding *material factors* such the legal and political pervasiveness of these decisions be taken into consideration but also the *associative factors* of discursive ascriptions of meaning, since 'both factors influence the behaviour of actors in the process of policy implementation' (Wiener 2001: 79, my translation). This chapter therefore argues that the actual significance of the integration process in foreign and interior policies cannot only be measured against the background of its incremental, piecemeal and overtly cautious nature on the 'material factors dimension'. Additionally, the associative function of constructing a new inside/outside dimension through substantive policies in both areas has to be accounted for. This analysis thus takes note of the insight that 'social order presupposes ... some underlying mental order based on fundamental distinctions between that which is included and that which is excluded' (Lapid 2001: 13). The institutional and actor-related cross-pillar linkages of EU foreign and interior policies cannot be sufficiently accounted for without an additional focus on the functional frame to which these policies relate, i.e. the social construction of the EU as a location of 'foreign' and 'interior' policies, thus ascriptions traditionally associated with the Westphalian state (Caporaso 1996). The characteristic features of this functional frame will be detected by analysing the way in which both areas have, from a substantive perspective, become firmly embedded at the EU level.

The emergence of an insider/outsider dimension of the EU is thus regarded as a critical juncture of EU politics since it introduces an additional notion of sovereignty, on top of rather than instead of a hitherto nationally defined understanding of 'foreign' and 'interior'. The integration of these two policy areas at the EU level, based on the 'associative factor dimension' of an 'inside' and an 'outside', has some far-reaching consequences which are more than the sum total of the *acquis* in both areas. Or, to use a phrase by Etienne Balibar, 'what can be demarcated, defined, and determined maintains a constitutive relation with what can be thought' (1998: 216).

The central role of this functional frame, which provides the discursive reference point for substantive decisions in both areas, in no way suggests that centralizing foreign and interior policies is a smooth, 'coherent' or predetermined process. On the contrary, the fundamental political significance of constituent policies renders integration of this policy type inherently difficult. Indeed, both foreign and interior policies are characterized by a gradual, cautious, often incoherent and highly incremental integration process. A focus on the general path of integration, however, supports the notion of a gradual centralization of both areas at the EU level, starting from an initially intergovernmental focus and progressing towards the consolidation of an explicit

EU framework. The role ascribed here to functional frames should, however, not be confused with (neo-) functional theories of European integration (Sandholtz and Stone Sweet 1998). While it can be argued that spill-over effects from market integration played a part in bringing foreign and interior policies onto the EU agenda, they cannot sufficiently account for the underlying dynamics within these specific areas. The functional perspective developed in this book is based on a different understanding of what the concept of 'function' entails. Function is henceforth defined as the 'policy logic' which stems from the functional frame within which specific policy areas are embedded, i.e. the functions a policy area has for a specific political system such as constituent policies (i.e. foreign and interior policies) for the EU as a political entity at large. By analysing EU foreign (Middle East) and interior (migration) policies from the Maastricht Treaty onwards, this chapter argues that when looking at the policy history of both areas a gradual increase in substantive cross-pillar linkages and a greater political significance of substantive decisions in both areas which underpin the insider/outsider distinction can indeed be observed. As already mentioned in Chapter 2, this approach resembles notions of 'path dependency' and 'cultural frames' as they have been put forward by historical and sociological institutionalism (Pierson 1996, 2000b; Fligstein and Mara-Drita 1996; Mahoney 2000). In a similar way, this book also argues that formal rules, institutions and actors do not operate in a vacuum, but have to be analysed in relation to the larger historical and functional dynamics which structure the way in which actors and institutions operate.

This chapter is divided into four main sections. The following part takes a look at the internal and external factors which initially brought foreign and interior policies onto the European policy agenda. It addresses both spill-over effects from market integration and external stimuli. While both factors certainly had some share in explaining why foreign and interior policies emerged onto the EC/EU policy agenda, they alone do not suffice to identify the ways in which the integration of both areas developed after they both became part of the EU political system with the Maastricht Treaty. The second section of this chapter then accounts for the way in which foreign and interior policies have become formally integrated at the Treaty level. It argues that constituent policies are characterized by a 'Treaty paradox'. The actual incoherence of foreign and interior policies on the institutional dimension, exemplified by the pillar divide, is matched by a coherence on the polity dimension, as provided for by the concept of the 'single institutional framework'. While changes to the initial Maastricht model of greater centralization have occurred, these changes have, at the Treaty level, been highly incremental. Third, and notwithstanding this observation, the *acquis* in both areas points to multiple substantive overlaps between the pillars. The development of these substantive cross-pillar linkages in both areas, which is more than just the accumulated stock of single decisions, can thus be conceptualized as the gradual consolidation and underpinning of the functional frame of constituent policies. Hence, while integration on the dimension of substantive policies has been cautious and rather piecemeal, a *notion of the common* has emerged in which the EU, through policy-making in foreign and interior policies, develops and fosters the insider/outsider distinction related to both policy areas (see also Cederman 2000; Huysmans 2000a; Neumann 2000; Leitner 1997). The final section then turns to the way in which the development of constituent policies at the EU level has impacted on the budget of the Union. It is shown that the general patterns in the integration of constituent policies have also left their mark on this dimension. While there has been a significant increase of budgetary resources in the two areas, this increase at the same time reflects the cautious and incremental approach of giving solid substance to both policy areas.

On the basis of these four key observations, this chapter therefore attempts to specify how the substantive cross-pillar linkages relate to the functional frame of an EU-specific insider/outsider distinction. Noting that this integration process is a highly incremental endeavour, the integration of foreign and interior policies into a 'single institutional framework' with the Maastricht Treaty can nevertheless be seen as a 'critical juncture' in EU history, not so much because these 'new' policy areas have in any way replaced national policies in foreign and interior affairs, or because these policies would be very efficient, but rather because the provision of policies in both areas at the Union level is a key element in the construction of a territorial and authoritative dimension of the EU.

Spill-over effects, external pressure and integration in foreign and interior policies

While this book argues that the integration of foreign and interior policies on the substantive dimension can be explained by focusing on the ways in which policies relate to the overall functional frame of constituent policies, there are, of course, important environmental factors which are relevant for the development of EU foreign and interior policies and in particular the original appearance of these policies on the EC/EU policy agenda. Two of these factors will be briefly outlined in this section, namely the internal context of spill-over effects from market integration and the external context of international developments.

Spill-over effects from market integration had a considerable impact on bringing both foreign and interior policies to the European policy agenda. As far as foreign policies were concerned, policies on the so-called 'low politics' dimension of foreign economic relations have gradually developed at the EC level. With some resistance, particularly from the French government, the Commission already in the late 1960s, for example, 'sought to enhance its status through formalizing diplomatic relations with missions from third states in Brussels' (Forster and Wallace 2000: 463). As Michael E. Smith has argued, the 'initial creation' of co-operation in the area of 'high politics' in the intergovernmental framework of the 'EPC could be viewed in part as a product of functional or sectoral "spillover" [since] it was intended to augment the expanding economic policies of the EC' by an intergovernmentally dominated setting (1998: 305). In time, various linkages between the EC and EPC frameworks developed and were somewhat codified by the SEA of 1986. However, the two settings were not formally integrated under one roof until the Maastricht Treaty of 1993. This also points to the limits of a mere neo-functionalist account of developments in European foreign policies. Thus, in spite of the spill-over potential, the economic and diplomatic settings of EU foreign affairs today reveal significant differences with regard to both institutional rules and the content of policies. In other words, developments 'can not be treated in terms of supranational institutionalism or federalism' (1998: 332). What can be argued, however, is that the institutionalization of 'an intensive transgovernmental network' in EPC and CFSP as well as the increase of linkages between these settings and the EC proper can be understood against the background of the various functional overlaps between the various parts of foreign policies stretching across quite divergent institutional settings (Forster and Wallace 2000: 489; M. E. Smith 1998: 311–15). Such arguments on institutionally fragmented yet functionally connected policies can also be brought up when looking at EU interior policies. Thus, as Geddes has pointed out, 'free movement is central to the contemporary EU, while immigration and asylum are not' (2000: 43). The functional logic can indeed account for linkages between economic policies and these two settings. Hence, the integration of interior policies into the EU framework has brought the EC setting on the one hand, and the intergovernmental or transgovernmental settings on the other, closer to each other. This movement, however, occurred 'against all the conventional wisdom of neofunctionalist theories, yet driven by functionalist imperatives' (den Boer and Wallace 2000: 518). Spill-over effects might have initiated and sustained integration across the pillars but cannot account for the direction, shape and speed of integration.

> Free movement chimes with the EU's fundamental market-making purposes, but has brought with it immigration and asylum policy co-operation and limited integration. These connections between free movement and immigration and asylum demonstrate the blurred distinction between 'low' and 'high' politics that arises because of the ways pressure can build for integration in policy areas that impinge directly on state sovereignty as a result of integration in areas where national sovereignty issues are less pronounced and where economic interdependence is more clearly evident.
>
> (Geddes 2000: 43)

It is to this limited extent that spill-over effects had a role in initiating the integration processes of constituent policies. Neo-functionalist accounts thus rightly point to patterns of sectoral coherence of specific policy areas but largely fail to reflect upon the specific functional features of different policy areas.[1]

It was not only developments within the EC or the EU that shaped the integration of foreign and interior policies. In addition, developments external to the EU also had an impact upon the policies of the Union. For example, the evolution of the Yugoslav crisis during the 1990s functioned as a 'painful learning process' for EU foreign policies and provided a reference point for subsequent internal reforms with regard to both policies and institutional provisions (Forster and Wallace 2000: 477). A similar impact of events in the 'outside world' on the shape of European policies can be observed in Middle East policies. Thus, because of objections from the Unites States and Israel to EC Middle East policies, mainly on the issue of the inclusion of the PLO in peace negotiations, the EC was kept on the sidelines throughout the 1980s (Greilsammer and Weiler 1988; Hollis 1997; Robin 1997). It was only after the Oslo Agreement between Israel and the PLO that the US and Israel softened their stance on a European role in Middle East politics. Indeed, the multilateral setting of the peace process, set up at the 1991 Madrid Conference, was the (economic) platform on which the EC and later the EU could place its efforts to increase its leverage in the region (Hollis 1994).[2] The external stimulus provided for by the peace process gave the EU various other opportunities to become engaged in Israeli–Palestinian relations (Peters 1996; Salamé 1994). EU policies on the Middle East are also affected by the actual state of bilateral relations with the United States (Watzal 1995). Volker Perthes has argued that 'US–European differences on the Middle East, and on Middle East policies, are largely linked to developments in the region' (2002b: 53). EU–US differences have in particular emerged in periods of stalemate for the peace process when the EU blamed the United States for not sufficiently using its alleged influence on Israeli politics (Hadar 1996; Marr 1994). In contrast, the EU had a modest political role in the peace process, in particular during periods of Israeli–Palestinian rapprochement when a policy consensus between the Union and the United States could more easily be evoked. This was the case prior to the drafting of the 1999 Berlin declaration of the European Council and during the establishment of the Mitchell commission in the year 2000 (Perthes 2002b: 54).

A similar impact of external developments can also be detected with regard to interior and migration policies (Collinson 1994). International migratory movements are not under the control of the EU, and due to its geographical and economic disposition 'one has to expect constantly high immigration pressure' towards the Union (Klos 1998: 21, my translation; Sassen 1996). Indeed, the various waves of intergovernmental co-operation on migration policies had 'over the two decades before Maastricht been largely responsive to perceived threats and public anxieties' as well as to 'changing patterns of migration [which] provided a second set of pressures for closer cooperation' (den Boer and Wallace 2000: 495). The fall of the Iron Curtain, as well as migratory pressures resulting from the Yugoslav wars, underline the significance of these external variables. But an increase in clandestine migration in southern regions of the EU, originating mainly from Arab countries, sub-Saharan Africa, Kurdish-populated areas and Albania, has also added another stimulus to previously less concerned member governments to seek co-operation on migration policy issues at the EU level (Baldwin-Edwards 1997).

The single institutional framework and institutional fragmentation

As has already been outlined in detail in Chapter 3, constituent policies are, on the Treaty level, characterized by the fragmentation of policies across quite divergent institutional regimes. Indeed, the pillar structure of the Maastricht Treaty splits up the two areas of foreign and interior policies into two main blocs – one located in the 'classical' EC pillar, one in the newly established 'intergovernmental' pillars of the CFSP and JHA.[3] EU foreign and interior policies are subject to an inherent tension which can be viewed as a paradox between the institutional fragmentation and the functional unity of both policy areas. The Treaties divided both areas into two (rather than three) separate pillars with the objective of avoiding a 'contamination' between the two separate 'pillar logics' (Denza 2002). At the time of the Maastricht Treaty, as far as foreign policies were concerned, external economic relations and developmental assistance measures were part of the EC pillar, whereas diplomatic foreign policies (and security measures) were integrated into the CFSP framework. In interior policies, economic free movement provisions and parts of visa policies belonged to the EC pillar, while asylum and immigration (as well as policing and judicial co-operation measures) were part of the JHA pillar. Subsequent Treaty reforms did not fundamentally alter this institutional division of the two functionally unified policy areas. Hence, the Amsterdam Treaty upheld the clear-cut division between the EC and CFSP in foreign policies. As regards JHA, migration policies did shift to the EC pillar but this area still resembles key features of the third pillar. While the pillar logic was thus to some extent weakened for interior policies – note that police and justice co-operation still belong to the third pillar – there is still third-pillar path dependency in migration policies (Majer 1999: 123–4). The Nice Treaty did not provide for further changes to this pillar divide and has had no further impact on the fundamental principle of a divergent policy framework for constituent policies.

The pillar metaphor refers to the principle of separate and independent institutional frameworks as they exist in theory (Moravcsik 1998: 449–52). The aforementioned objective to avoid cross-pillar contamination is even explicitly referred to in the Treaties. Hence, in the view of the drafters of the Treaty, ex-Articles L and M TEU provided for a clear-cut division between 'supranational' and 'intergovernmental' frameworks.[4] Ex-Article L TEU restricted the powers of the Court of Justice mainly to the EC pillar, with the only possible exception being conventions in the JHA framework, thus 'protecting' the second and third pillars from encroaching EC powers. In a similar way, ex-Article M TEU aimed to ensure the 'integrity' of the EC pillar by providing that nothing in the

TEU 'shall affect the Treaties establishing the European Communities or the subsequent Treaties and Acts modifying or supplementing them'. The Amsterdam Treaty changed these provisions only in detail. Thus, Article 46 TEU (ex-Article L) continues to limit the powers of the Court of Justice, most notably in the second pillar. The reach of the Court's jurisdiction was only marginally extended to cover, with clear restrictions, the remaining third pillar, the (newly incorporated) provisions on closer co-operation and the provisions of Article 6(2) TEC with respect to the EU on fundamental rights. The newly acquired competencies of the Court of Justice on migration policies were subject to considerable limitations, as discussed in Chapter 3. Finally, no changes to these provisions were made by the Nice Treaty.

This *pillarized framework* is, however, less solid and less exclusive than the pillar metaphor suggests. It stands in an inherent tension with the parallel concept of a *single institutional framework*. The provisions on this single institutional framework are set out in Article 3 TEU. This article states that 'the Union shall be served by a single institutional framework which shall ensure the consistency and the continuity of the activities carried out in order to attain its objectives while respecting and building upon the *acquis communautaire*'. This suggests that the separation of the pillars is less strict than it appears when looking at the aforementioned restrictive provisions only. Article 3 TEU establishes connecting points between the pillars on two dimension. First, on the policy dimension it calls for the 'consistency' of EU policies, independent of their Treaty base. While this provision applies to all pillars, it is elaborated further by the second paragraph of Article 3 TEU regarding foreign policies. This article lays out that 'the Union shall in particular ensure the consistency of its external activities *as a whole* in the context of its external relations, security, economic and development policies' (my emphasis). Second, on the institutional dimension the provisions of Article 3 TEU ensure the participation of various actors across the three pillars and refer to the European Council (Article 4 TEU) as well as the EP, the Council, the Commission, the Court of Justice and the Court of Auditors (Article 5 TEU). Moreover, Article 3 TEU provides for the joint responsibility of two different executive actors for EU foreign policies. 'The Council and the Commission shall be responsible for ensuring such consistency and shall co-operate to this end. They shall ensure the implementation of these policies, each in accordance with its respective powers.'

The concepts of the single institutional framework of the Maastricht Treaty and of the consistency of EU policies, first introduced in the EPC provisions of the SEA, were meant to solve co-ordination problems arising from this paradox between institutional fragmentation and functional unity (Nuttall 2000: 25–7). In contrast to the Maastricht Treaty, the provisions of the SEA on EPC were careful in clearly separating foreign policy co-operation from traditional EC tasks. However, it was already Article 30(5) SEA that addressed the problem of split competencies in foreign policies between EPC and EC frameworks, and which delegated to both the Presidency *and* the Commission the task of seeking and maintaining the 'consistency' of European foreign policies

(Macleod *et al*. 1996: 412). Consistency, thereby, took on at least three different connotations. First, policies in both settings should not be 'inconsistent with each other'; second, policies in both settings should be co-ordinated 'in the service of an overriding purpose' and, third, policies should reflect the ultimate authority on European policies and, therefore, ensure that 'EC external policies were to be subordinated to the political control of ... the Member States' (Nuttall 2000: 25–6). The Maastricht Treaty's provisions on interrelated but separate pillars did then not change the general problem of consistency, namely that 'there were still to be two modes of foreign-policy making' (2000: 181). However, in line with the aforementioned arguments in a slow but significant process of centralization of constituent policies at the EU level, the Maastricht Treaty provided for some important changes. First, in contrast to the SEA, the Maastricht Treaty brought the three pillars of the Union under one institutional heading, namely the EU. Second, in the area of foreign policies, the task of ensuring consistency was no longer the responsibility of the Presidency (a single member state) and the Commission but rather the joint responsibility of the Council (a collective European actor) and the Commission. This was more than a mere change in semantics and must, in the light of the arguments presented in Chapter 2, be seen as a further step towards the cautious centralization of EU constituent policies.

Having said this, it must be emphasized that the Treaties have not yet solved the paradox of two formally separate pillars which *at the same time* are part of a single institutional setting. Inconsistencies in the application of consistency not only occur in day-to-day policy-making in cross-pillar politics, as for example in the co-ordination of developmental assistance or in the use of economic sanctions, but have even led to obvious contradictions in the Treaties. Thus, Article 13 TEU, which sets out the responsibilities of the Council in CFSP, stands in marked contrast to the aforementioned joint responsibility of the Council and the Commission for the consistency of EU external activities as set out by Article 3 TEU. Thus Article 13 TEU states, surprisingly, that it is the Council alone that 'should ensure the unity, consistency and effectiveness of action by the Union'.

As this discussion on the Treaties' provisions show, the ultimate relationship between the pillar structure on the one hand, and constituent policies on the other, cannot be determined from mere Treaty exegesis. Treaty provisions are neither self-explanatory nor coherent. They rather institutionalize the aforementioned paradox between institutional fragmentation and functional unity without providing guidelines on how this paradox should be solved in practice. However, what the Treaties do is to recognise the indivisibility, from a functional perspective, of foreign and interior policies as an integral part of the political system of the EU. At the same time, the Treaties leave open the question of what the linkage between the pillars should look like in practice. This underlying tension thus points to the dynamic potential of EU foreign and interior policies. While a certain distinction between the two kinds of pillar has been codified and is upheld by the Treaties, the Treaties integrate all parts of both policy areas into the EU framework, thus formally ending the division of constituent policies into an EC setting and a strictly intergovernmental framework.

The policy history of EU Middle East and migration policies: fostering cross-pillar linkages

When looking at the policy history of Middle East and migration policies, three main features come to the fore. First, the pillar distinction shapes but does not determine the substantive policies in both areas across the three pillars. Second, a process of centralization of policies in both areas, as well as a modest convergence across the pillars, can indeed be observed on the substantive dimension. This has not culminated in a harmonization of policies into 'single' foreign and interior policies but has fortified the insider/outsider distinction and documents the consolidation of this functional frame of constituent policies. Third, the integration process is characterized by its incremental and piecemeal nature rather than by grand decisions.

European foreign policies towards the Middle East were, prior to the Maastricht Treaty, based on two only loosely connected policy tracks in the frameworks of the EC and the EPC. Moreover, the characteristic features of these two settings also provided the background against which Middle East policies within the 'single institutional setting' developed. Thus the origins of EU Middle East policies can be traced back to the 1970s. Two main approaches can be identified and this chapter argues that the noteworthy development of the post-Maastricht period was not so much the continuation of these approaches but rather the incremental process of integration across the pillars fostering the insider/outsider distinction.[5] The first policy approach was developed within the EPC setting and builds upon the 'classical' intergovernmental EPC method of declaratory policies. It is based on consensual agreement between member states and resembles working features typical of IOs, such as emphasis on consensus and declarations rather than concrete action. It not only defined the European approach to certain issues, but was meant to lead to the convergence of national interests in the area of foreign affairs. The second approach shows a striking similarity to what has been identified as a key feature of West German foreign policies prior to unification. Thus the EU is also characterized by its economic weight on the one hand, and its constrained political reach within the international arena on the other, and could, therefore, be described as an 'economic giant' and a 'political dwarf'. Indeed, bilateral relations of the EC with Middle Eastern countries were mainly based on trade relations, as well as 'cheque book diplomacy' via considerable financial assistance towards less-developed countries. Being set on this track, Middle East policies did not have to be reinvented after the Maastricht Treaty. What did, however, happen was that these different policies were gradually linked and synchronized, with the objective of establishing a centralized, common appearance of foreign policies emanating from the EU level.

Middle East policies already figured prominently on the European policy agenda prior to the Maastricht Treaty. Within the EPC framework, the Middle East has since the inception of EPC, been a key area for European foreign policies. It was in the immediate aftermath of the 1969 Hague Summit that member states were seeking to define priority areas for increased consultation and co-operation (European Parliament 1999e: 14–16). Following the Yom Kippur War of 1973, efforts among member states to develop a common position on the Middle East conflict increased. In an EPC resolution of 1973 member states for the first time 'recognised the need to take into account "the legitimate rights of the Palestinian people", and to no longer treat the Palestinian question solely as a refugee issue' (European Parliament 1999e: 14). Moreover, in the mid-1970s two interlinked institutionalized processes concerning the Middle East were established, namely the Euro-Arab Dialogue, which provided for action both in the EPC and EC frameworks, and the Global Mediterranean Policy (GMP) in the EC setting (Rhein 1999). However, action in both settings – the GMP was slightly reformed in 1989 and renamed the Redirected Mediterranean Policy (RMP) – has overall been criticized for producing little in actual results and only slightly improving the quest for a coherent common approach towards the region (Schumacher 2005). Consequently, both settings were depicted as manifestations of what Christopher Hill has termed the 'capability–expectation gap' of European foreign policies (1993; Hill 1998b; Regelsberger and Wessels 1996; Gomez 1998). Notwithstanding these shortcomings regarding the content of policies, the period prior to the Maastricht Treaty nevertheless documents the relative importance attached to the Middle East within the EC and EPC frameworks. Thus, between 1985 and 1992, 73 out of 742 working group meetings of the Council dealt with the Middle East, a total of almost 10 per cent. If the 22 meetings for the Euro-Arab Dialogue are added to that list, than about 15 per cent of all meetings dealt with this part of the world. No other policy area or region even approached these figures.[6]

The strong focus on the Arab–Israeli region reflected by various EPC statements, the Euro-Arab Dialogue as well as the GMP did impact on the European stance regarding the Israeli–Arab conflict and culminated in the Venice Declaration of 1980 which set out the major guidelines on European Middle East policies that prevail today. With this declaration, the EC was the first international actor to call for the inclusion of the PLO in future peace negotiations. On the one hand, the Venice Declaration has been severely criticized by Israel and the United States. Opposition from these two countries on the stronger political involvement of the EC and later the EU in the conflict can be related to their critical assessment of the content of European policies as expressed by the Venice Declaration (Greilsammer and Weiler 1988). On the other hand, the interest of Arab states and the PA in a stronger role for the Union in the peace process can only be understood against the background of trust created by, inter alia, the Venice Declaration.

Within the EC setting, the GMP and later the RMP were the most important frameworks. As part of the GMP, the EC concluded on a bilateral basis free trade agreements with all Mediterranean countries except Libya and Albania (Tovias and Bacaria 1999; Tovias 1997). The free trade agreement between Israel and the EC dates from 1975, while in 1986 the Community concluded an agreement for preferential trade for products originating from the Occupied Territories (Ahiram and Tovias 1995). These two agreements also included protocols on financial assistance, which were regularly updated throughout the 1970s and 1980s. Notwithstanding the significance of economic linkages between the EC and Israel, which made Israel increasingly dependent on imports from and exports to the Community, the political role of the EC in the region was hardly strengthened during that period (Ahiram and Tovias 1995; Giersch 1980).

It was an external event, namely the signing of the Declaration of Principles between Israel and the PLO, that provided a new access point for a collective European role on the political dimension (Anderson 1999). Hence, in the framework of the Madrid Peace Conference, which was convened after the Gulf War of 1991, the EC took over a key role in the framework of the multilateral dimension of the peace process. Europe remained excluded from the bilateral dimension in which the United States and, ironically, the small European country and non-member state of Norway, played an important broker role (Ries 2000). However, within the multilateral track the EC and later the EU chaired the working group on regional economic development (REDWG) which became the most active and ambitious segment of the multilateral setting (Peters 1996; Stetter 1997). The EU had a quite proactive interpretation of its mandate in REDWG. A permanent secretariat in Amman was established which comprised representatives from the governments of Egypt, Israel, Jordan and from the PA as well as a representative from the EU. A thick institutional framework of various working groups was established and several concrete multilateral projects on economic co-operation were developed. Yet, while the secretariat is still formally in operation, REDWG has effectively stopped producing results, in particular on the level of implementation, since the first major crisis of the Middle East peace in early 1996.[7]

The coming into force of the Maastricht Treaty did not change EU Middle East policies overnight, but rather created the institutional prerequisites that, supported by favourable external circumstances, allowed the Union to foster the linkages between its multiple policy frameworks towards the region and incrementally to provide for the further convergence and centralization of these policies. The first three years after Maastricht can be understood as a period of adaptation to the new institutional setting of the TEU. Initially, the EU made little use of the new instruments provided for by the Maastricht Treaty. For almost two years after the TEU came into force the Council only once adopted one of the new instruments provided for by the CFSP. And the Joint Action of 1994 in support for the Middle East peace process also remained declaratory and resembled an EPC statement much more than a legal act (Council 1994a; on the legalization of EU foreign policies see M. E. Smith 2001). This initial period furthermore bears similarities with another feature of the EPC period, namely the issuing of consensual declaratory policy instruments, such as Presidency declarations and statements. They still served the old EPC purpose of documenting and invoking consensus amongst member states rather than triggering a particular activity. The huge number of declaratory statements without any implementation aspects published by the EU in this initial period documents the lack of real political influence as well as the on-going internal quest for a common stance (European Parliament 1995).

Notwithstanding these shortcomings, the period from 1993 until 1996 also laid the foundations for more substantive cross-pillar foreign policies, and by the end of 1996 the EU had set in place the key institutional structures of its post-Maastricht Middle East policies. For example, in late 1995 the EMP was launched which, while being formally organized as a multilateral forum, mainly operates as an EU policy towards the region (Joffé 1999; Stavridis and Hutchence 2000). Moreover, by 1996 the EU had also become the biggest donor of financial assistance to the PA, while it has concluded two trade agreements with the PA and Israel which transcended the merely economic foci of prior agreements. Finally, by the end of 1996 the EU had also appointed, within the CFSP setting, a Special Representative to the Middle East peace process.

Leaving aside for a moment the actual success of these different policies, the significance of their mere consolidation at the EU level should not be underestimated. For example, the EMP is indeed a much more ambitious project than its predecessors. 'Having spent several decades as not much more than a preferential trade deal, the EU's new Mediterranean policy at least allows for the pursuit of economic *and* political goals in a reasonably coherent institutional framework', thus documenting the functional unity of cross-pillar foreign policies (Gomez 1998: 150, my emphasis; Edis 1998). It should, however, also be mentioned that the EMP did raise expectations, in particular on the southern shores of the Mediterranean, which could not be met by the constrained internal capabilities of the EU (Stetter 2003). Second, the remarkable financial assistance of the EU towards the PA was for some time an 'eminently political support' although it has ultimately not been able to stabilize the peace process. Yet it has established a division of labour between the United States and the EU. From that perspective, the EU has acted 'as the "payer" and the United States as the "player" in this region' (Sterzing and Böhme 2002: 39).

Third, the new Association Agreement between the EU and Israel had a substantially wider scope than all its predecessors and was supplemented by intensified scientific co-operation (Nathanson and Stetter 2005). Indeed, Israel is the only non-European country that has the status of a member state within the EU framework programmes for research and development. The Association Agreement is not restricted to covering EC foreign policy competencies but includes national competencies as well, thus pointing to further cross-pillar linkages. The Interim Association Agreement between the EC and the PLO has mainly a political significance and documents the indirect recognition by the EU of the PA as the government of a future state of Palestine (Paasivirta 1999). The intensification of economic relations did not, however, lead to an automatic increase of political weight. Finally, the appointment of the Special Representative has made EU policies in the framework of the CFSP more visible and documents the cautious integration process of EU foreign policies across the three pillars. However, the significance of this decision should, at the same time, not be overstated. As far as the internal dimension of the EU is concerned, the mandate of the Special Representative has been carefully circumscribed by the Council, while concrete results on the ground remained the exception rather than the rule.

Thus, by the end of 1996, EU foreign policies towards the Middle East were characterized by the establishment of various substantive cross-pillar linkages, which gave 'flesh' to the functional frame of an EU-specific insider/outsider distinction. Policies pursued within the EMP as well as the Association Agreement with Israel had such an explicit substantive cross-pillar design. Moreover, the mandate of the Special Representative was, on a practical level, also linked with the activities of the Commission in the first pillar. And assistance measures from the EU level had to be co-ordinated with parallel national assistance by member states. The precise shape of these various substantive cross-pillar linkages points to a cautious integration of EU Middle East policies, without a parallel abandoning of national competencies. The concrete policies that emerged out of these various institutional settings after 1996 resembled this piecemeal and cautious approach to integration. First, it was only by mid-1995 that the EU started to make consistent use of the new policy tools provided for within the CFSP framework. Until 2003, however, a total of 13 Joint Actions dealt with the Middle East. All of these Joint Actions directly deal with the implementation of policies, thus documenting the shift from the declaratory style of policy-making during the EPC and the early CFSP period towards a cautious yet active understanding of CFSP instruments. Two Joint Actions dealt with the establishment of a European Electoral Unit to oversee the first Palestinian elections of January 1996 and provided for a budget of €10 million to cover the expenses of the unit. The bulk of Joint Actions, seven in total, addressed the mandate of the Special Representative. This dates from November 1995 and has since then been prolonged on a yearly basis. The budget at the disposal of the Special Representative increased from €2.1 million in 1996 to €3 million in 1998 and €2.8 million in 1999 but then considerably diminished to €1.1 million in 2001, thus responding to the collapse of the peace process.

Notwithstanding this development, the mandate of the Special Representative has on several occasions been widened, mainly to enable the inclusion of security issues among his responsibilities. This corresponds with the mandate of the EU Special Adviser on counter-terrorism which was laid down by three Joint Actions in 1997, 1999 and 2000. Operating on a less visible basis than the Special Representative, the EU Adviser, who reports directly to the Council, has received budgetary resources of €13.6 million. Regarding the impact in the region, the appointment of a Special Representative did not fundamentally increase the amount of EU influence in the political process. 'While at least some Middle East leaders and diplomats involved in the process consider Moratinos [the Special Representative at that time] naive and inexperienced, it appears that thus far he has avoided making serious mistakes, and has contributed to the process within the modest parameters that he has defined for his mission.' While the Special Representative 'neither challenged American supremacy nor sought in any way to pressure Israel' he was not able to firmly establish the EU as an 'acceptable primary mediator' for the peace process (Alpher 2000: 198–201 and 1998; Heller 1997). Assessments of the work of the EU Adviser have been more enthusiastic than for the Special Representative but there are rare public accounts due to the secretive approach adopted by the EU Adviser (Economic Co-operation Foundation 2002).[8]

Second, on the dimension of declaratory Council statements the Berlin Declaration of April 1999 has been identified as a rare occasion of direct diplomatic impact by the Union. In order to prevent the Chairman of the PA, Yasser Arafat, from proclaiming a Palestinian state after the expiry of the Palestinian–Israeli interim agreement on 4 May 1999, for the first time an official EU document referred not only to the 'right of the Palestinians to exercise self-determination' but explicitly stated that this right 'includes the option of a state' (European Council 1999a). This declaration by the European Council is part of a long policy history in which the EC/EU's position in Palestinian statehood has developed over time. Thus the 1973 November Declaration of member states dealt for the first time with that issue and referred to the 'legitimate rights of the Palestinians', thus 'no longer treating the Palestinian question solely as a refugee problem'. In the London Statements of 1977, then, 'the right of the Palestinians to a homeland' was recognized, thus giving a territorial notion to the Palestinian cause. The Venice Declaration then 'emphasises the right of the Palestinians to self-determination' thus adding a notion of authority to prior positions. This support became more concrete after the Palestinian elections of 1996, and since then the EU has started to speak in official declarations of 'self-determination for the Palestinians, with all that this implies', without, however, specifying what it does imply. But the EU did not leave it to the fantasy of the addressees of these statements to find out what self-determination 'implies'. After the stalemate in the peace process in summer 1996 the EU became more explicit in its approach. One Council conclusion of 1997 referred to 'the right of the Palestinians to exercise self-determination, *without excluding* the option of a state' (my emphasis). It was, finally, the Berlin Declaration that directly recognized 'the right of the Palestinians to exercise self-determination, *including* the option of a state' (my emphasis). In the summer of 2000, expecting the success of the Camp David meeting, the EU already considered Palestinian statehood a *fait accompli* and supported US mediation efforts by ensuring its support for the 'viability of any resulting Palestinian state'.

This statement corresponded with a rare convergence of US and European approaches to Middle East policies between mid-1998 and the end of 2000 when, almost in parallel, a change of leadership occurred both in Israel and in the United States, which again estranged the transatlantic partners as well as the EU and the new Israeli government. However, in mid-1998, during the first major crisis of the peace process between 1996 and early 1999, 'the US administration became more responsive to Palestinian grievances and demands' thus inter alia documenting a convergence of perceptions from the EU and the US. 'US and European officials agreed, silently, in their wish for a change of government in Israel. They were also concerned about the possibility of a Palestinian declaration of statehood on 4 May 1999.' The Berlin Declaration is the visible product of this shared concern. 'US and European officials effectively co-ordinated their positions on the issue, with both sides working on Arafat to dissuade him from a state proclamation before the Israeli elections' (Perthes 2002b: 56).

Third, regarding the new mixed agreements between the EU and partner countries to the EMP, the Association Agreements with Israel and the PLO reflect the cross-pillar approach of EU foreign policies, since these (mixed) agreements address both political and economic issues of bilateral relations. Thus a member of the legal service of the Commission has argued that the EC–PLO agreement, although formally not a mixed agreement and being con-fined to first-pillar policies, fulfils 'political purposes' by assigning Palestinian self-administration the same status that otherwise only applies to states in the framework of the EMP (see Paasivirta 1999). Also the EU–Israel Association Agreement documents a politicization of cross-pillar foreign policies. It was the 1994 Essen European Council that proposed the establishment of a 'special relationship' between Israel and the EU (European Council 1994). However, rather than leading to the institutionalization of a coherent and comprehensive framework for bilateral relations, what seemed to be special in EU–Israeli relations was the dependence of economic relations upon the actual state of the peace process. In periods of Israeli–Palestinian rapprochement, economic rela-tions were smooth and led to the quick conclusion of agreements, such as, in 1995, the Association Agreement and the acceptance of Israel as a member state of the EU scientific framework programmes.[9] However, economic rela-tions suffered during crises in the peace process. Hence, the Association Agree-ment only came into force in February 2000, since the French and Belgian parliaments, supported by the Commission, had prevented ratification for political purposes. Also public quarrels between the Commission – supported by several member states – and Israel on an alleged breach of the rules of origin provisions of the agreement concerning imports to the EU of Israeli orange juice served such political purposes, according to a Commission official.[10]

Fourth, the significant financial assistance by the EU to Palestine has not been a smooth operation. On the one hand, as already mentioned, the EU has been the biggest donor to the PA. Indeed there is no other country in the world that has received a similar amount of assistance from the EU as Palestine

(Brynen 2000). When looking at the combined assistance from the EU and its member states to Palestine, the EU has during the period 1994–9 committed more than €2 billion, which covers approximately half of all international contributions (West Bank and Gaza 2000: 6). Moreover, the funds allocated in Palestine amount to more than 10 per cent of the overall MEDA budget in the framework of the EMP. This is by far the largest per capita support the EU grants to any country in the world, including those in central and eastern Europe. The ratio between per capita contributions to Palestine in comparison with the average per capita assistance for all Mediterranean countries is around 23:1. On the other hand, this remarkable assistance programme has come under criticism. It was neither able to prevent the collapse of the peace process and, subsequently, the demolition by the Israeli army of the largely EU-sponsored Palestinian infrastructure, nor to moderate the stance of the Palestinian and Israeli leaderships (Asseburg 2002a and 2002b). Moreover, as far as the internal dimension was concerned, charges of mismanagement and even of corruption within the Commission have obstructed the smooth allocation of funds. This has only added to the complex internal decision-making procedures which rendered the implementation of funding a painstaking exercise.[11] Moreover, further allegations that the monthly budgetary aid of €10 million, which the EU has paid to the PA since 2001, has been used by the PA to finance terrorist activities have further deteriorated the credibility of EU assistance. While these accusations have been rejected by the Commissioner responsible, they were never entirely refuted.[12]

Fifth, the EMP itself has a rather mixed record. On the face of it, the EMP is a success. Association Agreements have been signed and ratified with most partner countries, financial assistance to the region has increased and is also distributed to non-governmental organizations in these countries (Galal and Hoeckman 1997). Moreover, the thick institutional structure has remained intact in spite of the ups and downs of the peace process. Indeed, the EMP is the only international forum – besides the UN – in which Israeli officials participate alongside those from Mediterranean Arab countries, including Syria and Lebanon. On the other hand, however, the EMP has not fulfilled all expectations. The Arab countries perceive the economic focus as one-sided and serving EU interests in industrial exports and agricultural protectionism, while Israel considers the partnership as preventing the exploitation of the full economic potential of EU–Israel relations. The EMP has also not been able to significantly improve regional co-operation among partner countries which would be a prerequisite for the establishment of a Euro-Mediterranean free trade area by the year 2010 (Dessus and Suwa 2000; Zaafrane and Mahjoub 2000). It has also achieved quite ambivalent results with regard to the so-called third basket, dealing increasingly with issues of 'cultural dialogue' (Stetter 2005). Moreover, the EMP has not really stabilized the political relations between Israel and Arab countries, while the collapse of the peace process has halted progress on the political dimension of the EMP, for example with regard to the drafting of a Euro-Mediterranean security charter (Hollis 2000; Behrendt and Hanelt 1999).

Finally, the Common Strategy of the EU on the Mediterranean region of June 2000 reveals a mixed picture (House of Lords 2001). With this document the European Council recognized the Mediterranean as a region of prime strategic importance to the EU's interests, thus fostering a shared political identity amongst EU member states. The Common Strategy also acknowledged the multiple cross-pillar linkages of EU policies.[13] Yet at the same time it documented the limitations of EU foreign policies. The Common Strategy did not really add anything new to the objectives already contained in the multilateral Barcelona Declaration of 1995 (Hakura 1998). The only remarkable feature was that, while itself being adopted unanimously by the European Council, the Common Strategy allowed for subsequent decisions to be taken by qualified majority. However, this general rule does not apply to decisions on the Middle East. 'Apparently the member states are afraid that the "Common Strategy" could mean that decisions concerning the Middle East in the future ... could not be prevented by one member state with its veto.' It seems that 'the Israeli-Palestinian conflict bears potential for conflict within the EU as well' (Sterzing and Böhme 2002: 43).

Comparable to developments in EU Middle East policies, after the Maastricht Treaty migration policies witnessed an incremental centralization process at the EU level. Thus previously only very loosely connected policies, such as migration policies at the intergovernmental level, the EC level or within the Schengen co-operation, were cautiously merged, thereby underpinning the insider/outsider distinction related to EU interior policies (Favell 1998). This centralization process of interior policies can be documented by looking at the conclusions of the Tampere European Council as well as the concept of deploying a scoreboard for the regulation of migration policies.

Prior to the Maastricht Treaty there was only very limited action on migration policies in the EC framework, and most activities remained limited to provisions on the free movement of workers. These rules, however, only partially applied to TCN and were mainly directed towards citizens of the EC member states. As Geddes notes, 'the Treaty's provisions did not cover TCNs *qua* TCNs' (2000: 46). Attempts to link EC provisions with migration policy action, as they were pursued by the Commission and the EP, failed prior to the Maastricht Treaty. In 1976 the Council rejected a Commission proposal for a directive against clandestine migration and in 1985 the Court of Justice issued a judgement that prevented the adoption of migration-related matters under the social policy provisions of the TEC. As long as only the EC employment situation was concerned, the Court of Justice approved the policy of the Commission to collect national information regarding TCNs. Beyond the narrow confines of these free movement and employment provisions as well as the provisions in bilateral association agreements, 'the majority of developments remained intergovernmental' (Peers 2000: 66). This intergovernmental co-operation, which emerged from the Trevi setting, dealt primarily with issues related to free movement, terrorism and policing but did not, until the mid-1980s, tackle migration policies as such (den Boer 1996).[14]

It was then the SEA of 1986 that triggered intergovernmental co-operation also on migration policy issues (Lobkowicz 1994; Korella and Twomey 1993). The provisions of the SEA 'for the creation of a single market made it clear that free movement had unavoidable immigration and asylum implications' which, as most member states agreed, should be dealt with outside the EC setting (Geddes 2000: 67). Hence, linked with the Trevi setting, member states established in 1986 an ad hoc working group on immigration. However, actual results within this setting remained meagre and subsequent attempts to stream-line co-operation at the intergovernmental level, such as the establishment in 1988 of a group of co-ordinators, as well as the drafting of the Palma docu-ments of 1989 on priority action on free movement and migration issues, did not lead to extensive action.

Notwithstanding this development, the period prior to the Maastricht Treaty witnessed two important substantive developments at the intergovern-mental level, namely the Schengen framework on the one hand, and the elaboration of two conventions dealing with asylum and external border provisions on the other (Callovi 1992; Nanz 1995). The Schengen *acquis* was formally integrated into the EU framework by the Amsterdam Treaty in 1999. But prior to that date Schengen was also linked with the EC framework (Convey and Kupiszewski 1995). Against the background of the deadlock on achieving an abolition of internal border controls in the EC due to the resist-ance of some member states, five of the then 12 member states agreed in 1985 to move ahead with an early form of closer co-operation, with the abolition of internal border controls between them. In order to compensate for the loss of internal border controls, which was the main objective of Schengen co-operation, flanking measures were adopted which related to determining common principles governing the entry into *Schengenland*, such as rules on external border controls, the issuing of visas and entry and procedural issues concerning asylum seekers (Kostakopoulou 1998). Until the Amsterdam Treaty came into force all other member states except for the United Kingdom and Ireland, which were linked by the Common Travel Area, became member states of the Schengen agreement, which now forms part of the EU *acquis*.[15] Two non-member states, Norway and Iceland, participate in the Schengen co-operation, while the United Kingdom and Ireland have in the meantime opted in to most provisions of the Schengen setting.[16]

Second, the Dublin Convention of 1990 as well as the External Frontier Convention of 1991 were meant to establish common rules on asylum and external border policies, thereby putting in place flanking measures for the attainment of the free movement of person provisions of the SEA (Müller-Graff 1995). Both conventions documented the willingness of member states to establish joint provisions on migration policy issues but also revealed the inherent problems of intergovernmental co-operation. The Dublin Conven-tion, which took note of the objective raised by the Palma document to estab-lish 'a European system of responsibilities for the adjudication of asylum claims', was signed in 1990 but only came into force in 1997 when at last it was ratified by the French Assemblée Nationale (Guild 1996; Hailbronner 1998). The Dublin Convention became the 'core' of the EU asylum policy regime and set out a 'hierarchically ordered catalogue' which defined criteria for determining the exclusive responsibility of one member state to consider an asylum application (Hailbronner 2000: 385; Hailbronner and Thiery 1997). Notwithstanding the slow ratification process, between 1993 and 1997 the Council adopted several legal acts related to the convention, most of them linked to its implementation.[17] Prior to the Maastricht Treaty, member states had already agreed on asylum-related matters in the 1992 London Resolutions, which built upon provisions contained in the Dublin Convention, and set up clearing houses to deal with information exchange on asylum (CIREA) and immigration (CIREFI). When compared with the already protracted implementation of the Dublin Convention, the External Frontier Convention fared even worse. Although the principal agreement was ensured by 1991, the ratification process was permanently halted, since the United Kingdom and Spain disagree over the application of the convention with regard to the status of Gibraltar, while some member states raised objections regarding the Commission's proposals on the role of the Court of Justice in the framework of the convention.

For the first time the TEU brought all migration policy issues within a formally Europeanized framework (Weber-Panariello 1995; Baldwin-Edwards and Schain 1994; Butt Philip 1994). Indeed, in the time between the Maastricht and the Amsterdam Treaties, member states made regular use of the instruments provided for by the first and third pillars. Table 5.1 depicts all decisions adopted with regard to migration policies during this period and reveals the number of legal acts concluded (all from the third pillar except for one decision on visa policies adopted in 1999 in the EC framework). The number of legal acts adopted increased when compared to the pre-Maastricht period. Moreover, in this period the Schengen member states adopted additional migration-related measures in this intergovernmental setting.

Table 5.1 also indicates a decline of formal decisions following the Amsterdam Summit in June 1997 at which member states agreed upon the new Treaty. This relates to the informal agreement to shelve the adoption of some legal acts from the third pillar until the first pillar setting of Title IV TEC of the Amsterdam Treaty came into force. Notwithstanding the considerable number of 46 formal decisions on migration policies, which highlights the incremental increase of substantive decisions on EU migration policies, the

Table 5.1 Number of decisions on migration policies, 1994–1999

Year	1994	1995	1996	1997	1998	1999 (May)	Total
Number of decisions	9	8	10	10	6	3	46

Source: Own collection from *Official Journal*, various issues.

Maastricht Treaty framework did not really operate smoothly. As an illustration, Table 5.2 lists the content of all formal decisions on migration policies from 1993 until May 1999, separated according to issue areas.

Table 5.2 allows us to draw several conclusions regarding the way in which migration policies were addressed within the 'single institutional framework' prior to the Amsterdam Treaty. Thus the 46 decisions relate to a wide array of different issues and document an increase of substantive decisions in this policy area. On the other hand, however, the piecemeal character of legislation, as well

Table 5.2 Substantive decisions on migration policies, 1994–1999

Number in issue area	Legal base	Issue	Legal form	Year of adoption
Institutional affairs				
1	JHA	Application of article K.9 TEU	Conclusion	1994
2	JHA	Commission communication	Conclusion	1994
3	JHA	Organisation of CIREA and CIREFI	Conclusion	1994
4	JHA	Implementation of third-pillar acts	Recommendation	1995
5	JHA	Publication of third-pillar acts in *Official Journal*	Decision	1995
6	JHA	Setting up of 'Sherlock' training programme	Joint Action	1996
7	JHA	Priorities of action	Resolution	1996
8	JHA	Priorities of action	Resolution	1997
9	JHA	Setting up of 'Odysseus' training programme	Joint Action	1998
Free movement for TCN/admission				
1	JHA	Admission of TCN for employment	Resolution	1994
2	JHA	Travel for pupils from member states who are TCN	Joint Action	1994
3	JHA	Admission of TCN who are self-employed	Resolution	1994
4	JHA	Admission of TCN for study purposes	Resolution	1994
5	JHA	Monitoring implementation on admission	Decision	1995
6	JHA	Status of TCN who are long-term residents	Resolution	1996
7	JHA	Provisions on unaccompanied minors	Resolution	1997
Asylum seekers/refugees/displaced persons				
1	JHA	Minimum guarantees for asylum procedures	Resolution	1995
2	JHA	Burden-sharing on displaced persons	Resolution	1995
3	JHA	Emergency procedure on displaced persons	Decisions	1996
4	JHA	Definition of term 'refugee'	Joint Position	1996
5	JHA	Implementation of Dublin Convention	Conclusion	1997
6	JHA	Monitoring implementation of Dublin Convention	Decision	1997
7	JHA	Projects for asylum seekers and displaced persons	Joint Action	1997
8	JHA	Projects for asylum seekers and refugees	Joint Action	1997
9	JHA	Dublin Convention	Convention	1997
10	JHA	Implementation of Dublin Convention	Decision	1997
11	JHA	Implementation of Dublin Convention	Decision	1997
12	JHA	Projects for asylum seekers and displaced persons	Joint Action	1998
13	JHA	Projects for asylum seekers and refugees	Joint Action	1998
14	JHA	Implementation of Dublin Convention	Decision	1998
15	JHA	Emergency measures for Kosovo refugees	Joint Action	1999

Table 5.2 Continued

Number in issue area	Legal base	Issue	Legal form	Year of adoption
Expulsion/readmission/illegal immigration				
1	JHA	Standard travel document for expulsions	Recommendation	1994
2	JHA	Specimen readmission agreement	Recommendation	1994
3	JHA	Principles for protocols to readmission agreements	Recommendation	1995
4	JHA	Co-operation on expulsion	Recommendation	1995
5	JHA	Combating illegal immigration	Recommendation	1995
6	JHA	Combating illegal employment	Recommendation	1996
7	JHA	Monitoring implementation of expulsion	Decision	1996
8	JHA	Exchange of information on repatriation	Decision	1997
Visa/residence permits				
1	JHA	Airport transit visa	Joint Action	1996
2	JHA	Consular protection	Recommendation	1996
3	JHA	Uniform format for residence permits	Joint Action	1996
4	JHA	Sharing costs for uniform residence permits	Decision	1998
5	JHA	Common standards for uniform residence permits	Decision	1998
6	JHA	Detection of false visa	Recommendation	1999
7	EC	Positive visa list	Regulation	1999

Source: Own compilation from *Official Journal*, various issues.

as the fragile legal status of decisions, reveals the reluctance of most member states to harmonize migration policies. The bulk of the decisions, namely 15, was taken on matters related to asylum and refugee issues. The Dublin Convention indeed required the adoption of further legislative acts specifying some of its provisions. Furthermore, even those member states that were resisting an abolition of internal border controls agreed with common provisions regarding asylum. However, it should also be noted that the Dublin Convention as well as its various implementing decisions did not provide for integration on the substance of asylum procedures or conditions for the reception of asylum seekers (Klos 1998; see also European Parliament 2000d).

A cautious step towards a Europeanized setting with regard to the substance of asylum provisions was provided for by the Joint Position of 1996 on a harmonized application of the term 'refugee'. The act establishes common rules with regard to the question of which refugees qualify as asylum seekers in the framework of the Geneva Convention. The 1995 Council resolution on minimum guarantees in asylum procedures already seemed to assume the existence of such an approximation of policies when stating that asylum decisions must 'be taken on the basis of equivalent procedures in all Member States and common procedural guarantees' (Council 1995b; Peers 2000: 119). However, the Council acts referred to in Table 5.2 also reveal the obstacles with regard to the establishment of a Europeanized setting on asylum policies. Among the

46 legal acts on migration policies that were published in the Official Journal between 1994 and May 1999, only one act was adopted within the first pillar, namely a Regulation on a common visa list. All other acts were adopted within the framework of the third pillar and had, consequently, 'soft law' character.[18] Member states were not bound by these decisions and implementation could not be invoked either by other supranational actors or EU citizens. Even more striking, most decisions were not adopted on the basis of the legal instruments provided for by ex-Article K.3(2) TEU. This article referred to Joint Positions, Joint Actions and Conventions. However, among the 45 third-pillar acts, only 12 were adopted with such a clear legal basis, and all other decision were termed conclusions, recommendations, decisions and resolutions, none of which had a Treaty base. Only in the area of asylum policies, thus an area in which a general consensus for further legislation existed after the Dublin Convention had been signed in 1990, was there a somewhat equal balance between explicit third-pillar instruments and even softer forms of soft law.

It is also striking that in the area of visa policies, the only migration policy issue that had already been transferred to the EC pillar with the Maastricht Treaty, only one first-pillar measure came into force. In fact, after the Maastricht Treaty the provisions of the first pillar on migration policies became a field of inter-institutional wrangling. A Regulation of 1995 on a uniform format for visas was annulled by the Court of Justice after the EP had filed a charge against the measure. This decision by the Court of Justice effectively halted further decisions on visa policies prior to the Amsterdam Treaty. The cautious approach to the integration of migration policy issues is also well documented by the Joint Action of 1996 on airport transit visas. Member states chose to adopt this measure in the framework of the third pillar, although on the face of it visa policies belonged to the EC setting. The Court of Justice rejected an annulment charge by the Commission, arguing that the Council was justified in adopting this measure under ex-Article K TEU.[19] In the area of expulsion, readmission and illegal immigration not a single measure was adopted under an official third-pillar legal instrument, while on admission policies only one out of seven measures was based on the TEU's provisions. No single decision on external borders was published in the Official Journal in this period, thus providing evidence of the deadlock in this area caused by the dispute on the External Frontiers Convention.

The period of JHA co-operation on migration policies from 1993 to 1999 thus reveals a mixed picture regarding the substantive developments in migration policies. On the one hand, the number of decisions increased considerably when compared with the co-operation prior to the Maastricht Treaty. The incremental process of developing a European migration regime, which started in the late 1980s, therefore gathered speed after 1993. Moreover, the development of a whole set of policies dealing exclusively with TCNs provided substance to the creation of an 'insider/outsider' distinction at the EU level, thus underlining the political significance of integration in this area. On the other hand, the legal form of these decisions, the piecemeal approach to the various issues, the lack of an overarching framework on migration policies and the lack of progress on external border policies demonstrated the limits of the centralization of this policy area. The Schengen co-operation did not really present an alternative to an EU migration policy regime, not so much because Schengen co-operation as such was not working – indeed, for many issues, such as external border provisions, visa policies or asylum rules Schengen functioned as a 'laboratory' for measures which would later be adopted at the EU level (Hailbronner 2000: 141; Monar 2001). Yet,

> the ongoing 'widening' and 'deepening' of Schengen, as its organs made a number of decisions implementing the [Schengen] Convention, meant that the cross-over between Schengen and JHA co-operation was con-tinuingly increasing. The convergent geographical and material scope of official European integration under the EU-Treaty and 'black-market' Schengen integration led some Member States to suggest that the two processes should be formally reconciled.
>
> (Peers 2000: 36)

While following the coming into force of the Amsterdam Treaty the integra-tion of migration policies at the EU level thus gained momentum, the general pattern of incremental integration did not substantially change (Hailbronner 1998). Notwithstanding the significance of the semi-communitarization of migration policies and the 'Treaty monument of the area of freedom, security and justice', actual progress on migration policies lagged behind the deter-mination suggested by this ambitious formula (Chalmers 1998: 1). On the one hand, the commitment to establishing the area of freedom, security and justice, as well as the more comprehensive approach to dealing with migration policy issues as expressed by the setting up of a scoreboard, point to the rele-vance of migration policies as a key policy area at the EU level. On the other hand, however, the lack of progress on the detailed legislative objectives formulated in this area documents disagreement on crucial institutional and substantive issues among member states.

The new 'focal point' of establishing an area of freedom, security and justice initially triggered the expectation that following the coming into force of the Amsterdam Treaty EU migration policies would move beyond the patchwork approach of previous third-pillar co-operation. Being aware that the 'miscel-lany of achievements' in migration policies so far did not form 'a single concept', several initiatives from the Commission, various Presidencies and from the Council level aimed to predefine what a 'comprehensive' overall migra-tion strategy should look like (Commission 1998a; European Council 1998). The Vienna Action Plan of December 1998 aimed to set the guidelines for EU migration policies under the Amsterdam Treaty rules.[20] The Action Plan was particularly ambitious with regard to asylum and refugee issues. It even referred to the need to establish a 'single European asylum procedure', thus linguistically underlining the centralization dynamics of this area. However, the notion of 'single' policies was abandoned as quickly as it appeared. The Tampere European Council Conclusions of October 1999 more cautiously referred to the establishment of a 'common European asylum system' (European Council 1999b; House of Lords 1999). It should, however, also be noted that the Tampere meeting was the first European Council summit fully devoted to EU interior policies, thus once more underlining the potential provided for by the Amsterdam Treaty. In the Tampere conclusions, the European Council enumerated the main areas on which action should be taken within the framework of, inter alia, Title IV TEC. This included action on partnership with countries of origin, a common European asylum system, fair treatment of third-country nationals (including admission and residence) and management of migration flows. These 'Tampere priorities' as well as the specific objectives formulated by the European Council on these various areas, were subsequently taken up by the Commission when drafting the scoreboard. The Tampere provisions structure the scoreboard which had the goal of ensuring the legislative adoption by May 2004 of those migration decisions needed in order 'to attain the objectives set by the Amsterdam Treaty and Tampere European Council' (Commission 2002b: 2).

Yet, as indicated by Table 5.3 actual progress on adopting the necessary legal measures enumerated at length in the Amsterdam Treaty, the Vienna Action Plan, the Tampere Council conclusions and the scoreboard lagged behind the widely accepted ambition of giving 'flesh' to the concept of an area of freedom, security and justice. Legislation on migration policies issues after the Amsterdam Treaty continued to reflect the highly incremental and piecemeal character of policy-making. Thus in the period under consideration not a single legal measure was adopted regarding the admission and residence of TCNs, while provisions on borders and visa issues remained mainly restricted to highly technical operational provisions, such as adaptation to the Schengen common consular instructions (House of Commons 2002). Progress was only achieved on those issues on which there was already some first-pillar legislation prior to the Amsterdam Treaty, namely visa lists and the uniform format for visas. Highly visible projects such as the establishment of EURODAC or the ERF do document some institutional centralization of migration policies at the EU level but cannot cover the lack of overall substantive integration of migration law.

Such a sceptical evaluation regarding the implementation of the repeatedly endorsed objective to establish a comprehensive migration policy framework at the Union level was recognized by both the European Council and the Commission. However, appeals from both institutions to speed up the adoption of legislative measures in order to meet the 2004 deadline did not bear fruit. The Laeken European Council of 2001 was critical of developments in migration policies arguing that 'progress has been slower and less substantial than expected' and that 'a new approach is therefore needed' (European Council 2001). An evaluation from the Presidency became more specific (Council 2001d). Various obstacles, such as the highly technical nature of some measures

Table 5.3 Substantive decisions on migration policies, 1999–2002

Number Issue in sub-group		Legal form	Year of adoption
Countries of origin			
1	Implementation of action plans	Report to European Council	2000
Asylum			
1	EURODAC	Regulation	2000
2	EURODAC application rules	Regulation	2002
3	Minimum standards for refugee status	Conclusion	2001
4	Temporary protection for displaced persons	Directive	2001
5	European Refugee Fund	Decision	2000
Illegal immigration, readmission, external action			
1	Combating illegal immigration	Plan	2002
2	Combating illegal immigration by sea	Conclusion	2002
3	Harmonization of laws on carrier's liability	Directive	2001
4	Readmission agreement with Hong Kong	Agreement	2001
5	Minimum standards on repatriation	Directive	2001
6	Combating trafficking in human beings	Undertakings	2001
7	Repatriation programme	On basis of a Green Paper	2002
Visas and internal and external borders			
1	List of exemptions from visa requirement	Regulation	2001
2	Amending the list of exemptions from visa requirement	Regulation	2001
3	Implementation of visa applications	Regulation	2001
4	Updating of Common Consular Instructions	Decision	2001
5	Amendment to Common Consular Instructions	Decision	2001
6	Amendment to Common Consular Instructions	Decision	2002
7	Uniform format for visa	Regulation	2002
8	Uniform format for forms for affixing the visa	Regulation	2002
9	Travel on a long-stay visa	Initiative	2001
10	Detection of false documents: exchange of information	Decision	2000
11	Implementing powers on border checks	Regulation	2001
12	Amending Common Consular Instructions	Decision	2002
13	Amending Common Consular Instructions	Decision	2002
14	Development of SIS II	Regulation and Decision	2001
15	Management of external borders	Plan	2002

Source: Own compilation from *Official Journal*, various issues.

proposed by the scoreboard, 'real differences on the scope of the instruments to be adopted' and 'Member States' reluctance to go beyond the confines of their national laws' all hampered the integration of migration policies beyond the general will expressed in Amsterdam, Vienna and Tampere on 'formulating common policies' (Council 2001d: 4). In fact, the Presidency identified the on-going unanimity requirement in the Council on most migration policy measures as a 'serious hindrance to progress' (2001d: 5). However, the call by the Laeken European Council to 'make good delays' on the implementation of migration policy issues enlisted in the scoreboard did not change the overall slow process of integration on the substantive dimension.

Hence, one year after the Laeken European Council the Commission could conclude that the appeal by heads of state and government did not change the cautious approach in the Council. Thus, 'the backlog referred to by the Laeken European Council has not been cleared in some areas, notably as regards the common policies on asylum and immigration' (Commission 2002b: 4). The considerable divergence of national migration policies, often intensified by *new* legislative measures from member states, the complex institutional provisions of Title IV TEC and uncertainties stemming from the 2004 enlargement, as well as a potential legislative congestion in the migration policy pipeline prior to the 2004 deadline, were identified as major stumbling blocks to the establishment of more than piecemeal, often technical legislative acts (2002b).

The budget in foreign and interior policies from Maastricht to Nice

The financing of constituent policies within the single institutional framework has been a contested issue between the Council, the Commission, Parliament and the Court of Auditors. What will be of interest in this section is further substance to the claim that foreign and interior policies since 1993 have been characterized by a cautious and incremental, yet on-going centralization process, which anchored this 'new' policy type at the EU level. This is not a mere discussion of figures. 'Budgets matter politically, because money represents the commitment of resources to the provision of public goods', such as, in this case, constituent policies (Laffan and Shackleton 2000: 212).

As has already been discussed in Chapter 3, one of the practical consequences of the single institutional framework has related to the financing of cross-pillar policies. Thus, ex-Articles J and K TEU provided for the financing of CFSP and JHA activities from two different budgetary sources. On the one hand, so-called 'administrative' expenditure had to be charged to the EC budget, whereas 'operational' expenditure could be charged to the EC budget by unanimous agreement of all member states. Otherwise, 'operational' expenditure had to be charged to the member states. In the first years following the coming into force of the Maastricht Treaty, the financing of the second and third pillars was a contested issue both within the Council and between the Council, the Commission and Parliament.

Following the establishment of the second and third pillars, some member states were reluctant to make recourse to the EC budget for the financing of these policies, fearing that this might lead to a creeping communitarization of foreign and interior policies. However, the failure of member states to credibly commit themselves to finance 'intergovernmental pillar' activities out of national budgets soon led to such a recourse to EC budgetary resources (Monar 1997b). Table 5.4 provides data on the development of the foreign and interior

Table 5.4 Budget expenditure foreign and interior policies, 1992–2003 (€ million)

Year/area	1992	1993	1994	1995	1996	1997	1998	1999	2000	2001	2002	2003
Foreign policies	2,433	2,873	3,070	3,410	3,874	3,835	4,223	4,725	4,201	5,043	5,085	4,949
(CFSP)	(0)	(14)	(10)	(83)	(61)	(24)	(23)	(37)	(38)	(39)	(35)	(48)
Interior policies	0	0	0	3	2	7	8	36	80	148	145	154
Total budget	58,857	65,269	59,909	66,758	77,454	80,003	81,637	84,268	82,868	106,924	95,655	99,686

Source: Own calculations from Budget (1992, 1993, 1994, 1995, 1996, 1997, 1998, 1999, 2000, 2001, 2002, 2003).

policy budgets in relation to the total EC budget for the years from 1992 to 2003.[21] Moreover, Table 5.4 includes data on expenditure in the second pillar, enlisted for each consecutive year, and for third-pillar expenditure up until 1998. It should be noted that data on interior policies from 1999 onwards relate to the cross-pillar budget for the creation of an 'area of freedom, security and justice' and mainly comprise first-pillar migration policy expenditure. A comparison of expenditure on CFSP and JHA measures reveals the greater reluctance of some member states to finance interior policy measures from EC budgetary resources than those involving external action (Monar 1997b). This correlates with the aforementioned reluctance to use Treaty-based legal instruments, such as Joint Actions, in particular in the JHA setting. Thus the small amount of legislative activity is mirrored by reluctant recourse to the EC budget.

The financing of foreign and interior policies also affected inter-institutional relations. Thus Parliament has also been keen to ensure its 'power of the purse' on non-compulsory expenditure with regard to the financing of CFSP and JHA from the EC budget, and has opposed attempts by the Council to 'elude parts of Communitary budgetary principles in decisions on the introduction and the implementation of EC funding for measures within the intergovernmental pillars' (Monar 1997b: 77). Thus in both areas Parliament has pushed for the conclusion of inter-institutional agreements that regulate the relations between the different arms of the budgetary authority. While for the CFSP such an agreement was ultimately agreed upon in 1997 and amended in 1999, no agreement between the Council and Parliament could be reached for JHA, again documenting the reluctance of some member states for legislative and budgetary commitments in the third pillar (Inter-institutional Agreement 1997 and 1999). These inter-institutional agreements contained a declaration of intent that the institutions 'shall annually assure' (agreement of 1997) or 'endeavour' (agreement of 1999) to agree on the amount of operational expenditure to be charged to the EC budget. Moreover, they agreed that funds will not be entered in a reserve, which escapes the control of Parliament, and that for urgent actions a maximum of 20 per cent of yearly CFSP expenditure will be entered in the budgetary heading. While under the EC budgetary provisions the Commission was responsible for the implementation of all expenditure, and thus also those from the CFSP and JHA entries, it did not have a political responsibility for acts adopted within these areas. This led to a 'blurring of responsibilities' and rendered the Commission 'a mere "cashier" of intergovernmental co-operation deprived of political responsibility but nevertheless accountable to the European Parliament' (Monar 1997b: 77–8). As will be discussed in the following chapters, accusations by the Court of Auditors, which were taken up by Parliament, on the maladministration of budgetary resources, mainly those of first-pillar foreign policies, led in 1999 to the resignation of the entire college of Commissioners.

The functional relevance of the EC budget for the integration of constituent policies comes to the fore when looking at the expenditure in both areas since 'the budget is a useful yardstick to measure positive integration' (Laffan and Shackleton 2000: 213). The absolute figures in Table 5.4 reveal the differences made in the cautious yet significant use of CFSP expenditure and the extremely reluctant recourse to finance JHA from the EC budget. It was only the semi-communitarization of migration policies with the Amsterdam Treaty that caused a major increase of expenditure on interior (migration) policies. This expenditure has been mainly earmarked for the ERF.

Figures 5.1 and 5.2 illustrate the anchoring of constituent policies at the EU level. Thus Figure 5.1 shows a steady increase in the combined expenditure on both areas for the years 1992 to 2003. In proportion, however, only a tiny amount of expenditure related to interior policies, with the bulk of budgetary resources spent on first-pillar foreign policies, in particular aid. For example, in the 2002 budget on foreign policies €1.3 billion was spent on co-operation with countries in central Asia and the Balkans. Commitments of €0.9 billion were devoted to food and humanitarian aid, co-operation measures in the framework of the Lomé Convention and co-operation with Mediterranean countries participating in the EMP. Budgetary resources were, furthermore, committed to the promotion of democracy (€100 million) and other measures (Budget 2002).

Figure 5.1 reveals that there has been a steady increase in foreign and interior policy expenditure but no major change that would point to a dramatic juncture. This is also reflected in Figure 5.2 which relates expenditure in foreign and interior policies to the total EC budget. As can already be seen in Table 5.4 it was not only foreign and interior policy expenditure that has modestly increased since 1993 but the total size of the EC budget (Laffan and Shackleton

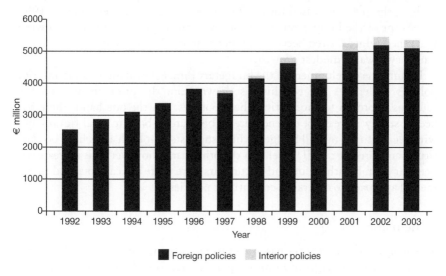

Figure 5.1 Total expenditure in foreign and interior policies, 1992–2003.

Source: Own calculations (see Table 5.4).

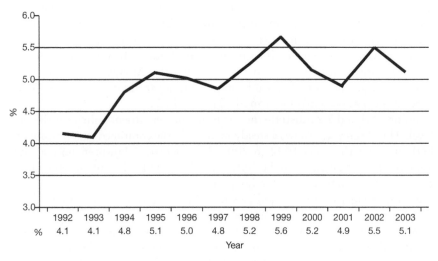

Figure 5.2 Share of foreign and interior policies in comparison to total EU budget, 1992–2003.

Source: Own calculations (see Table 5.4).

2000). Figure 5.2 relates the increase in foreign and interior policies expenditure to the increase in the total EC budget. An incremental and small but nevertheless visible increase of the relative share of constituent policies vis-à-vis other policy types within the overall EC budget can be detected. While in 1992 and 1993, the two years prior to the coming into force of the Maastricht Treaty, the share of foreign and interior policies was 4.1 per cent of the total EC budget, the share increased until 1995 to more than 5 per cent and by 1999 6 per cent of the budget was spent on constituent policies. In the following years the budget floated between 4.9 per cent and 5.5 per cent with an overall tendency towards modest growth.

In sum, the development of the budgetary dimension of foreign and interior policies underlines the conclusions drawn from the prior analysis on the cautious approach to integrating these policies. On the one hand, there has been a steady increase of expenditure in both areas, both in total figures and with regard to the overall budget, which suggests that both areas have become firmly anchored at the EU level. On the other hand, however, this increase has been far from breathtaking and documents once more the cautious and incremental approach to centralize constituent policies.

Conclusion

The analysis of this chapter has aimed to provide substance to the claim that the study of EU foreign and interior policies has to include considerations of the way in which the integration process of constituent policies on the substantive dimension has fostered the functional frame around which these policies evolve. Integration in both areas is subject to conditions that differ from those applying to other policy types, given the direct linkage of constituent policies with notions of sovereignty. However, notwithstanding the overall cautious approach to integration, the substantive developments in foreign and interior policies have been characterized by a gradual increase in the depth and width of substantive decisions, as the two case studies of Middle East and migration policies illustrate. Yet the policy history is also a history of highly incremental and piecemeal measures which did not culminate in a 'comprehensive', let alone exclusive, EU framework. This lack of comprehensiveness has been emphasized, rather than accommodated for, by the ambitious objectives formulated in both areas, such as the Common Strategy on the Mediterranean region or the Tampere European Council conclusions. What has, however, emerged in the process of integrating both areas at the EU level has been an increase of substantive cross-pillar linkages, thus at least to some extent providing flesh to the functional frame of constituent policies, namely an EU-specific insider/outsider distinction. Arguably, the substantive decisions made in both areas since 1993 have underpinned and consolidated the political pervasiveness of this distinction.

Part III

Policy-making in cross-pillar settings

Actor preferences and policy-making dynamics

6 The divergent policy preferences of supranational actors in foreign and interior policies
Tackling the myth of supranational unity

Introduction

Supranational actors are more than passive recipients of primary and secondary capabilities which have been delegated to them by member states' governments. Making use of these capabilities they do not only develop specific preferences in the two areas of foreign and interior policies but also actively channel these preferences, as part of their day-to-day involvement in EU foreign and interior policies, into the policy-making process. This chapter accounts for the way in which the preferences of the Commission, Parliament, the Court of Justice, the Court of Auditors and the Council Secretariat have developed with regard to foreign and interior policies in general, and Middle East and migration policies in particular. This chapter, inter alia, tackles the following questions.

How can the preferences of supranational actors in the two areas be explained? What is the relationship between these preferences on the one hand, and the specific capabilities of each actor on the other? Moreover, are preferences stable or dynamic? To what extent do they converge or differ between the various actors? And how do these preferences relate to the dynamics of constituent policies?

This analysis is based on two key propositions which both challenge those conceptualizations which assume self-interested, (bounded) rational actors with fixed preferences (Moravcsik 1998; Dowding 2000). Thus, in the analysis of this chapter, preferences are not regarded as exogenously given. Instead, it will be shown that the preferences of supranational actors can best be understood against the background of the functional characteristics of the specific policies they relate to. In other words, preferences are analysed as relating to a complex environment which actors constantly have to make sense of. Moreover, as will be shown, preferences are not based on rational choices but rather on functionally induced processes of preference formation. Thus the empirical data show that the preferences of supranational actors are quite dynamic, often unstable, and subject to changes over time.[1] This does not exclude the possibility of lock-in effects regarding these preferences. Yet lock-in effects should be studied as the result of a temporary accommodation with the functional and institutional environment of a given policy setting rather than as an inherent ideational feature.

A key proposition advanced by this chapter is that the functional features of constituent policies set the frame within which actor preferences evolve. The preferences of supranational actors in the two areas thus stand in a much more dynamic relationship with the institutional and functional features of both areas than often assumed. The patterns of interaction between national and supranational actors, which emerge out of the interplay between these three dimensions, will then be discussed in Chapter 7. The key results stemming from the analysis of this chapter is that the preferences of supranational actors in the two areas do not fit into a simple intergovernmental/supranational dichotomy. As much as supranational actors perform quite different institutional roles, they also developed divergent preferences which cannot be subsumed under one integrationist heading.

The preferences of supranational actors in Middle East and migration policies can be understood when addressing the relation of these preferences with the functional characteristics of foreign and interior policies. Thus preferences are not given, but are constructed against the background of a specific functional frame. This argument does not, however, imply that preferences are completely dependent upon policy functions. Yet these functions render certain sets of preferences more likely than others and help to identify the individual and often divergent nature of the preferences of supranational actors rather than assuming an allegedly institutionally determined division between 'intergovernmental' and 'supranational' logics (Moravcsik 1998).

The analysis of the preferences of supranational actors in foreign and interior policies reveals four main insights. First, all actors share the characteristic that they had to develop their individual preferences on the two areas against the background of the formative period of EU foreign and interior policies following the Maastricht Treaty. With little institutional and policy history on stock, this early period can, therefore, also be understood as a period of *preferences formation* in which supranational actors had to draw for themselves a 'picture' of the two fields.[2] Lacking both solid 'institutional data' and organizational experience, preferences in this period were primarily shaped by the functional requirements of providing the EU with its own internal and external identity. This explains the initially quite similar preferences of most supranational actors. This observation directly leads attention towards the second main argument which relates to the dynamic nature of preferences. Learning processes as part of day-to-day policy-making, as well as constant adaptation to the requirements stemming from the functional dynamics of both areas, required supranational actors to adjust their preferences. This adaptation went hand in hand with a lock-in effect. Thus the preferences of supranational actors stabilized as a result of constant interaction with other actors in the policy-making process, an accommodation with the own institutional role and the establishment of internal organizational structures. Due to the quite different institutional roles and experiences in the policy-making process, it can finally be shown that the preferences of supranational actors vary considerably. It is this divergence that will be particularly emphasized throughout this chapter.

Preferences in the two areas are not primarily driven by a supranational/ intergovernmental divide, which would put supranational actors in collective opposition to national governments, but rather by a complex accommodation process in which supranational actors – and also national governments – develop and constantly adapt their specific policy preferences (Tallberg 2002: 33–6). This does not exclude the occurrence of shared interests between supranational actors but does emphasize the divergence of preferences which often prevails over shared integrationist tendencies. Therefore, the institutional feature of a dominance of executive actors in foreign and interior policies also leaves its mark upon the preferences of supranational actors. Consequently, the preferences of the Commission and the Council Secretariat are strongly related to the executive roles performed by both actors. Being part of the same 'epistemic community', subject to similar and shared learning exercises and in constant professional exchange, the preferences of these executive supranational actors and national governments reveal important similarities (Richardson 1996a; Sebenius 1992).[3] These *executive preferences* can then be differentiated from the *control preferences* of Parliament, the Court of Justice and the Court of Auditors.

In sum, this chapter argues that the preferences of supranational actors have to be understood against the background of the functional characteristics of constituent policies. While the shared preferences in terms of a shared interest of supranational actors for a communitarization of both areas do indeed lead to some convergence, this trend is at the same time countered by a divergence of preferences between supranational actors which relate to their different institutional capabilities.

This chapter analyses the preferences of supranational actors from three different angles. It firstly looks at the *policy preferences* of supranational actors in Middle East and migration policies, thereby exploring how these actors have developed specific 'lenses' with the help of which they observe the two areas. It will be asked what kind of objectives they have in both areas, what kind of action they propose for pursuing these objectives and how these objectives are subject to change and adaptation. In a second step these policy preferences are then put in context with their *long-term preferences* in foreign and interior policies. Therefore, the proposals of supranational actors for institutional reform, as they were tabled during the 1996 and 2000 Intergovernmental Conferences as well as during the Convention for an EU constitution, are analysed. Finally, this chapter looks at the *internal organizational structures* of each actor in foreign and interior policies in an attempt to detect how they have responded to the organizational requirements stemming from the integration of constituent policies. The first part analyses the preferences of executive actors, starting with the Commission, followed by a study of the preferences of the Council

Secretariat. Accordingly, the second part accounts for the preferences of 'control actors', namely Parliament, the Court of Auditors in Middle East policies and, finally, the Court of Justice in migration policies.

The considerable divergence of preferences of supranational actors in the areas of foreign and interior policies in general, and Middle East and migration policies in particular, results from the different roles performed by these actors in both areas. The differences between the preferences of executive actors on the one hand, and actors which control executive policy-making on the other, should, however, not lead to the conclusion that within these two groups preferences will be the same. As this chapter shows, the preferences of the Commission are on several crucial dimensions different from those of the Council Secretariat, while Parliament, the Court of Justice and the Court of Auditors also have significant differences with regard to the main interests in both areas. Balancing this divergence, there is some convergence among supranational actors regarding their jointly shared long-term objective of the further centralization of foreign and interior policies at the EU level. These similarities in preferences were visible in the early period after the Maastricht Treaty in particular, as well as in the proposals of supranational actors for Treaty reforms.

When in 1993 the Maastricht Treaty came into force, supranational actors had already developed certain preferences regarding both areas as part of their involvement in policy-making in EC foreign and interior policies at the Community level, as well as their (marginal) roles in the intergovernmental EPC and Trevi co-operation frameworks. The Maastricht Treaty introduced an element of change, since supranational actors – as well as member states – had to adjust their preferences to the new functional and institutional environment of constituent policies. In this early formative period, preferences on Middle East and migration policies were shaped by shared perspectives of supra-national actors on the functional need to establish 'comprehensive frameworks' for both areas at the EU level. As a result of adaptation to their quite different capabilities, however, divergent preferences soon counter-balanced this partial convergence. This accommodation process can well be detected when looking at the ways in which these actors have developed their internal organizational structures in both areas in order to meet their institutionally defined roles in foreign and interior policies.

The Commission's preferences in Middle East and migration policies have shifted from an initially quite ambitious and political perspective on both areas to a more technical and managerial approach. The Commission's preferences reveal a strong focus on its entrenched first-pillar capabilities and those issues that it regards as being largely consensual among member states. Notwith-standing this accommodation of the Commission with the cross-pillar design of both areas, its proposals for Treaty reforms reveal a tension between its short- and long-term preferences. The Council Secretariat's preferences are a different matter and have to some extent been separated from those of other supra-national actors, since the Secretariat does not have the same autonomy in the policy-making process as the other four actors. Its traditional function as an apolitical secretariat has, thus, characterized the Secretariat's preferences from the outset. Notwithstanding the persistence of these preferences, the politicization of the Secretariat following the establishment of the offices of the Special Representative and the High Representative led to an emergence of more independent preferences that can no longer be defined as being the mere reflection of the joint will of all member states.

Parliament's preferences point to its high degree of autonomy from member states as well as from executive policy-making in both areas. Consequently, the formulation of alternative policy agendas, as well as fundamental criticism about the institutional features of cross-pillar politics, has been the prime characteristic of Parliament's perspective on both policy areas. Yet a gradual decrease of opposition to official EU foreign and interior policies can over time be observed. Moreover, in both areas Parliament has developed a specific self-understanding as a provider of a platform for representing the interests of those 'outsiders' affected by EU foreign and interior policies, namely third countries and third-country nationals. The Court of Justice issued two important judgements in the area of migration policies in the years under consideration and these judgements bring to the fore preferences which emphasize the ECJ's interest in fostering the legal unity of both areas across the three pillars. The Court of Auditors, finally, has been active in the area of foreign policies and has scrutinized the administration of EU funds by the Commission and member states. Like those of the other 'control actors', the preferences of the Court of Auditors reflect a much more comprehensive approach in addressing the functional unity of both policy areas when compared with the Commission and the Council Secretariat.

The policy preferences of the Commission: accepting a managerial role

The preferences of the Commission in Middle East and migration policy are directly linked to its involvement in the executive 'epistemic community' of member states, Commission and Council Secretariat (Haas 1992). Yet the preferences of the Commission in both areas have been subject to significant changes over time. Thus, in the formative period following the coming into force of the Maastricht Treaty, the preferences of the Commission in Middle East and migration policies were primarily based on a *functionally unified understanding* of what the concept of the single institutional framework entailed. Preferences revealed a quite ambitious and political approach to policy-making in both areas, based on the assumption that the single institutional framework would lead to comprehensive policies which stretch beyond the pillar confines, thereby ensuring a dominance of first-pillar policies. This orientation, however, soon gave way to a more managerial and cautious approach. The Commission's preferences shifted to a more pragmatic understanding which recognized that the cross-pillar institutional setting implied significant limitations to its own executive capabilities. In this adaptation period the Commission's preferences shifted to a more moderate focus on its entrenched first-pillar powers, whereas in the second and third pillars emphasis was put on fostering its role as an 'associated member' within the Council-dominated working structures of these two pillars, thus acknowledging the lead taken in these institutional settings by member states. Notwithstanding this development, an uneasiness regarding the overall institutional design of EU foreign and interior policies has been expressed by the Commission in the various Treaty reforms. This reveals an underlying tension between the long-term normative preferences on the one hand, and policy preferences on the other. In sum, in both areas the Commission has developed preferences which reflect its acceptance of the political primacy of the Council and member states, combined with a co-operative, administrative approach regarding its own role in the policy-making process rather than political assertion.

In September 1993, coinciding with the coming into force of the Maastricht Treaty in November of that year, the Commission published two communications in which it outlined its agenda for EU Middle East policies. It advocated an ambitious political perspective for EU foreign policies in the region, while the suggested instruments were mainly directed towards the 'economic front', in other words those areas in which the Commission possessed considerable capabilities and prior experience (Commission 1993b: 1). As part of this political assertion, the Commission claimed to set out the guidelines for a 'longer-term approach' to Middle East policies (Commission 1993a: 1). It suggested centring EU Middle East policies on the promotion of 'economic integration' in the region, thereby developing 'regional cooperation and institutions (for example water and energy management)' (Commission 1993a: 4). Against the background of the EU's own history, the Commission proposed a 'progressive institutionalisation' of the Middle East (Peres 1996: 104–11; d'Alançon 1994). It considered the Regional Economic Development Working Group (REDWG), which includes officials from Israel, Palestine, Jordan and Egypt and whose permanent secretariat is based in Amman as the nucleus for a creation of supranational working methods in the Middle East (Commission 1993a: 3; Peters 1996).[4] The focus on economic policies was further emphasized by the Commission's proposal to establish a huge financial assistance programme to the nascent Palestinian Authority, consisting of €500 million in aid for the period 1994–8. With regard to the Union's relations with Israel, the Commission suggested giving priority to an upgrading of the 1975 Free Trade Agreement and equipping the Commission with a negotiating mandate which covers 'a wide range of sectors' (Commission 1993b: 5). This linkage between regional institutionalization, trade policies and financial assistance also characterizes the Commission's proposal for a new design for Mediterranean policies, with which the EU should pursue its strategic interests in the region. Thus a network of Association Agreements linking the EU with all non-member states in the Mediterranean, both on a political and an economic level, the establishment of a Euro-Mediterranean Free Trade Area by the year 2010, an assistance package of €5.5 billion and support for regional integration are the main policies proposed by the Commission (Commission 1994b). In an attempt to foster its own central role in relations with the Palestinian Authority, the Commission stressed that the 'Commission's representative in the territories should take up his position shortly' (Commission 1993b: 3). Indeed the Commission, for political reasons, considered the opening of this office a key objective and engaged in month-long negotiations with the Israeli authorities until the opening of a representative office of the Commission in East Jerusalem, with the main administrative task being to oversee the allocation and implementation of aid, was finally accepted.[5]

The political ambitions of the Commission were, however, soon challenged by both external and internal developments. While the political crisis of the Middle East peace process since the mid-1990s rendered the link between economic support and political influence less strong than hoped for, the impact of cross-pillar institutions within the EU foreign affairs system brought to the fore the limits which the Commission faced in defining the overall direction of EU policies (Monar 1998 and 2000). As a result of this learning process, the Commission adapted its preferences and developed a more cautious approach to its own role in policy-making. The Commission acknowledged that trade and assistance measures are not a substitute for diplomatic foreign policies, thus an institutional arena of EU politics in which member states continue to take the lead. The Commission consequently concluded that although the Union's economic involvement in the region 'had a very important political result' such as the political survival of the Palestinian Authority or the 'decisive [financial] support for modernisation' in Arab countries, it nevertheless 'seems to have failed to achieve its original goals' (Commission 1998b: 7). The vulnerability of its own ambitious agenda for Middle East policies from external developments also affected the Commission's preferences on Mediterranean policies when it argued that the EMP 'has increasingly faltered since it was based on the implicit assumption that the peace process would at least remain on track' (Commission 1998b: 14). While the Commission mainly blamed external factors, such as Israeli closures, as 'preventing the success' of its policies, the modification of preferences was also the result of an adaptation to EU internal developments (Commission 1998b: 16). While somewhat defiantly arguing that economic policies were the main policy of the EU whereas only 'in parallel ... the Union maintained its *supportive complementary* role' on the political level, the Commission's preferences in the area adapted to the recognition of an internal division of powers which foresaw political guidance of the Council and the pursuit of diplomatic activities by the Special Representative and, later, the High Representative (Commission 1998b: 3, my emphasis). Thus, 'diplomatically and politically', the Union should – 'complementary ... to the US' – be represented by the 'Ministerial level and through its Special Envoy' (1998b: 22–3).

The adaptation of preferences was mitigated by the Commission's experiences within the executive system of EU foreign relations. On the one hand, this system guaranteed a permanent involvement of the Commission in policy-making, for example in the working groups of the Council or the Middle East working groups of the Special Representative.[6] On the other hand, the Commission realized that the political dimension of foreign policies and the definition of overall objectives would not be its own task (Gomez 1998). This adaptation to the recognition of its own limited cross-pillar capabilities in foreign policies also becomes visible when looking at the way in which the Commission was involved in the drafting of the Common Strategy on the Mediterranean region. Thus the Common Strategy was drafted jointly by officials from the Council Secretariat and the Commission, the Commission taking the lead for those aspects related to the first pillar while the Secretariat was responsible for those devoted to the second pillar *and* the overall object-ives.[7] The Commission thus had a seat at the table but had to pay the price of accepting political guidance by the Council. This adaptation has also affected the preferences of the Commission with regard to the EMP. Not forgetting to emphasize its own pivotal role within the institutional structures of the EMP, the Commission reluctantly consented to the political leadership of the Council in this cross-pillar institutional setting. 'The Common Strategy of the European Union on the Mediterranean region was adopted to *guide* the policies and activities of the Union' (Commission 2000d: 5, my emphasis). This statement documents the adaptation of preferences to the specific institutional features of constituent policies. Whereas in the early period the Commission viewed policies almost exclusively from the economic, first-pillar perspective and attempted to define a political agenda for EU Middle East policies, learn-ing experiences within the cross-pillar institutional setting, as well as an accommodation with the prerogatives of the member states and the Council Secretariat on both the wider cross-pillar political dimension of EU foreign policies and the more narrow second-pillar policies, led to an adaptation of preferences towards a more cautious stance which devises for the Commission an administrative role mainly on the economic dimension.

It is against the background of these changed preferences that the reforms of the internal organizational structures of the Commission must be understood. It was in 1996 that the Commission started a major restructuring process of its internal organization in foreign policies. The suggested reforms relate to several layers. First, 'the internal structures of the External Relations (RELEX) DG were reformed and adapted to comply with those of the second pillar, inter alia through the creation of a separate CFSP Directorate and a Conflict Prevention and Crisis Management Division' (European Parliament 2001f: 17). Second, in 1999 the Commission merged the three foreign policy DGs into one (Allen 1998). Third, it set up a cross-DG unit, named EuropeAid, that had the task of improving the implementation of assistance measures, which remains the Commission's main foreign policy instrument (Santiso 2002). Fourth, the Commission initiated a long-term process of reforming the entire external service structures with the objective of establishing an 'integrated External Service' (Commission 2000c: 2). These new structures should guarantee that the Commission's organizational structures, which initially were set up to 'represent the Commission in trade negotiations and in some industrialised countries', respond better to the 'broad scope of EU external relations as well as the new profile and potential of CFSP' (Commission 2001a: 2–3). The reform of the external service, which focuses mainly on an improvement in the co-ordination of policies between the Brussels headquarters and the more than 120 Commission delegations in third countries, in particular regarding aid management, documents both the adaptation to the cross-pillar institutional setting as well as a shift of orientation towards a stronger focus on its traditional first-pillar capabilities. Thus these reforms are meant to enable 'the Commission to contribute at all levels to the CFSP. It also enables it to tailor its actions under the First Pillar so as to be coherent with the EU's wider political objectives' which, however, are set by the European Council (Commission 2000c: 6). The reform of the external service includes, finally, a professionalization of internal structures. The Commission plans to establish structures for career planning within the its external service, the regular alternating of staff between headquarters and delegations, and the establishment of specialized training structures.

While it is true that on the dimension of executive policy-making the Commission has adapted to the cross-pillar institutional setting, it did not entirely refrain from proposing far-reaching changes to the structure of the Union's foreign relations. Leaving its day-to-day preferences largely unaffected, the Commission proposals during Treaty reforms reveal an underlying tension of these preferences with the preferences held on the long-term design of EU foreign affairs. Thus, during the 1996 IGC the Commission fundamentally criticized the cross-pillar setting.

> The very fact that two different working methods – the Community approach and the intergovernmental approach – coexist in the same Treaty is a source of incoherence. Experience has confirmed the fears previously expressed on this subject. The single institutional framework which was supposed to ensure harmony between the various 'pillars' of the Treaty has not functioned satisfactorily. The proper lessons have to be drawn.
>
> (Commission 1995b: 2)

The reform proposal of the Commission did, however, not amount to a complete communitarization of foreign policies. Rather than directly proposing institutional reforms, the Commission focused on the functional dimension of policies. It urged tackling the 'disappointing' performance of the common foreign policy which was described as being 'inherent in the existence of separate "pillars"' (1995b: 69). Accordingly, the Commission and member states should foster the linkages between the pillars in an attempt to ensure a better management of the two-pillar architecture within the single institutional framework. By doing so, they would then concentrate on improving the effectiveness of policies. Thus, while emphasizing the objective that 'the

Union must be able to present a united front', the Commission did not propose major institutional changes, besides greater recourse to qualified majority voting and providing the Union with legal personality (Commission 1996). A similar reform perspective was then again put forward by the Commission at the 2000 IGC. It explicitly stated that all proposals work 'on the assumption that the pillar structure will be kept' (Commission 2000b: 4). It was only in the framework of the Convention that the Commission became more explicit about its general criticism of the pillar architecture of EU foreign policies and called for an abolition of the cross-pillar institutional setting. Somewhat intricately, the Commission argued that in 'certain relatively new policy fields', such as foreign affairs, 'we need to create systems to agree and implement policy which reflect the effectiveness and legitimacy of the Community method' (Commission 2002a: 4). Regarding foreign policies, the Commission suggested a 'stepwise institutional change' that would ultimately result in an exclusive usage of the Community method of decision-making. The Commission not only proposed introducing qualified majority voting in foreign policies but also gradually providing the Commission with the sole right of initiative. As a first step in that direction, the Commission supported the idea of merging the offices of the High Representative and the external relations Commissioner into the office of a 'Secretary of the European Union' and proposed locating the Secretary within the Commission. For that purpose the foreign policy services of the Council Secretariat, the Commission and the delegations should merge into a 'single administration'. The Secretary should be appointed jointly by the Council and the President-designate of the Commission. The right of initiative would rest with the Secretary, shared with member states during the transitory period, and at the end of this period solely with the Secretary – after a vote by the Council with an enhanced qualified majority. Moreover, the Secretary would also be responsible for representing the Union abroad and implementing common decisions (Commission 2002a).

The Commission's preferences in interior policies reveal many parallels with the aforementioned developments in foreign affairs. Thus a similar adaptation process from an initially ambitious and political agenda, which was based on a functionally unified approach to migration policies, was replaced by a more managerial, issue-orientated attitude. This adaptation was triggered by an accommodation with the constraints posed by the cross-pillar institutional setting (Myers 1995). Notwithstanding the stabilization of these preferences, the Commission continues to uphold its long-term preferences for a complete communitarization of this area.

In the immediate aftermath of the Maastricht Treaty, the Commission's preferences were guided by its ambition to develop a functionally coherent model with the help of which migration policies could become embedded within 'a European area without internal borders' (Commission 1994a: 23). Elaborating on a quite assertive understanding of its role in policy-making, the Commission deliberately looked 'beyond the existing work programme of the

Union' set by the European Council (1994a: foreword). And indeed its political
ambitions were reflected in the objective of 'providing a general framework
within which a European immigration and asylum policy can be developed'
(1994a: 5). This 'comprehensive approach' was only marginally affected by
considerations about the impact which the cross-pillar institutional setting
might exert on policies (1994a: foreword). On the contrary, the framework was
based on 'the wisdom of a comprehensive multi-disciplinary approach' which
combined three main policies which, if implemented, would have stretched
across all three pillars (1994a: 11). Thus, the Commission's approach consisted
of reducing migration pressure through first- and second-pillar policies, controlling migration flows through first- and third-pillar measures and, finally,
integration policies for legal immigrants through a combination of first- and
third-pillar policies. The Commission recognized that the realization of this
'combination of policies ... requires the co-ordination of traditional areas of
activity, such as social policy, aspects of common foreign and security policy
and trade, co-operation and development instruments as well as migration and
migration management policies' (1994a: 5). Nevertheless, the Commission
was optimistic with regard to prospects for rapid implementation and argued
that 'the TEU brings all of these policies within a single institutional framework and therefore creates new possibilities for the development of the
comprehensive approach which is now required' (1994a: 5). Possible obstacles
were not addressed and hence the Commission was also confident that the pre-
Maastricht approach of 'approximation rather than harmonisation' could be
overcome (1994a: 9). Suggesting a far-reaching transfer of first-pillar method-
ologies and concepts to this new EU policy area, the Commission argued that
the overall objective now would be to 'harmonise immigration and asylum
policies' (1994a: 20). In this early period after the coming into force of the
Maastricht Treaty, the preferences of the Commission on migration policies
showed little concern for the impact of the cross-pillar institutional setting and
were based on the assumption of a 'Treaty *obligation* to co-operate within a
single institutional structure' (1994a: 2, my emphasis).[9]

The political ambition to set out a 'comprehensive' agenda for migration
policies was, however, soon confronted with the complexities of policy-making
in the area. In a process of adaptation to the cross-pillar institutional setting of
constituent policies, the Commission adjusted its preferences and shifted to a
narrower focus on those parts of asylum and immigration policies which
promised a realistic chance of being adopted at the Council level (den Boer and
Wallace 2000: 508).[10] This adaptation is well documented in the way in which
the Commission dealt with the application of ex-Article K.9 TEU, which
provided for a transfer of parts of migration policies from the third to the first
pillar. Whereas in 1994 the Commission regarded a transfer of migration
policy matters quite positively and proposed considering the application of
Article K.9 'to asylum policies ... in the light of experience', the Commission
subsequently shifted to a more cautious approach (Commission 1994a: 6).
Thus, when readdressing the question of a transfer, the Commission concluded

that the 'article did not at present seem ... to be the most appropriate instrument, not to say an impossible one' (Commission 1995a). In particular, the Commission referred to the complex decision-making procedures in the Council with regard to an application of ex-Article K.9:

> The procedure laid down is cumbersome and requires the Member States' unanimous approval and ratification in accordance with their respective national constitutional provisions. In one Member State this means that a national referendum will inevitably be triggered if Article K.9 is invoked.
>
> (Commission 1995a)

This adaptation to the incremental decision-making procedures of cross-pillar politics as well as of the political dominance of member states in this area led the Commission to readjust its preferences in migration policies towards a managerial, issue-orientated approach. The Commission ultimately acknow-ledged that 'the JHA acquis ... is different in nature from other parts of the Union's acquis' (Commission 1998a: 4). On the issue of policy-making, the Commission stressed the need of 'interinstitutional cooperation', since in the area of migration policies 'more than in others it will therefore be necessary to continue a constructive dialogue between the Member States and the Commission' (1998a: 3). It also qualified its own approach to making use of its right of initiative. Thus the Commission 'will, of course, make use of its right of initiative, but in doing so it will set priorities which take account of the timetable fixed by the Treaty itself', rather than suggesting, as previously announced, a 'comprehensive' framework (1998a: 6). Finally, no longer is the harmonization of migration policies described as the objective but rather the goal is 'to develop more similar approaches and closer co-operation' of member states (1998a: 6). The Commission, thus, became aware of the 'admittedly real difficulties of adjusting national approaches to these sensitive issues' (Com-mission 2001b: 5). Self-restraint and increased awareness of the constraints posed by the cross-pillar institutional setting for autonomous action are the main characteristics of this adaptation period. Hence 'the Commission regards the design and implementation' of migration policies as a 'joint effort with the Council' and will only make use of its 'existing know-how, before developing specific know-how in areas in which hitherto the Commission had no formal powers' (Commission 1998a: 10).

    The stabilization of these preferences can be exemplified by looking at the Commission's approach to policy-making in the aftermath of the Amsterdam Treaty. The Commission no longer pursued an ambitious political agenda but rather accommodated a more managerial role within the EU executive. The political guidance of the Council on the policy agenda in migration policies was accepted and the Commission pointed out that in policy-making 'the starting point has to be the elements already endorsed by the European Council' (Commission 2000a: 4). The shift towards a more managerial and less political definition of its own role is well documented by the Commission's focus on the scoreboard. Thus the Commission defined its own role in this process as one of 'implementing the necessary measures and meeting the deadlines' (Commission 2000e: 3). It refrained, for the time being, from developing a 'comprehensive' agenda for migration policies. Indeed, by prioritizing the management of the scoreboard, it does 'not attempt any comprehensive coverage of the potentially vast area of legislation' as was, for example, outlined in the 1994 communication on asylum and immigration (Commission 2000a: 6). The narrowing down of its executive activities into pre-defined bits and pieces, as they are entailed in the scoreboard, has shifted the Commission's focus towards the mechanisms that guarantee the proper functioning of the various initiatives contained in it.[11] This shift towards a greater emphasis on the short-term perspective nurtured the Commission's demand that the scoreboard, at least, 'must be sufficiently detailed and structured that precise targets to be reached by the end of each calendar year are clearly identified and visible', thus reflecting the hope that proper technical management would trigger political dynamics at the Council level (Commission 2000a: 5). Yet actual experiences with the implementation of the scoreboard brought disillusionment.

> It would be satisfying to report to the European Council that the 'pillar switch' has led to a greater sense of urgency and flexibility than was the case before the Amsterdam Treaty came into force, particularly in the light of the clear deadlines set at the highest political level. Unfortunately, that is not yet the case.
>
> (Commission 2001b: 6)

It should be mentioned that the Commission has not entirely abandoned its ambition to develop a 'comprehensive' approach to migration policies. However, it has adjusted these preferences to the constraints posed by the cross-pillar institutional setting of constituent policies. Thus for all measures that go beyond the initiatives listed in the scoreboard, and which entail a combination of policies beyond its narrow legislative agenda, the Commission came up with the concept of an 'open method of co-ordination' (Caviedes 2004; Tallberg 2002; Hodson and Maher 2001). The Commission envisaged that the open method of co-ordination, as it was suggested for both asylum and immigration policies, would be managed by the Commission itself and, essentially, provide for the removal of certain (cross-pillar) policies from legislation in order to establish, in the long run, non-legislative, administrative 'flanking measures and techniques for convergence' (Commission 2001c: 3; Commission 2001b). This method, which again documents the adaptation to more managerial preferences, should, by providing for administrative co-operation between the Commission and member states, and a regular exchange of information and reports, 'provide the necessary policy mix to achieve a gradual approach to the development of an EU policy, based ... on the identification and development of common objectives to which it is agreed that a common European response is necessary' (Commission 2001a: 5).

The Commission's internal organization in migration policies has changed fundamentally since the Maastricht Treaty and has gone hand in hand with the overall centralization process in this area. Thus in 1992 the Commission established a nucleus administrative unit on Justice and Home Affairs located within the Commission President's office. This unit consisted of three officials only and was later slightly upgraded to a total staff of five. Following the coming into force of the Amsterdam Treaty, a DG for Justice and Home Affairs was established. However, small staff numbers in this setting were also perceived by the Commission as a major hindrance to efficient action. Thus the two units dealing with migration issues comprised a staff of 10 officials with regard to free movement and borders and 16 in the area of immigration and asylum. While the semi-communitarization of migration policies, as provided for by the Amsterdam Treaty, was perceived as 'positive for us', the personnel situation was depicted as putting the Commission in 'an awkward position'.[12] The almost exclusive concentration of the Commission on ensuring progress in the implementation of the narrow, albeit extensive legislative horizon sketched out by the scoreboard corresponds with the small number of officials working within the Commission on this agenda.

Notwithstanding the accommodation of the Commission with its managerial role in migration policies, an entire communitarization of this area, and thus the abolition of the semi-communitarized institutional setting, continues to be the long-term preference of the Commission. Seen from that perspective, the Amsterdam Treaty reforms were only a first step away from the heavily criticized policy-making processes under the Maastricht Treaty. During the 1996 IGC, the third pillar was described as being based on 'outdated methods and resources'. The Commission criticized in particular the 'ineffectiveness and the absence of democratic and judicial review' and argued 'that the best way of attaining all these objectives would be to transfer justice and home affairs to the Community framework' (Commission 1996). There were thus three main demands from the Commission. Since 'the unanimity requirement is probably the main reason why Title VI has proved ineffective' the Commission proposed the introduction of qualified majority voting for all migration policy issues. Moreover, since legislation in this area 'directly affects individual rights' it also requires – in opposition to foreign policies which 'has to deal with fluid situations' – the transfer of jurisdiction to the Court of Justice. Finally, communitarization is also deemed necessary because

> in complete contrast to foreign policy, where the same arrangements apply, the option of charging expenditure to the Community budget has not been exercised as it has proved impossible to secure unanimous agreement of the very principle of using the Community budget in this area.
>
> Commission 1995b

During the 2000 IGC as well as in the Convention, the Commission was even more precise regarding its long-term preferences. It proposed the introduction of an entirely communitarized institutional setting in this area, i.e. the sole right of initiative for the Commission and qualified majority voting in the Council on all decisions as well as the across-the-board introduction of the co-decision procedure (Commission 2000a; 2002a).

The Commission has undergone a noteworthy adaptation of its preferences in Middle East and migration policies. As part of this process it had to adjust its political ambitions to the limitations posed by the cross-pillar institutional setting. It should, however, also be noted that the incorporation of the Commission into executive policy-making across the pillars provides the Commission with the opportunity to develop skills and knowledge beyond the narrow confines of its main responsibilities. It is against this background that the Commission's approach to developing specific 'labels' for EU policies can be understood. Thus the Commission attempted to develop 'cultural frames' for both Middle East and migration policies in a similar way to what happened in the framework of the Single Market Programme (Fligstein and Mara-Drita 1996; Fligstein and Stone Sweet 2002). If successful, the European dimension of a particular policy area will be identified with these 'cultural frames' and, inter alia, foster the role of the Commission as an 'indispensable' actor within the institutional setting established for implementing these frames. Indeed, in both areas there exist institutionalized, executive-biased structures, which are built around such 'cultural frames' and which are strongly promoted by the Commission. In foreign policies, for example, the Commission reveals a strong focus on the frame of 'Barcelona', and since 2003 the 'neighbourhood frame' in the context of the ENP. In that context, the debate about who could rightly claim 'ownership' of the EMP is an intriguing example of the Commission's approach to become associated with such institutionalized frameworks. While some argue that the Barcelona process was initially designed by the Spanish and French governments, in an attempt to establish a counterweight to the effects from Eastern enlargement, Commission officials strongly insist that the origins of 'Barcelona' come from within its own ranks (Barbé 1998; Gomez 1998; Rhein 1999).[13] In a similar way, the Commission has associated itself with the concept of an 'area of freedom, security and justice'.

The emergence of the Council Secretariat as an autonomous actor

It is not usual to analyse the preferences of the Council Secretariat as an autonomous variable. Given the traditional public invisibility of the Secretariat, 'it might be tempting to view the General Secretariat as nothing more than the notary of the Council'. However, 'this rather limited view would belie the reality of the situation' (Hayes-Renshaw and Wallace 1997: 102). Indeed, in Middle East and migration policies, the preferences of the Secretariat cannot simply be derived from knowledge of the interests of member states

(Christiansen 2002). This section addresses two features which structure the Secretariat's preferences. First, it looks at those preferences which are derived from the 'traditional' role of being a professionalized, facilitating secretariat of the Council. Second, it discusses the increase of autonomy in preferences which accompanied the centralization process of constituent policies and the subsequent establishment of two new offices in the Secretariat in the area of foreign policies, namely the offices of the Special Representative and the High Representative.

The traditional public invisibility of the Council Secretariat has, at least in the area of foreign policies, given way to a particular visibility. Media coverage of the activities of the Special Representative for the Middle East peace process since 1996, and after 1999 of the High Representative for the Common Foreign and Security Policy, has intensified significantly.[14] But it was also within the Secretariat itself that the establishment of these two offices was perceived as a significant change. An official dealing with the CFSP compared the new General Secretary of the Council to his predecessor and argued that 'Solana is something completely new. Trumpf was invisible.' What was perceived as new was not only the personalization of the EU foreign affairs systems as a result of this institutional innovation, but also changes to the operating structures of the Secretariat in foreign policies. Thus, several officials from the Secretariat noted that there has been an increase of autonomy of the Secretariat. One official from the Special Representative's staff concluded that she was 'not sure that member states understood this consequence of their decision' to establish these two offices.[15] Overall, the internal perception was that, due to these changes, the 'role of Secretariat is in flux'.[16]

These new features must, however, be distinguished from the continuity regarding the way in which the Secretariat still deals with many of its traditional functions such as writing agenda notes, assisting the Presidency, suggesting compromise proposals, drafting Joint Decisions or co-chairing working group meetings without attempting to acquire an autonomous role in the decision-making process. These long-established features guarantee a high degree of continuity, and consequently foster the solidity of the linkage between the Secretariat and member states (Forster and Wallace 2000).

Nevertheless, institutional innovation has also led to the emergence of more autonomous preferences of the Secretariat in EU foreign policies. Yet, unlike the Commission, the Secretariat does not put in question the cross-pillar design of the EU foreign affairs system, but rather works on the assumption that it is to the 'advantage' of the EU that the Commission is responsible for the first pillar and the Secretariat for the CFSP.[17] The pillar division is, thus, not perceived as an obstacle for 'coherent' policies but as a guarantor of the Secretariat's newly acquired capabilities. It is against this background that the Secretariat does not seek a full-scale harmonization of foreign policies. The High Representative could, therefore, argue 'that ours is a common foreign policy, not a single one' (Council Secretariat 2002a: 3).

This cautious approach is nurtured by the sometimes painstaking experiences of both the Special Representative and the High Representative in developing common positions jointly with the member states. The Special Representative, for example, must take these practical difficulties into consideration although they might hamper the effectiveness of his mandate. In the words of one advisor, 'the main problem is: what messages he has to present. He cannot move without full support of member states, this reduces his speed.'[18] While there is, thus, criticism about the cumbersome procedures of the CFSP, this view is balanced by the interest of the Secretariat in maintaining the two-pillar design of foreign policies, which in turn allows the Special Representative and the High Representative to perform executive tasks independent of the Commission. This also explains why the Secretariat has not come up with proposals for overall Treaty changes in foreign policies. During the 2000 IGC, the Council Secretariat made suggestions for reforms but 'none of them requiring an amendment of the Treaties' (Council Secretariat 2002b: 2).

It is, however, not only with regard to Treaty provisions but also on the dimension of concrete policies that the Secretariat puts less emphasis on institutional architecture than does the Commission. In Middle East policies this has, for example, supported the formation of the quite divergent preferences of the Secretariat and the Commission on the priorities for action. While the Commission attempted to keep the EMP separated from problems in the peace process, hoping that the Palestine–Israeli conflict would not lead to a blockage of the Barcelona structures in which the Commission had invested considerable resources, the Secretariat was less concerned with such considerations. During the second EMP meeting of foreign ministers in Malta in 1997 the Special Envoy brokered a meeting between the Israeli Foreign Minister David Levy and PA chairman Yasser Arafat. This meeting was perceived by the Secretariat as a signal both of the increased diplomatic importance of the EU and as a step towards overcoming the 'artificial separation of Barcelona and the peace process'; the Commission considered this event as an infringement upon its own institutional terrain and 'since then tries to keep the Special Envoy out of Euro-med'.[19] This 'protectionization' by the Commission of the EMP has met with harsh criticism by officials from the Secretariat and was regarded as being detrimental to the overall strategic objectives of the EU while serving the institutional interests of the Commission only (Peters 1998).[20] Since the Secretariat shows little interest either in sustaining a particular institutional frame for EU Middle East policies or in encroaching on Commission prerogatives in the first pillar, its interests lie mainly in the diplomatic arena. Both the Special Representative and the High Representative regard their role as an open 'talking mandate' rather than as being embedded in a particular institutionalized setting.[21] The diplomatic initiatives of the Special Representative and the High Representative have affected the EU internal equilibrium in foreign policies. While both have emphasized their close relationship with member states and accepted their prerogatives in the second pillar, a diplomatic assertion from within the Council Secretariat can also be observed. Thus an official from the Secretariat pointed out that some 'member states do not push for a political role of the EU' in foreign policies. Yet it is this political role which the Special Representative and the High Representative have repeatedly claimed to represent.[22] Both the Special Representative and the High Representative have on several occasions referred to themselves as the people behind the single EU telephone extension Henry Kissinger always asked for: 'The EU now has a phone number' (Council Secretariat 1998). Even more than that, only one person picks up the phone and the EU now speaks with 'one voice' (Council Secretariat 2002a: 3).

The preferences of the Secretariat regarding its own role in international politics complemented this 'one-voice' perspective. Thus visible acts of diplomacy as well as formal and informal contacts with third parties are perceived by Secretariat officials as the key elements of EU Middle East policies pursued by the Special Representative or the High Representative. The acceptance by Palestinians and, surprisingly, by Israel and the United States that the Special Envoy should be actively involved in the 1997 Wye River Agreement was repeatedly cited as one of these diplomatic successes which documented the 'advantages of complementarity' of US and EU approaches to Middle East policies (Perthes 2002b: 52).[23] Similarly, the participation of the High Representative in the Mitchell Commission or the Middle East quartet could be cited as such examples of diplomatic assertion. Being represented by 'one voice' also allowed the Special Representative and the High Representative to develop personal relations with actors from the United States and the Middle East. Officials from the Secretariat perceive this as an important value added of their own activities and as contributing to the overall effectiveness of EU policies. In Middle East policies, they highlighted the intense contacts with the Palestinian Authority. Thus an advisor to the Special Representative pointed out that – prior to the Al Aqsa Intifada – 'every second week he [the Special Representative] meets Arafat. Our asset is access to Arafat' and we 'get a lot of information from the PA'.[24]

Less visible than these meetings between Middle Eastern politicians and the Special Representative, but not necessarily less efficient, were the diplomatic initiatives of the EU Special Advisor who was responsible for security relations with the Israeli army and the Palestinian security forces. Regular personal contacts between the Security Advisor, who had a professional army background, with his Israeli and Palestinian counterparts, together with mediation efforts, have paved the way for an 'informal EU involvement' on the security dimension of the conflict, which arguably formed the basis for developments at a later stage, such as the EU role in the security operations at the Gaza Border Crossing since summer 2005. This is noteworthy, since in public statements by the Israeli government such involvement by the EU is often rejected (Economic Cooperation Foundation 2002: 22). The professional, issue-orientated approach of the Special Advisor has convinced an initially quite sceptical Israeli army establishment of the usefulness of EU involvement. This approach has been contrasted with – in the Israeli perspective – the less successful public shuttle diplomacy of the Special Representative.[25] A vivid description of this secretive approach was given by the Special Advisor himself, when referring to his contribution to the implementation of a ceasefire after a Palestinian suicide attack in Israel:

> It was a process that we did on a daily basis. I went down to see the [Palestinian] security leaders in order to deal with particular security problems, then went back to Arafat every night with a list of problems, and then returned to the field with Arafat's endorsements/instructions. Was a very time-consuming effort.
>
> (Economic Cooperation Foundation 2002: 2)

The establishment of the offices of the Special Advisor, the Special Representative and the High Representative has not only led to an readjustment of the preferences of the Secretariat but has also triggered organizational adjustments. Prior to this institutional change, Middle East policies were, on the Council level, exclusively dealt with by the Middle East and Maghreb-Mashrek working groups, in which officials from the Secretariat performed their 'traditional' administrative tasks (Regelsberger 1997). Parallel to these working groups, the Special Representative had set up two autonomous task forces on Middle East issues. These task forces, on water issues and refugees, were chaired by an official from the Special Representative's unit and co-chaired by the Commission (Peters 2000). They had the objective of developing proposals for post-conflict concepts on these two issues, but, in practice, serve the purpose of providing a 'think thank' for the Special Representative on Middle East policies at large. The bulk of the budget of these task forces is spent on expert briefings and consultants' reports.[26] According to officials from Directorate General E (CFSP), the Special Representative has been successful in shifting the agenda-setting power within the Council away from the 'traditional' CFSP working groups into these task forces.[27] The considerable size of his unit has been jealously referred to by officials from other (CFSP) units.[28]

In addition to this internal reorganization of the Council Secretariat's structures, three other new institutional structures, on the bilateral level, are worth mentioning. The EU–Israel Forum in Tel Aviv, whose first chairman was an advisor to the former Prime Minister Benjamin Netanyahu, has the task of providing information about the EU in Israel and of initiating debates about bilateral relations.[29] Largely unrecognized in Europe, this debate has gained momentum in recent years and led to intense discussions in the Israeli media, academia and politics – with the active participation of the EU–Israel Forum – about the future relationship between Israel and the EU, inter alia discussing the issue of possible membership (Schael 2002; Nathanson and Stetter 2005).[30] Second, the EU Special Advisor directs the aforementioned European–Palestinian Security Committee. Last, four European–Israeli working groups were established by the Special Representative to deal with the economic needs of the Palestinian population in the Occupied Territories. They focused on issues such as the passage of goods and people, finance, labour and the long-term economic development of Palestine. These working groups meet in Israel and bring together officials from the Special Representative's staff, from member states' embassies, the Commission delegation and officials from the respective Israeli ministries.

In migration policies the capabilities of the Council Secretariat are more limited than in foreign affairs. Its tasks are mainly based on the traditional function of being the Council's bureaucracy. These capabilities also shape the preferences of the Secretariat in migration policies (den Boer and Wallace 2000: 504). Therefore, political assertion is not sought by the staff of DG H, the SIS unit and the legal service, which together comprise approximately 15 officials. They describe their role as being 'a service provider for Council meetings', whereas on the political dimension 'there is no Secretariat agenda'.[31] Assessments of their own impact on migration policies are modest. An official concluded that 'an influence is there, but it is not enormous and works mostly through [assisting] Presidencies'.[32]

This cautious approach does not, however, impede the development of specific preferences on migration policies, which are not necessarily consensual with all member states. Thus the Secretariat has quickly adapted to the semi-communitarized institutional setting of migration policies. An interesting institutional explanation for this adaptation was offered by a Council official who argued that when compared with the Commission 'the Council Legal Service is even more progressive [on migration issues]. We can do that since we not need to be so careful.'[33] Thus, when discussing new approaches to migration policies following the Amsterdam Summit of 1997, it was the Secretariat which 'told member states that they should not continue pre-Amsterdam Conventions' ratification. But the Commission did not dare to say that.'[34] Somewhat transcending the role of a mere neutral service provider, the objective of the Secretariat is therefore to 'explain' to member states what kind of consequences the shift of migration policies to the first pillar has had. As one official pointed out, 'member states are slow in understanding EC competence' in migration policies.[35] While being convinced that 'the Community method is in the end the only way to get somewhere' a pragmatic and patient strategy was preferred over a more pro-active one. Since the path of integration had already been entered, there was no perception of a particular hurry. It was rather suggested that they should slowly 'let the Community law develop'. On this path of integration the role of the Secretariat would then be one of a scout or a sign post. 'We make member states accustomed with that', an official concluded.[36]

There are marked differences with regard to the preferences of the Council Secretariat when the two areas of migration and Middle East policies are compared. In the former area, the Secretariat continues mainly to perform the classical, administrative function of a bureaucracy. In contrast, the latter is characterized not only by the emergence of new institutional structures but, in the wake of these, a change of preferences towards a more political and autonomous understanding. Note, however, that this change of preferences is stronger for those officials directly attached to the offices of the Special Representative or the High Representative than for those working on foreign policies in DG E, where much of the traditional close working relationship with the member states in general, and the Presidency in particular, continues to shape preferences. The Secretariat has to shift between these two kinds of preferences. While in both areas the dominant role of the Council and member states is generally accepted (this also shields the Secretariat from executive competition by the Commission), there is strong evidence that in foreign policies the Secretariat has developed new kinds of preferences which are based on an active understanding of its role in the policy-making process.

Formulating alternative policy agendas: the role of Parliament

The preferences of Parliament in Middle East and migration policies are shaped by its rather weak position vis-à-vis the EU executive within the cross-pillar institutional setting of constituent policies. As a result of its marginal role, Parliament has often focused on voicing harsh criticism about the substance of EU policies in both areas and, consequently, on developing alternative policy agendas. Since this critical approach is related to both Council and Commission it has fostered the executive/control divide in EU foreign and interior policies. The focus on alternative agendas can be observed on three dimensions. First, by putting emphasis on the issues of democracy and human rights, Parliament has combined its alternative policy agenda with an underlying normative frame.[37] Second, Parliament has given a particular voice to the way in which it perceives the interests and demands of those affected by EU policies, be they the southern Mediterranean countries in the EMP in general, and Israel and Palestine in particular, with regard to foreign policies; and be they migrants or third-country nationals in the area of migration policies. Third, Parliament has not stopped at criticizing the content of policies but has proposed an alternative institutional setting and – also in its day-to-day operations – demanded a complete abolition of the pillar structure in both areas. Parliament legitimized this demand by arguing that the need for efficiency, coherence and strategic outlook of EU policies requires this overall communitarization.

The scepticism of Parliament in the area of Middle East policies relates to the perceived lack of political results, both in the framework of the EMP and in the EU's efforts in the Palestinian–Israeli conflict. Moreover, the strong focus of official EU policies on trade and assistance measures meets with certain reservations and Parliament emphasizes the shortcomings of this narrow economic focus of policies.[38] Against this background, Parliament criticizes the results of the EMP and argues that 'the progress achieved to date and described by the Commission ... is in actual fact much less obvious than the Commission appears to believe' (European Parliament 2001c: 16). Parliament links this critique regarding the substance of policies with an analysis of what it considers to be weak instruments of EU foreign politics which in turn lead to a lack of political strategy. Accordingly, it argues that shortcomings are the result of 'Member States' inability to give practical effect to the common foreign and security policy'. This inability then translates into actual policies. For example, the Common Strategy on the Mediterranean region is criticized because it only 'reproduces' the Barcelona Declaration, while

> nothing is said about how the measures and instruments to be set in motion under the new strategy will be financed [and] strangely, the long list of specific initiatives to be launched under the Common Strategy is followed merely by a scanty set of provisions relating to instruments and institutions.
>
> (European Parliament 2001b)

These inefficiencies are, according to Parliament, the main factor which accounts for the secondary role which the EU plays in international politics. This becomes obvious in the Middle East in particular where 'the European Union is not involved in the discussions on the political future of the region' while all it 'has done is to inject money without having any clear strategy and without drawing adequate benefits therefrom, such as the recognition of the fact that it has a special role to play in this area' (European Parliament 1999a).

As a result of this scepticism regarding the substance of EU policies in the Middle East and the wider Mediterranean area, Parliament has focused on developing alternative policy agendas which are not dealt with as extensively by other actors. A main focus of this alternative agenda has been the area of democracy promotion and human rights (Gillespie and Youngs 2002; Youngs 2002). In these areas Parliament has been able to make use of its capabilities in the budgetary process and, for example, succeeded in 1994 in including the 'European Initiative for Democracy and Human Rights' into the EU budget out of which, for example, MEDA Democracy projects had been funded (Stetter 2003).[39] Less successful was the attempt to establish, within the Commission, a European Centre for Democracy and Human Rights, which would bundle all human rights-related activities that had previously been spread over 19 different units and DGs (European Parliament 1997e). While Parliament introduced a specific budget heading referring to this centre in 1995, it has never been set up. The focus on democracy and human rights is furthermore reflected in Parliament's follow-up activities to the implementation of the Association Agreements with Israel and Palestine. In a resolution of April 2002 Parliament called for sanctions against Israel and a suspension of the EU–Israel Association Agreement because of Israeli military action in Palestine and the human rights situation there (European Parliament 2002a). Although this resolution was not binding and the call for sanctions was later rejected by the Council and also, albeit with some hesitation, by the Commission, Parliament's decision was widely covered both in Arab countries and in Israel. In the former case the decision was praised as providing a counter-agenda to US policies; in the case of the latter the decision was largely rejected and portrayed as being a proof of traditionally anti-Israeli or even anti-Semitic policies in Europe. Indeed in many reports the resolution was presented as the new policy of the EU, thus confirming the observation made by one parliamentarian that often 'abroad they do not differentiate between Parliament, the Commission and member states'.[40]

The focus on alternative policy agendas has also rendered Parliament more receptive to those demands from third countries which are not covered by official EU policies. Thus Parliament combines its criticism of the EMP with an emphasis on those items which are regarded by southern Mediterranean countries as being neglected within the Barcelona framework and, at a later stage, the ENP. This is particularly true for Parliament's approach to the economic provisions on free trade, which apply mainly to industrial products, and which are perceived as being biased in favour of the EU. Indeed, there is widespread critique by southern Mediterranean governments of the exclusion of agricultural products from free trade arrangements, although this is one of the few areas where these countries could provide considerable exports to the EU. This critique has been taken up by Parliament which demands 'the rapid liberalization of trade in agricultural products' (European Parliament 1997b). Parliament has also called for a more liberal approach to migratory movements, termed 'organised free movement of persons' (European Parliament 2001b; Hakura 1998). Regarding relations with Palestine, following the coming into force of the 1997 Interim Association Agreement with the PLO, Parliament argued that there is 'still a need to extend the scope of trade concessions for agricultural products of which the Palestinians have special requirements' (European Parliament 1996e). In other areas Parliament has also provided a platform for policy demands from Middle Eastern countries. Thus, since the mid-1990s, calls for Palestinian statehood have become a regular feature of Parliament's Middle East policies, whereas the Council, much more cautiously, only adopted this position at the Berlin European Council of May 1999 (European Parliament 1996a; Peters 2000). Largely unobserved by European media, but widely covered in Israel, an initiative of some MEPs has brought up the issue of possible Israeli membership in the EU. A petition in support of this issue has been signed by more than 50 MEPs – around 10 per cent of all members of Parliament – as well as several members of the Israeli Knesset (Tovias 2003).

It is not only with regard to policies that Parliament has been a forum for alternative agendas. On the issue of the institutional design of EU foreign policies Parliament has also maintained a sceptical stance. It views the institutional setting in foreign policies as being largely insufficient and argues that EU decision-making is blocked by 'the intergovernmental nature of its foreign policy' which is why 'the Union has not yet succeeded in playing a credible role in the Middle East' (European Parliament 1996e). Indeed, Parliament argues that the 'intergovernmental method ... threatens to paralyse totally the operations of the CFSP' (European Parliament 1997d). These efficiency-related arguments are then linked with a normative argument, namely that the main problems faced by EU foreign politics is the democratic deficit caused by the intergovernmental setting. Against this background, Parliament has called for the introduction of 'Community procedures' in all areas of foreign policies (European Parliament 2001d). This demand comprises the introduction of qualified majority voting in the Council, exclusive use of the EC budget and the consultation of Parliament on all issues (European Parliament 1997d). With regard to the Commission, Parliament has suggested the creation of a 'common diplomacy', inter alia supported by the establishment of a College of European Diplomacy and the transformation of Commission Delegations into 'Community delegations' (European Parliament 2001d). Parliament is explicit about its main objective in this institutional reform, and therefore pledges 'at least in the long term ... overcoming the three pillar structure' (European Parliament 2002d). With regard to more immediate reforms, as they were proposed during the 2000 IGC, Parliament came up with separate proposals for the first and second pillars, yet expressed its hope that these reforms would 'progressively diminish' the pillar divide. Thus, in the area of external economic relations, in which Parliament's capabilities are much less developed than in developmental assistance, the introduction of the co-decision procedure, as well as an involvement of Parliament during trade negotiations between the Commission and third countries, is demanded. As a major reform of the entire area of foreign affairs, Parliament has suggested that the Commission be delegated implementing powers for all non-military decisions, while the office of the High Representative should be fully integrated into the Commission, rendering the appointment procedure the same as the one for the election of the Commission President (European Parliament 2000c). These reforms were meant to pave the way for even further integration, ultimately resulting in the 'integration of all "pillars" into the Community structure' and the creation of a 'European Foreign Office' (European Parliament 2000b).

When turning, finally, to the internal organization of Parliament in Middle East policies, two main features characterize Parliament's organizational structures. First, Parliament has developed organizational structures with a strong focus on interparliamentary co-operation both in the EMP and in relations with Israel and Palestine. The lack of inclusion in the setting up of the Barcelona conference was heavily criticized and Parliament demanded from the Commission and the member states a stronger involvement in these frameworks (European Parliament 1999d). While Parliament was initially quite optimistic that the establishment of the Euro-Mediterranean Parliamentary Forum would provide a counter-weight to the executive dominance in the EMP, these hopes did not ultimately materialize (Stavridis 2001). Consequently, the agenda of these meetings has shifted from a general focus on the entire Barcelona process to a narrower, more issue-oriented approach in which the EP and the southern Mediterranean parliaments mainly focus on issues related to the aforementioned alternative policy agenda.

Regarding its internal organization in Middle East policies, two parallel structures have been established, namely parliamentary delegations on the one hand, and 'Inter Groups' on the other. Delegations deal with the official relations between Parliament and parliaments in third countries. Only for 'important countries' – and Israel and Palestine are considered by Parliament as such – is there a single delegation, whereas most delegations cover wider regions.[41] Inter Groups, on the other hand, are lobby groups in favour of a particular issue or country. Doubling the already established relationship of the delegations with Israel and Palestine, the Israel Inter Group was founded in 1992. This step was described as being a response to the existence of the Inter Group for Peace, which was set up in the 1980s and which supported the cause of the Kurdish People's Party (PKK) and the PLO. While the delegations, except for yearly visits with their counterparts from the Knesset or the Palestinian Legislative Council, 'do not work very strongly', the Inter Groups do take a 'more proactive approach'.[42] They have strong preferences on defending the interests of 'their' country. It is hardly surprising, therefore, that the establishment of the Israel Inter Group was based on a joint initiative by several MEPs and the former ambassador of Israel to the EU. Occasionally, the quite divergent preferences between these two Inter Groups get carried into the plenary. An initiative by the Inter Group for Peace to agree on a parliamentary resolution condemning Israeli policies on the rules of origin provisions for Israeli products originating from settlements in Palestine has failed to gain the necessary support 'due to pressure from the Israel lobby' in the Israel Inter Group.[43] Membership numbers in both Inter Groups are similar. The Inter Group for Peace comprises some 60 members, whereas the Israel Inter Group consists of around 80 MEPs.[44] The activities of these Inter Groups did not, however, only relate to external relations. Thus the head of the Israel Inter Group referred to a successful motion for a resolution to establish a European day for Holocaust remembrance as the most noteworthy initiative from the Inter Group. Another member of the Israel Inter Group stressed the usefulness of Inter Groups for information-gathering. He referred in particular to several expert briefings prior to the conclusion of the Science and Technology agreement between Israel and the EU. Being a member of the Committee on Industry, External Trade, Research and Energy, he acknowledged the quality of three meetings organized by the Inter Group at which MEPs were briefed on these agreements. He pointed out that, when compared to the information received in the Inter Group meetings, the 'Commission briefing was weaker'.[45]

Turning to migration policies, Parliament's preferences show a remarkable similarity to those outlined on foreign policies. The lack of direct influence over executive policy-making has led Parliament to adopt a general scepticism with regard to the overall policy agenda in migration policies. Yet a certain shift in Parliament's preferences towards less fundamental opposition to the official policy agenda of EU migration policies following the Amsterdam Treaty and a greater focus of its critique on the institutional structures in this area points to the integrative dynamics of the semi-communitarized institutional framework as well as to an anticipation of a wider introduction of the co-decision procedure in May 2004.

Following the establishment of the third pillar, Parliament initially adopted a very sceptical stance towards the executive, member states and Commission alike (Monar 1995). The preferences of Parliament regarding policy-making in migration policies related to two main dimensions. First, it opposed the policy agenda pursued in this area by criticizing the policy priorities set, which were regarded as one-sidedly serving the security interests of national governments.[46] Arguing that 'Member States are far more interested in police co-operation and the exchange of information than in citizens' rights' has led, according to Parliament, to a biased design of policies (European Parliament 1997c). Member states, the prime decision-makers in the third pillar, are thus portrayed as 'overemphasizing ... migration-limiting policies and the maintenance of order' (European Parliament 1997a). For example, Parliament blames the Council for having adopted 'a restrictive interpretation' of the rights of asylum seekers and refugees (European Parliament 1998). This general critique about the content of policies is strongly interwoven with an opposition to the very decision-making mechanisms in migration policies. Parliament, thus, not only complains that 'Member States are curtailing the right to asylum' but 'has been critical of the way in which decisions on asylum and immigration are taken behind closed doors'. Decisions are described by the chairwoman of the responsible committee as lacking 'any form of democratic accountability' due to the lack of parliamentary and judicial control mechanisms and termed 'pseudo-legislation [being] unacceptable as forms of Union legislation' (European Parliament 1996c).

Following the coming into force of the Amsterdam Treaty, Parliament modified its stance somewhat and the content of legislative proposals from member states and the Commission became subject to more constructive criticism. While parliamentarians still warned that some measures 'do not appear to strike the right balance between security and integration', it was acknowledged that Council and Commission have became more receptive to proposals from Parliament (European Parliament 2000a). While criticism regarding decision-making structures continued to figure prominently, Parliament often put this critique in the form of a warning not to repeat the 'mistakes' of the pre-Amsterdam period. Parliament could thus attack 'the illegal behaviour of the Council in the past' but emphasize that due to a more open attitude of Council and Commission it would now be 'prepared to pass over this' (European Parliament 1999c).

Notwithstanding these changes in the inter-institutional climate, Parliament still regarded the detection of those decision-making practices, which reflect a 'thinking and working typically associated with intergovernmental cooperation', as one of its main responsibilities (European Parliament 2000e). While Parliament occasionally referred to the perceived democratic deficit in EU migration policies, the focus of institutional critique shifted to more subtle observations. First, Parliament began to detect the implementation problems of EU migration policies rather than those directly related to decision-taking. It pointed out that migration policies differ from other areas of the first pillar to the extent that the Council attempts as a rule to circumvent the implementing rules of Article 202 TEC. 'No convincing reason has been given by the Council for departing from this principle and reserving the most important implementing powers for itself' (European Parliament 2000g). Second, Parliament criticized the 'inchoate way of legislating' on migration policies, the reasons for which were related to the piecemeal strategy in legislation prescribed by the scoreboard approach (European Parliament 2002b). The reasons behind such an approach of 'artificially dividing' the interrelated aspects of migration policies have finally been seen as being inherent in the provisions of the Amsterdam Treaty institutional rules (European Parliament 2000h). It is against this background that Parliament has been more receptive to legislative proposals from the Commission than to several proposals tabled by member states, although it did not object the content of these proposals.

Regarding its own policy agenda, Parliament has focused on two main aspects, these being an emphasis on the cross-pillar characteristics of migration policies and – similar to the way in which Parliament provides a forum for views from third countries in foreign affairs – a representation of the interests of third-country nationals vis-à-vis national and European executives. Prior to the Amsterdam Treaty, Parliament stressed the cross-pillar dimension of migration policies by linking third-pillar policies with the free movement of people as it is provided for by the TEC.[47] Arguing that ex-Article 7a TEC would transfer a direct legal obligation on member states to abolish all internal border controls by the deadline of 1 January 1993, Parliament sought to speed up the parallel development of rules on migration policies. While noting 'that measures required for the functioning of the internal market, comprising an area without internal frontiers, may not under any circumstances be dependent on a measure which has to be taken on the basis of Title VI', it was clear to Parliament that prior to the attainment of this objective member states would insist on the establishment of flanking measures in the area of migration policies, such as external border controls, visa policies or asylum and refugee issues (European Parliament 1996b). Noting, however, that member states and the Commission were not willing to implement these internal border provisions without the establishment of prior legal measures on migratory issues, and recognizing that there was no legal support from the Court of Justice on Parliament's interpretation of a direct effect of ex-Article 7a TEC, its policy proposals consequently focused on demanding a 'comprehensive' and 'holistic' approach to migration policies (European Parliament 2000h and 2002c). Challenging the scoreboard approach of Commission and Council, Parliament suggested that they should 'seek overall solutions regarding immigration and asylum, thus avoiding piecemeal measures' (European Parliament 2000g). Such a 'comprehensive' setting would not only include cross-pillar linkages with both first- and second-pillar foreign policies but also cover social or employment issues.[48] As far as migration policies in the narrower sense were concerned, Parliament asked the Commission and the Council to come up with 'a future consolidated proposal, covering all the arrangements applying to the right of asylum, temporary protection, and subsidiary protection' into one single legal instrument laying down the rules of an EU migration policy regime (European Parliament 2000f).

By arguing that executive policy-making in migration policies leads to many shortcomings on the rights dimension of this area, Parliament has from the outset laid particular emphasis on providing a platform for the perspective and interests of migrants. It has warned against creating 'new forms of discrimination between citizens of the Union ... against citizens of third countries' (European Parliament 1997a). Asylum seekers, for example, are subject to a 'shaky legal status' which renders their daily life very difficult (European Parliament 1996c). Authorities should also be more aware that for individual asylum seekers 'the decision in question can be of great importance [and] can make the difference between life and death', and, therefore, to do everything to avoid them 'fall[ing] victim to a game of ping-pong contemptuous of their humanity' (European Parliament 1997f and 1999b). Authorities should recognize that asylum seekers are 'invariably desperate people who have taken many risks in order to find safety' and that European society should be prepared to ensure their 'integration into social and economic life' rather than keeping them separate (European Parliament 2001e and 1998).

As already mentioned, Parliament has been highly critical of the institutional setting of migration policies, not least because of its own marginal role therein.[49] From the establishment of the third pillar onwards, Parliament has, therefore, called for steps helpful in 'attaining our ultimate objective, i.e. the "communautarization" of the third pillar' (European Parliament 1996d). During the 1996 IGC, Parliament demanded that migration policies 'should no longer be artificially distinguished from closely related policies within the full Community domain' and that, consequently, they 'must be progressively brought within the Community domain'.[50] This demand comprised the strengthening of the rights of Parliament, the Court of Auditors and the Court of Justice as well as overcoming the unanimity requirement in the Council (European Parliament 1995). While noting that the Amsterdam Treaty has provided for some improvements, Parliament's main demands have not been subject to change. During the 2000 IGC it again called for steps to ensure that the institutional framework of migration policies 'be substantially simplified'. Its proposals included full jurisdiction of the Court of Justice 'by removing the limitations and restriction in force', abolishing the time limit on both parliamentary opinions and amendments in the framework of the co-decision procedure, extending the scope of the (first-pillar) Schengen provisions to all member states while re-negotiating their current exemptions and, last but certainly not least, the introduction of the co-decision procedure as well as qualified majority voting in the Council for all legal measures to be taken on migration policies (European Parliament 2000b and 2000c). It was, finally, also in the framework of the Convention that Parliament tabled proposals for a future EU migration policy regime, thereby demanding additional steps for a full communitarization. Thus, within the catalogue of competencies drawn up by the Convention, Parliament foresees the free movement of persons as well as the 'legal basis for the common area of freedom' to be amongst the Union's exclusive fields of competence. According to Parliament's proposals, the focus for migration policy would, therefore, shift from the national to the EU level. 'Immigration policy and other policies linked to the free movement of persons' would, according to Parliament's proposal, be a shared area of competency, meaning that member states could only act within the 'limits defined by Union legislation' (European Parliament 2001a).

More so than in foreign policies, Parliament has been affected by the impact of the 1999 European elections and the shift towards the centre-right. This has also affected the composition of the Civil Liberties and Internal Affairs committee in which the European Peoples' Party (EPP) was the strongest party after the elections, replacing the Party of European Socialists (PES), which came in second. This change in the balance of power has, according to MEPs, also influenced the policy agenda pursued by Parliament (see on voting in the EP also Viola 2000). Thus, while Parliament is united in claiming more rights in the policy-making process vis-à-vis the executive, on a policy level an increase of divergence has been perceived. As one liberal MEP argued, on 'content there are differences. They get more pronounced.'[51] An official of Parliament agreed with that view and suggested that the committee 'after '99 has become more conservative than ministers'.[52] Conservative MEPs argued, on the other hand, that the changes were necessary in order for them to be taken more serious by Council and Commission and, in this perspective, the 'Council expects more than exaggerated proposals which often could not be implemented'.[53] Another explanation has been offered by a Socialist MEP, who argued that the reason behind the more moderate position of Parliament in the fifth legislature is that there has been a shift within the PES away from the aforementioned alternative policy agenda approach. 'More socialists [are] in government and Parliament gets more responsible', since a grand coalition of EPP and PES effectively dominates the committee. Hix reminds us that 'even without a common EP interest vis-à-vis the Council, an oligopolistic relationship between the two largest groups is enforced by the absolute-majority requirement' when voting on legislative proposals. Therefore, 'the PES and EPP must cooperate to ensure legislative coherence and protect their partisan interests and policy goals' (Hix 1999: 84).[54] The arguments presented in this chapter about a decrease in emphasis on alternative policy agendas largely support the argument that there has been a shift in Parliament's stance on migration policies closer to the executive agenda.

To summarize, the preferences of Parliament in Middle East and migration policies are, as has been shown, significantly influenced by the cross-pillar setting of EU constituent policies. Parliament's preferences in both areas are shaped in particular by the executive/control dimension, which has been identified as the main institutional characteristic of these two areas. Accordingly, arguments on Parliament's often assumed closeness to the Commission has not confirmed by research on the two cases analysed here. In both areas Parliament perceives its own role as being a provider for alternative policy agendas to official EU policies as they are pursued by the EU executive. It is, however, true that Parliament and the Commission do share some similarities regarding the long-term objectives for both areas in which they both push for largely communitarized settings. Notwithstanding this element of convergence between supranational actors, its impact on the overall actor constellations in this area remains quite small. Comparing Parliament's preferences on the two areas, a striking difference comes to the fore. While in Middle East policies Parliament's virtual exclusion from directly shaping the policy agenda, save developmental policies, has contributed to an on-going focus on an alternative agenda, this is not true to the same extent in migration policies. The perspective of a wholesale introduction of the co-decision procedure has contributed to a more co-operative attitude between Parliament and the executive. It seems, however, that this process has not been one sided. While Parliament has come closer to the executive agenda on migration policies, a greater acceptance of Parliament on the side of the Council and the Commission can also be observed in the decision-making process.[55]

The Court of Auditors: ensuring transparency

Both the Court of Justice and the Court of Auditors have made active use of their capabilities in foreign and interior policies and their actions have not been marginal to policy-making in either area. While the Court of Justice has issued two key judgements on migration policies in the period under consideration, which addressed the relationship between the pillars, the Court of Auditors has, in several reports, scrutinized EU policies in Middle East and foreign policies.

The Court of Auditors has on several occasions scrutinized the implementation of those parts of foreign policies which involve expenditure from EU budgetary resources. While, over time, an improvement in the quality of implementation is acknowledged, this progress has been slow and the Court of Auditors has pointed to various inefficiencies within the decision-making structures of both the Commission and the Council. The strongest criticism was raised in 1996 in a report on the implementation by the Commission of the MED programmes on decentralized co-operation (Giammusso 1999). As mentioned in the previous chapter, this report contributed to the corruption charges against the Commissioner responsible and aggravated tensions between Parliament and Commission, which ultimately resulted in the resignation of the college of Commissioners in 1999. In its report, the Court of Auditors accused the Commission of being responsible for a situation in which 'at all levels of the financial management of the MED programmes there are serious shortcomings and irregularities'. The Court of Auditors was bothered in particular by 'insufficient analysis' by the Commission of the means and instruments for successful implementation, and has argued that the 'structure and procedures of the Commission to oversee and monitor the implementation ... were inadequate and deficient'. Therefore, the overall success of policies themselves was questioned, since 'on the basis of the data currently available and its own observations in the field, the Court considers that the impact of the MED programmes remains to be proven'. However, the critique went even further and transcended mere disapproval of the decision-making practices in the Commission. The Court of Auditors pointed the finger at a 'serious confusion of interest' which the Commission, although being aware of it 'from the outset', did not 'put an end to in a timely manner'. The Court of Auditors referred to the delegation by the Commission of almost all the implementing powers for MED programmes to a private contractor and to the fact that 'in spite of several warnings, this de facto delegation of powers was not revoked' (Court of Auditors 1996).[56]

While corruption charges were not repeated in other reports, the Court of Auditors nevertheless remained highly critical of the way in which the Commission implemented policies in foreign affairs. The argument put forward by the Commission, that the lack of staff or unfavourable external circumstances in third countries were the main reasons behind implementation problems, was not accepted by the Court of Auditors. On the contrary, the Court argued that the problems related primarily to the way in which the EU executive worked. First, implementation problems in developmental assistance could generally be related to 'the very cautious approach adopted by the national authorities [of EU member states] in this field'. Second, as far as the EU level was concerned, 'the way in which humanitarian aid is organized by the institutions' had to be blamed (Court of Auditors 1997). Regarding this internal dimension the Court of Auditors emphasized organizational problems within the Commission which could not all be related to its precarious personnel situation. Thus the Commission did not take the necessary steps to overcome the 'lack of clarity in the division of tasks between the departments and of competencies between the Commission's headquarter in Brussels and the Delegations' (Court of Auditors 1998). Adding up these serious co-ordination problems between the DG and the Delegations, the Court of Auditors criticized the organizational structures of the Commission in Brussels. It pointed to the way in which the Joint Service (SCR) – which was established by the Commission to provide an organizational roof to all assistance measures – operated.[57] Thus, while the 'implementation of projects is the responsibility of the SCR ... project preparation remains the responsibility of the various RELEX DGs' (Court of Auditors 2001a). According to the Court of Auditors, the Commission was not able to handle its internal organization, thus severely hampering the impact of EU policies.

This has also affected Middle East policies. A report on the implementation of assistance in Palestine once more emphasized that within the Commission 'decision-making is heavily centralised, slow and cumbersome'. While it was acknowledged that 'the Commission's implementation of assistance to

Palestinian society has had positive results' such as the support for the peace process through funding the Palestinian Authority or the positive effects on educational and infrastructure programmes, the 'impact of these programmes has been reduced by structural weaknesses in the Commission's programming and management procedures and systems' (Court of Auditors 2000). Thus, contrary to consultancy reports sponsored by the Commission, which emphasized the heavy control by member states on the Commission's implementing powers as the main reason for these shortcomings, the Court of Auditors had a much more critical perspective on the internal operations of the Commission (MEDA 1999; MEDA Democracy 1999).

The Court of Auditors did not only scrutinize developmental assistance but also budgetary expenses from the second pillar, and in one report dealt directly with the CFSP. While recognizing that steps had already been taken by the Council towards an intensified application of first-pillar budgetary rules such as the setting up of particular budget headings on CFSP expenses, 'the creation of a budget line for preparatory costs', the 'abandoning of budgetary reserve', and the setting up of employment conditions for Special Envoys, the Court of Auditors demanded additional changes.[58] In particular, it criticized the fact that 'the question of the definition of administrative and operational expenditure', i.e. whether expenses are covered by the EC budget or by member states, 'is still not resolved' (Court of Auditors 2001b). As far as the implementation of measures was concerned, the Court of Auditors finally made a plea for a stronger role for the Commission.

The Court of Justice: constructing rights across the pillars

In spite of the letter of the Maastricht Treaty, which allegedly provided for an exclusion of the Court of Justice from having a role within the institutional setting of EU policy-making in the third pillar, the Court, surprisingly, adopted a pro-active approach on this issue and constructed rights across the pillars in a way not foreseen by member states in the Maastricht Treaty negotiations. While the ECJ had already ruled, for example, in the *Demirel* case on first-pillar-related aspects of migration policies, such as the rights conferred on third-country nationals by Association Agreements, the Maastricht Treaty sought to prevent the ECJ from developing legal doctrines for asylum and immigration policies.[59] However, in its two judgements of 1997 and 1998 on *Visa Lists* and *Airport Transit Visas*, the Court fostered the legal dimension of EU migration policies, thus providing yet another example for the 'legal autonomy approach' (Oliveiro 1999; Alter 1998; Mattli and Slaughter 1998).[60]

In *Visa Lists*, the Court of Justice dealt with the inter-institutional balance between Commission, Council and Parliament in the decision-making process. In this case, Parliament filed an annulment charge against a Regulation on a common visa list which was adopted by the Council of 25 September 1995 on the grounds that Parliament was not re-consulted after the Council had introduced some amendments to the Commission's original proposal on which

Parliament had been initially consulted (Peers 2000). The Court of Justice then indeed annulled the Regulation and fostered both the Community dimension of migration policies and the control of the executive in migration policies. The ECJ criticized the fact that the Regulation 'departs from the aim of harmonization in the matters of visas', since the Council had excluded a time limit for the expiry of parallel national visa lists as it was originally provided for in the legislative proposal by the Commission. However, 'any discontinuity in the harmonization of national rules of visas' should be avoided. Based on this observation, the Court of Justice considered the changes by the Council to the original proposal as being substantial. Since 'the text finally adopted, taken as a whole, differs in essence from the text on which Parliament has already been consulted' a fresh consultation was seen as being 'essential to the maintenance of the institutional balance intended by the Treaties'. The argument by the Council that re-consultation would result in the tacit introduction of a second reading in the consultation procedure was rejected by the Court. 'To accept the Council's argument would result in seriously undermining that essential participation ... and would amount to disregarding the influence that due consultation of Parliament can have on the adoption of the measure in question.'

Limiting the discretion of member states in the legislative process in migration policies has not been the only doctrine established by the Court of Justice. Thus, while visa issues were the only part of the migration policy *acquis* that had already been integrated into the first pillar with the Maastricht Treaty, this judgement went beyond the narrow confines of the first pillar. The opinion of the Advocate-General, although not repeated in the judgement, directly questioned the factual validity of the pillar divide in migration policies. The Advocate-General hinted that the case brought up the issue of 'the role of the Court in interpreting the Treaty on European Union', arguing that – in spite of the explicit exclusion of judicial review in the two 'inter-governmental' pillars by ex-Article M TEU – a 'parallel reading' of provisions from the first and the third pillars could become necessary. It was pointed out that for considering the

> scope of Community competence under Article 100c [TEC], the Court of Justice will look at that provision in its Treaty context and cannot, in my view, qualify or restrict that interpretation by reference to a provision which it is expressly prohibited from interpreting.

Somewhat paradoxically, while being excluded from any interpretation of Title VI TEU, at the same time 'the Court were entitled to have regard in a general way to the existence and content of Title VI'. This opinion of the Advocate-General, which was not rejected by the Court of Justice, sent out shock waves to some member states and was an invitation for supranational actors to challenge, at the next opportunity, a third-pillar measure. This happened only a few months later on 4 March 1996 when the Commission appealed against a Council Joint Action on Airport Transit Visas. The Commission announced, to the surprise of the Council, in a meeting of COREPER that it would challenge this third-pillar act in court, arguing that the measure should have been adopted in the framework of the visa provisions of the first pillar. The Commission based its appeal on the arguments of the Advocate-General, a former Commission official, as they were set out in *Visa Lists*. In an attempt to defend the separation of the pillars, the national governments argued that 'by virtue of Article L [TEU] the Court does not have jurisdiction to hear and determine the Commission's application'. Indeed, the Court of Justice upheld the legality of the adoption of the Joint Action in the framework of the third pillar, arguing that Airport Transit Visas were not visas in the definition of ex-Article 100c TEC, since they did not, in a legal sense, provide for the crossing of the EU's external borders. In contrast to regular visas, Airport Transit Visas did not give their holders the right of movement in the internal market and were only meant for movement in the international areas of EU airports. Notwithstanding the rejection of the Commission's appeal on the case in question, the judgement itself resulted, in the view of officials in the legal service of the Council Secretariat, in a 'clear victory for the Commission'. This is because the Court of Justice rejected the opinion by member states that it was not entitled to rule on the case due to the legal base of the Joint Action in the third pillar. Opposing this perception, the Court of Justice pointed out that it is its own task 'to ensure that acts which, according to the Council, fall within the scope of Article K.3(2) [TEU] do not encroach upon the powers conferred by the EC Treaty on the Community'. From that, 'it follows that the Court has jurisdiction'.[61]

In *Airport Transit Visas* the Court of Justice thus undermined the dominant legal opinion of a strict separation of the pillars. From this perspective the provisions on the judicial review of migration policies, as they appear in the Amsterdam Treaty, do not merely comprise an autonomous decision by national governments, but have to some extent already been autonomously codified by the case law of the Court of Justice, thereby challenging key intergovernmentalist assumptions. Moreover, *Airport Transit Visas* also tackles the institutional design of migration policies from another angle. The Court of Justice followed the argument of the Advocate-General to apply the 'functional approach' of legal reasoning, thereby looking 'at content and effect rather than form'. This approach of an institutional division within a functionally defined policy area such as migration policies has met with criticism from the Court of Justice on other occasions as well. During the 1996 IGC the Court voiced its criticism of the pillar structure, arguing that the 'sometimes artificial compartmentalization entailed by the system of three pillars ... run[s] counter to the need for transparency and put citizens of the Union in an unsatisfactory position from the point of view of legal certainty' (Court of Justice 1995).

This argument, finally, points to the potential impact of *Airport Transit Visas* on the institutional design of EU foreign and interior policies at large.

Thus the Commission or Parliament are able to challenge acts in the second and the (remaining) third pillar if they are able to show that, in the words of the Advocate-General, certain 'matters more properly fall within the Community sphere'. Take, for example, a second-pillar decision such as the Common Strategy on the Mediterranean Region, which includes mainly policies and instruments from the first pillar. While the provisions on the common foreign and security policy indeed refer to the adoption of common strategies by the Council, it could be argued that – looking 'at content and effect rather than form' – this measure should have been adopted in the framework of the first pillar – a view also held in the Council Secretariat.[62]

Conclusion

The preferences of supranational actors in foreign and interior policies cannot adequately be described by reference to the intergovernmental/supranational dichotomy. As this chapter has shown, the preferences of supranational actors can rather be understood against the background of their different capabilities. This has fostered rather than undermined the dominant executive/control dimension and has only occasionally been countered by shared preferences between supranational actors, which all, to different degrees, perceive the pillar design as impeding the emergence of a 'comprehensive' approach to foreign and interior policies. Against the background of the analysis put forward in this chapter, the questions raised in the introduction can now be readdressed.

First, the preferences of supranational actors in foreign and interior policies relate mainly to their cross-pillar institutional capabilities in constituent policies rather than an a priori preference for overall communitarization. While all supranational actors consider the need for locating both areas firmly at the EU level as important, the precise shape of their individual preferences cannot be covered by such a grand supranational perspective. This explains why the preferences of the Commission and the Council Secretariat reveal some important similarities, whereas Parliament, the Court of Justice and the Court of Auditors have developed quite different preferences. The incorporation of the Commission into the Council's working structures, and daily co-operation between the actors, have fostered a managerial approach by the Commission to policy-making. The Commission limits its activities to those areas in which it already holds executive powers and only cautiously challenges the overall political guidance of the Council. It is only beyond the daily policy-making process, by submitting long-term reform proposals during Treaty reforms, that the preferences for an overall communitarization are clearly expressed by the Commission. The Council Secretariat has, in particular in the area of foreign policies, only just started to develop autonomous preferences. The High Representative and the Special Representative, thus, not only provide an institutional counter-weight at the EU level vis-à-vis the Commission, but also highlight the linkage between authority delegation and the emergence of autonomous preferences vis-à-vis the member states (Tallberg 2002).

There is a marked difference in the preferences of executive actors and those controlling the executive. This can be explained by the marginal position of these 'control actors' in most institutional settings of foreign and interior policies. The pillar structure of both areas and the high degree of discretion of the executive have been heavily criticized by Parliament, the Court of Justice and the Court of Auditors. It is noteworthy that this criticism has not merely been directed towards the member states or the Council, but has covered the Commission's role in both areas as well. To summarize, although supranational actors indeed share some preferences on further centralization of constituent policies at the EU level, this does not undermine the omnipresence of the institutional divide between executive preferences on the one hand, and the preferences of 'control actors' on the other.

7 Patterns of policy-making in EU foreign and interior policies
Executive dominance and co-ordination problems

Introduction

As the previous chapters have shown, European integration in foreign and interior policies is a complex endeavour, subject to quite contradictory developments between the extremes of centralization and incrementalism. Hence centripetal dynamics stemming from the functional requirement of providing the Union with an insider/outsider dimension are constantly balanced by the incremental process of giving concrete substance to policies within an institutionally highly fragmented policy setting. While supranational actors have an autonomous and important role in the policy-making process, they remain constrained by manifold institutional limitations. The arguments of this book on specific functional dynamics that shape policy-making in constituent policies suggest that characterizations of 'intergovernmental' or 'supranational' logics are hardly sufficient to account for the dynamics of policy-making in both areas. Thus the integration in foreign and interior policies is not a zero-sum game in which integration at the EU level necessarily translates into power losses for national governments. As the analysis in the previous chapters has shown, 'European' and 'national' are not antagonistic entities. Neither member states nor supranational actors are homogenous blocs with quasi-identical, fixed and mutually exclusive preferences.

As a result of these insights, any categorization of patterns of interaction in EU foreign and interior politics has to take account of these complexities rather than trying to reduce them to a point of invisibility, as is often inherent in ascriptions of 'supranational' or 'intergovernmental' logics of European integration (Moravcsik 1998; Stone Sweet and Sandholtz 1998). This chapter argues that the analysis of functional, institutional and substantive cross-pillar overlaps in foreign and interior policies allows a typology of the main patterns of interaction in the policy-making process to develop in both areas. It proposes a categorization of policy-making in both areas based on the main characteristic features of interaction in EU foreign and interior policies as they have been identified in the previous chapters. This chapter thus focuses on the patterns of interaction between executive and non-executive actors as well as on the main mechanism of inner-executive co-ordination (and co-ordination problems).

First, as the arguments put forward in the previous chapters have emphasized, the main dividing line in EU foreign and interior policies is not located on the intergovernmental/supranational dimension but rather on the level between executive and non-executive actors. The governments of member states, the Council and its Secretariat as well as the Commission jointly hold the key institutional resources in the policy-making process and their respective cross-pillar capabilities often tend to overlap, thus necessitating a co-operative approach to policy-making within the EU executive. The capabilities of Parliament, the Court of Justice and the Court of Auditors are indeed limited. This combination of constraints to parliamentary and judicial control and a high degree of autonomy of the executive has primarily structured policy-making in EU foreign and interior affairs. Hence this chapter looks at the policy-making process in foreign (Middle East) and interior (migration) policies from the viewpoint of this dominant dichotomy.

Second, such an assertion does not imply that these two main blocs are in any way homogeneous. Indeed, an analysis of inner-executive co-ordination reveals not only the considerable degree of overlap between the capabilities of the Commission, the Council Secretariat and the member states, it also brings to the fore manifold co-ordination problems, divergent preferences and various deadlocks in decision-making and implementation.

Patterns of policy-making I: executive dominance

Interaction between the various actors involved in policy-making in EU foreign and interior policies is heavily shaped by the cross-pillar institutional setting of constituent policies. This does not set the main dividing line in EU foreign and interior policies on the supranational/intergovernmental axis but cross-cuts this dimension along the distinction between executive actors (Commission, Secretariat, Council and member states), on the one hand, and those actors controlling the executive (Parliament, Court of Justice and Court of Auditors), on the other. The distribution of power on the two sides of this executive/control dimension is, however, not balanced. While executive actors jointly hold the main institutional resources in the policy-making process, the powers of Parliament, the Court of Justice and the Court of Auditors are, as has already been outlined in previous chapters, much less pronounced. This pattern has, in turn, impacted interaction between the two sides on four main dimensions.

First, in most institutional arenas of foreign and interior policies there is actually only very limited interaction between the two sides, and this lack of joint decision-making mechanisms enables both executive actors and 'control actors' to pursue quite different policy agendas. The effect of these different spheres into which executive and non-executive actors are embedded is threefold. Thus both the EU executive and 'control actors' have been able to pursue their respective policy agendas with a considerable degree of autonomy. Yet actual policy-making is characterized by a strong dominance of executive actors while the influence of 'control actors' on day-to-day decision-making has been rather weak. Last, successful assertiveness by 'control actors' against the executive is rare and often takes the form of quite confrontational measures, such as referral to the Court of Justice or even threatening the Commission with a motion of censure. It is striking that in those rare instances in which 'control actors' have jointly confronted the executive they have been able to exert some influence on policy-making.

As far as the legislative process is concerned, Parliament's role in both foreign and interior policies remains limited. It is only with regard to budgetary issues that Parliament has been able to regularly assert its role in the policy-making process. However, recourse to the budget cannot conceal the overall limited impact on the substance of EU policies, given the small overall size of the budget. Even more limited is the role of the Court of Justice and the Court of Auditors. Their involvement in the policy-making process largely depends upon recourse made to them by other actors, which has in practice mainly meant the European Parliament. Yet recourse to the Court of Justice is a costly weapon, whose deployment has to be exercised cautiously since the 'hierarchical direction' of judgements by the Court renders this option a rather confrontational step (Scharpf 1997: 171–94). In migration policies, Parliament has on two occasions made use of this option. In the *Visa Lists* case Parliament has been successful in annulling a Council act after Parliament felt that its institutional prerogative of consultation in the legislative process was neglected by the executive. Indeed, after this judgement, member states and the Commission have become much more willing to consult Parliament on legislative proposals.[1] The threat of having recourse to the Court of Justice on an alleged failure to act by the executive regarding the abolition of internal border controls has led a hesitant Commission to finally make legislative proposals on that matter (Peers 2000: 75). A confrontational stance was also taken by Parliament in its motion of censure against the college of Commissioners in 1999 when Parliament came up with corruption charges against the Commission following allegations made by the Court of Auditors.

It is noteworthy that on all these occasions when Parliament adopted a confrontational stance it was not acting alone but based its action on support from other 'control actors'. Moreover, a look at policy-making in foreign and interior policies reveals another approach used by Parliament, namely pressurizing mainly the Commission in order to ensure its greater involvement in the decision-making process. The reluctance of some member states to delegate further capabilities in the two areas to the Commission can, inter alia, be related to this susceptibility of the Commission to bow to pressure from Parliament. This susceptibility is smaller for other executive actors, such as the Council Secretariat. This helps to explain why it was the Council Secretariat which in the area of foreign affairs has emerged following the Maastricht Treaty as the supranational actor that has been delegated the greatest number of new capabilities.

Notwithstanding these examples, direct interaction between executive actors and 'control actors' is limited, due to the institutional rules in both foreign and interior policies. The small number of joint decision-making institutions that include both the executive and 'control actors' has also left its mark on the policy preferences of these actors. Thus, not only do the capabilities within the executive often overlap, but so do the preferences on concrete issues in the policy-making process. These collective executive preferences are, however, not developed jointly with Parliament, let alone the other 'control actors'. While these 'different spheres' of communication have met widespread criticism about the lack of parliamentary control in EU foreign and interior policies, they have also provided Parliament with the space to develop an alternative agenda of EU politics in both areas.

The small amount of interaction between Parliament and the executive has been emphasized by several officials. Thus a member of the Commission's legal service pointed out that by focusing on an alternative policy agenda in the area of Middle East policies, such as human rights and democracy issues, 'Parliament is leading a different life'.[2] These 'different lives' of Parliament on the one hand, and the executive on the other, has also affected relations between the two sides. A member of the Special Representative's team argued that 'Parliament is an outside actor', while a member of the Council Secretariat pointed out that 'with Parliament we have almost no contact'.[3] These limits to interaction between the different spheres have been similarly pronounced in migration policies. An official from the Secretariat has confirmed that 'contacts with Parliament are sporadic and mainly one way, if Parliament needs something like documents or legal advice'.[4] This lack of interaction has to be contrasted with the regular, institutionally induced, day-to-day interaction between Council and Commission. Officials from the legal service of the Council Secretariat, dealing with migration policy, have thus held that 'the institutional interplay is closer with the Commission. With Parliament contact hardly exists. We do not know our counterparts [there].'[5] Another official from the Secretariat added laconically that 'there are many meetings with the Commission legal service. Parliament's legal service we only met in the Court of Justice' during the *Visa Lists* case.[6]

Second, these different spheres of action must not be considered to be synonymous with a fairly equal division of powers between actors. In fact, patterns of interaction between executive actors and 'control actors' in EU foreign and interior policies are characterized by an unequal distribution of powers regarding their capabilities in the policy-making process. With most institutional arenas in foreign and interior policies exhibiting limited space for effective parliamentary or judicial control, the dominance of the executive looms as one of the most characteristic features of constituent policies. It should, however, also be noted that executive dominance, at least as far as foreign policies are concerned, is also quite a common feature of national politics. Along these lines, a member of the British House of Commons has also argued, comparing the powers of the European Parliament with those of national parliaments, that 'the influence of the House of Commons on foreign policies is small and only indirect'.[7] Within the cross-pillar institutional setting of constituent policies, the dominance of the executive reaches beyond foreign policies and covers interior affairs as well. An MEP involved in the area of migration policies blatantly conceded this lack of impact. 'Influence from Parliament? For God's sake there is none.'[8]

Only in those instances when Parliament has been able to bring a certain issue onto the official (executive) EU agenda can a limited impact on policy-making be detected. According to another MEP this has been the case in migration policies, with Parliament's insistence for many years that the issue of the abolition of internal border controls must be tackled more actively by the executive. While the SEA originally set the deadline for achieving the free movement of persons by 1 January 1993, this deadline passed without an abolition of internal border controls. Subsequently, interaction between Parliament and the executive in the years 1993 to 1995 on interior policy issues was dominated by Parliament's repeated calls for action to be taken particularly in this area.[9] Parliament specifically pressured the Commission to initiate legislation on that issue and ultimately brought an action on the Commission's alleged failure to act before the Court of Justice. It was only after the Commission had presented the three so-called 'Monti Directives' on an abolition of internal border controls in March 1995 that the Court of Justice issued an opinion on Parliament's request in which the court argued that there was no need to rule on the EP's request. Parliament subsequently continued to push for action in this area but refrained from filing another failure-to-act charge, although the Council did not vote on the Commission's three proposals. This once again points to the approach by Parliament of pressuring the Commission in particular when demanding action from the executive.

This unequal distribution of powers has also affected executive/control relations in EU foreign policies. As a Head of Unit from the Commission specified, 'Parliament's influence is small and its focus is on political projects. There is more co-operation between us and the Council.'[10] As in interior policies, Parliament's impact on policy-making remained limited to voicing its alternative policy agenda, hoping that some of its demands might be taken on board by the executive. An MEP confirmed that 'our influence is mainly through information and debates'. Yet overall she had 'little belief in Parliament besides resolutions' which over time might convince the executive of the need to deal more intensively with a certain issue in the policy-making process. As a concrete example of such continuous insistence could be mentioned Parliament's long-standing record of focusing on issues such as the rules of origin provisions with regard to Israeli products originating from the Occupied Territories. 'Commission and Council seem to pay more attention to our views and we should [therefore] keep the pressure.'[11] Another example of this emphasis on alternative issues is Parliament's call to deal openly with the allegations that EU funds, managed by the Commission, are used by the PA to sponsor terrorist activities. While the Commission has tried to keep this issue off the agenda, Parliament has organized several debates, supported by intense media coverage, in which it has questioned the allocation of funds by the Commission in Palestine. Once this case was publicized, a further concealment by the Commission was no longer possible and the case was formally investigated by the EU fraud office.

Third, a permanent, institutionally regulated interaction between executive actors and 'control actors' (in particular Parliament) has been established with regard to budgetary issues. An official from the Middle East Unit of the Commission conceded that 'Parliament has in particular its budgetary powers. Concrete examples are the blocking of financial co-operation with Turkey. Parliament wants a say over every single operational decision of the CFSP.'[12] Moreover, Parliament has used its budgetary powers to create new budget lines, such as in 1994, when the MEDA Democracy funds were established following a proposal by Parliament. A committee chairman consequently argued that 'our main role is the budget' and that within the MEDA budget Parliament had been able to ensure greater consideration for funding human rights-related projects with NGOs in third countries without direct governmental involvement.[13] Similarly, an official from the parliamentary Administrative Service on migration policies regarded the budget as the 'big force of Parliament', for example regarding the establishment of the ERF.[14]

The way in which this limited impact, which Parliament can exert through its role as one of the budgetary authorities of the EU, is used meets with mixed emotions from the executive. Being otherwise largely unaffected by parliamentary involvement, not all officials feel that 'Parliament was correct in pressing us to include also financing of human rights projects' since these projects were very difficult to implement.[15] Commission officials hence complained that Parliament's demands were often unrealistic. 'The Commission cannot deliver what Parliament wants in the human rights budget line', one official argued.[16] And in the area of migration policies a deputy Head of Unit from the Commission pointed out that 'many projects were put on us by Parliament' against the will of the executive.[17] Commission officials were particularly concerned at being trapped between non-reconcilable expectations by member states on the one hand, and by Parliament on the other. 'The problem is that the Commission is often in the middle between Parliament and the Council'.[18] Moreover, Commission officials complained that Parliament uses its budgetary authority as a political tool against the EU executive in general, and the Commission in particular. Thus one Commission official compared Parliament to other 'control actors' and considered that when compared to Parliament, 'the Court of Auditors is more balanced. We are not afraid to be under scrutiny but the way in which it is done matters.'[19]

Fourth, the overall limited direct impact on policy-making in both areas has occasionally rendered attempts to use 'hierarchical direction', either through the Court of Justice or the Court of Auditors, Parliament's main instrument in executive/control interaction (Scharpf 1997: 47). The search for allies against executive dominance is based on Parliament's scepticism 'with the Commission's willingness' to seriously consider parliamentary demands and the perception that the Commission is 'member states oriented' (on variations in supranational influence see also Tallberg 2000).[20] It has already been pointed out that in the area of migration policies Parliament has brought a charge against the Commission relating to the free movement of persons. Another example of this quest for hierarchical direction is the *Visa Lists* case of 1997, which has already been discussed in the previous chapter. It seems that Parliament has been able to foster its role in the policy-making process as a result of its successful intervention with the court. Officials from the Council Secretariat confirm that following this case 'we pay more attention to Parliament. We re-consult them generously on a couple of files.'[21] This perception of a gradual increase in interaction between executive actors and Parliament is also shared by MEPs themselves. An official from Parliament, dealing with migration policies, argued that 'openness increases from the Council and member states', a perspective which also pertains to interaction on foreign policies.[22]

The use of 'threat' instruments did not increase overall trust between the two sides. The aforementioned failure-to-act charge by Parliament was seen by officials from the Council as 'a political decision of Parliament' lacking serious legal backing, and this decreased their willingness to share powers with Parliament in the policy-making process.[23] Relations in Middle East policies were even more strained when in 1999 Parliament, supported by corruption charges against a Commissioner responsible for financing projects in the framework of the EMP, brought up by a report by the Court of Auditors, called for the resignation of the entire college of Commissioners. A Commission official accused Parliament of running a politically inspired 'campaign'. 'There was no corruption with EU money', he argued, and maintained that 'Parliament acted irresponsibly', its only goal being to foster its role vis-à-vis the executive in the policy-making process.[24] This perspective, although not shared by most parliamentarians, points nevertheless to an inherent dilemma in the executive/ control relations of EU foreign and interior policies. The overall impact of 'control actors' remains limited and often 'threat', such as repeatedly filing charges with the Court of Justice or threatening the Commission, remains the only option for Parliament to get heard by the executive. This option, however, is costly since it undermines the development of co-operative working relations between the two sides. Moreover, Parliament has to be cautious in using this option since future delegation of additional capabilities in both areas depends on the goodwill of member states which can, of course, only be ensured if Parliament is considered 'responsible' – whatever that might entail.

To conclude, patterns of interaction between executive actors and 'control actors' are structured by an unequal distribution of capabilities between these actors in constituent policies. Both sides often act within different spheres, the executive being involved in day-to-day decision-making while Parliament focuses on an alternative policy agendas. Constant interaction remains mainly limited to the budgetary dimension of foreign and interior policies, where Parliament has some influence to establish budgetary headings for some of its policy preferences. The lack of significant parliamentary control in most institutional arenas of both areas has rendered the option of threat one of the few, albeit costly, fields of interaction. Due to these costs, however, this option has only been used by Parliament in small doses. While the willingness of Commission and Council to deal with parliamentary demands has, according to statements from both sides, slightly increased, the unequal distribution of capabilities within the policy-making process remains the characterizing feature of interaction in EU foreign and interior policies.

Patterns of policy-making II: the challenge of inner-executive co-ordination

As has been outlined in the previous section, executive actors dominate the policy-making process in EU foreign and interior policies. Notwithstanding their considerable capabilities for autonomously shaping policies in both areas, the powers of the different executive actors nevertheless vary, thereby, inter alia, affecting the autonomy of the Commission. These variations in power do not, however, mainly emanate from parliamentary or judicial control, but rather from a complex system of inner-executive checks and balances between the Commission, the Council Secretariat and member states' governments. Policy-making in most institutional arenas of EU foreign and interior affairs is highly dependent upon negotiated, consensual and often unanimous agreement within the executive. Inner-executive co-ordination takes place at all levels of the policy-making process and applies to the initiation of legislation, the adoption of legislative acts and the implementation of policies on the ground. Thus the strong joint decision-making mechanisms serve a particular function for centralizing areas as closely related to sovereignty as constituent policies. Inner-executive co-ordination in constituent policies is characterized by intense patterns of consensual policy-making and deadlocks with regard to policy initiation, decision-taking and implementation resulting from these joint decision-making mechanisms. The remainder of this chapter looks at these deadlocks in greater detail. It should, however, be emphasized that deadlocks in a strong joint decision-making system, such as EU foreign and interior policies, often serve a systemic function, namely to reinforce the functionalist features of the 'consensus principle [which] is to let all of the important parties share executive power in a broad coalition' (Lijphart 1984: 23).

There is a strong sense among executive actors about the need for such a consensual co-ordination and this understanding results not least from the assumption that without strong inner-executive co-ordination too many deadlocks would ultimately block policy-making. An official from the Council Secretariat pointed to the requirement for inner-executive co-ordination by emphasizing the extent of overlapping competencies in constituent policies. Thus, while the Council is responsible for political foreign affairs, 'the Commission is a heavy actor in Middle East policies due to its knowledge and administration of funds' and these two tracks have constantly to be co-ordinated.[25] A less positive but nevertheless similarly intriguing assessment has been put forward by members of the Special Representative's staff. One official argued that 'the Commission is very important' but deplored the fact that the 'Commission is not willing to share information with us and also the delegation do not. So the Special Envoy and the Secretariat are little informed', thus pointing to possible frictions in inner-executive co-ordination.[26] Similar arguments have been expressed by officials in the area of migration policies. Members from the legal service of the Council Secretariat have argued that 'the Commission has a lot of power' and that 'working parties are often dominated by Presidency and Commission'.[27]

As far as the initiation of legislation by the executive is concerned, both areas are characterized by a cautious approach by the Commission to make use of its right of initiative. The main reason for this caution obviously relates to the difficulties in getting proposals adopted due to the considerable divergence in the preferences of member states, which in most areas vote on legislative proposals by unanimity. Thus the Commission has been extremely cautious in proposing new legislation, fearing that some member states would oppose a too active use of the right of initiative. As has already been outlined in previous chapters, the main goal of the Commission has been to become accepted by member states rather than to develop an assertive attitude regarding its own policy preferences. While the Commission did, for example, propose long-term visions for the development of EU migration policies, such as in the 1994 communication, it has usually refrained from suggesting controversial pieces of legislation. This cautious attitude did not fundamentally change after the Amsterdam Treaty came into force. It is quite telling that the Commissioner for Justice and Home Affairs, prior to the publication of the first scoreboard in December 1999, conducted a tour of capitals in which the concrete measures to be listed in the scoreboard were hammered out piece by piece between the Commission and each national interior ministry. Being aware that the shared right of initiative as well as the predominance of unanimous decision-making practices could potentially provoke a stalemate in policy-making in this area, the Commission's main focus was directed towards intense inner-executive co-ordination prior to the initiation of (consensually agreed) legislation.

It should be noted that while the Commission is quite cautious in proposing new legislation, member states, in both areas, have been much less reluctant to make use of their right of initiative. It has been the changing Presidencies in particular that have sought to bring certain issues onto the EU agenda. In migration policies, these member states' proposals have not always been consistent with the commonly agreed scoreboard priorities. A similar tendency can also be observed in foreign policies. A Commission official argued, referring to the Common Strategy on the Mediterranean Region, that the 'Council tries to limit the Commission. More proposals come now from member states.' Being aware of this importance that member states attach to (diplomatic) foreign relations, 'the Commission plays a cautious role in political relations'.[28]

The joint decision-making mechanisms at the stage of initiating legislation are further intensified by the consensual patterns of concrete decision-taking. This is underlined, for example, by the difficulties into which the actual translation of the scoreboard into concrete decisions has run. Indeed, decision-taking on migration policies has been a painstakingly slow process. For example, notwithstanding the five-year period for the adoption of all scoreboard measures, key legislative proposals on migration policies got stuck in the legislative pipeline due to continuing disagreement among member states. Hence the scoreboard of December 2002 states that, contrary to the dates of adoption originally set in 1999, 'only a few of the objectives defined for the establishment of a common asylum and immigration policy have been met' (Commission 2002b: 5). The Commission's hope that yet another call from a European Council to accelerate the speed of decision-taking would cut the Gordian knot had decreased. Disappointment is only scantily covered when the Commission points out that 'the Seville European Council did endeavour to accentuate the dynamism flowing from the Laeken European Council' (Commission 2002b). In the very same document, however, the Commission expresses its scepticism about the significance of this 'flow of dynamism' much more openly and argues that 'the backlog referred to by the Laeken European Council has not been cleared in some areas, notably as regards the common policies on asylum and immigration, though the necessary proposals are all before the Council' (Commission 2002b: 4).

The final stage in which the virtues and perils of strong inner-executive co-ordination have become visible relates to the implementation of policies. These inner-executive co-ordination mechanisms can well be exemplified by looking in greater detail at the implementation of developmental assistance by the Commission. Thus several detailed reports from external consultants have scrutinized the implementation of EU developmental assistance in the Mediterranean region in general, and Palestine in particular. These reports have mainly dealt with the responsibilities of the Commission, but also touched upon the issue of the co-ordination of assistance between the Commission and member states within specialized committees, such as the MED committee. Indeed, these reports highlight a multitude of implementation problems emanating from within the institutional structure of the EU foreign affairs system, mainly from cumbersome procedures regulating the relations between the Commission and member states (Stetter 2003).

Such an analysis of a gap between the ambitious political goals of the EU as they were defined, for example, in the Common Strategy, and the actual implementation of MEDA assistance measures by the EU on the ground should, however, not lead to the conclusion that problems of inner-executive co-ordination could be avoided completely. Politics, after all, is a process of complex interaction and is necessarily time-consuming and this is particularly true for a sensitive area such as constituent policies. Nevertheless, observations from the case of developmental assistance show that some of the problems in implementation could have been avoided without harming the inter-institutional balance between the European and the national levels. While the improvements of EU assistance in the framework of the EMP, when compared with the period prior to the Barcelona Conference, has been generally ack-nowledged by these reports, MEDA assistance was nevertheless severely hampered by a very slow disbursement of assistance in partner countries (MEDA 1999; COWI 1998: 42). Thus, in the period from 1995 to 1998, only 25 per cent of promised assistance was disbursed to partner countries. Figures for Palestine were significantly higher, reflecting the priority the EU attached to Middle East policies, although they did not exceed 48 per cent. While some of the shortcomings in implementation can be related to deadlocks in bilateral negotiations or resistance from partner countries to engage in political and economic reforms, EU internal features help to account for most of these implementation problems.[29]

The implementation of EU assistance had already been criticized for its slow disbursement of funds during the protocol period, which predated the EMP. Thus it is striking that the much more demanding procedures for EU assistance under the new MEDA regime did not go hand in hand with a streamlining of inner-executive co-ordination. On the contrary, more complex programmes were added to the Commission's workload without consideration of how this would affect the operation of projects. The MEDA Regulation stipulates three different levels at which the member states within the MED Committee are involved in the implementation of aid by the Commission. These are on the strategic level of annually updated Regional and National Indicative Programmes, the operational level of individual, country-related Financing Decisions and Financing Protocols and, finally, the implementation level concerning concrete tendering procedures.

When deciding on National and Regional Indicative Programmes, the MED Committee approves, at the Commission's suggestion, 'sector priorities for a Project [as well as] portfolio according to country-specific and regional sector policy criteria' (MEDA 1999: 21). While the co-ordination between member states and the Commission at the strategic level is important to ensure the achievement of the overall objectives of EU developmental policies, this is not valid to the same extent for involvement of member states at the oper-ational and implementation level. Thus, with regard to commitments of the Commission concerning individual projects, the specific involvement of the MED Committee created many significant delays in implementation (MEDA 1999: 36).

Problems at the operational and implementation level are exacerbated by the lack of co-ordination between EU and member state developmental assist-ance to partner countries (MEDA 1999: 37). Moreover, the demand from the MEDA Regulation to define priority sectors on a national or a regional basis applies only to the EU level and not to member states' policies, hence further decreasing the effectiveness of policies.

Overall, the commitment procedures of the MEDA Regulations created a time-consuming workload of information and communication exercises for both the Commission and the member states. The outcome of this process is questionable since member states were in practice only informed about the 'intermediary status' of projects and were not able or willing to really engage in discussion on 'substantial, policy-related issues' (MEDA 1999). Nevertheless, this information exercise took the form of huge reports prepared by the Commission, requiring a heavy input of human resources which were consequently not available for reducing the time delays in negotiating and implementing the necessary agreements for launching MEDA assistance.

Moreover, the involvement of the MED Committee has resulted in often inefficient 'extra operational work-load' for the Commission (MEDA 1999: 39). This has actually hampered the effectiveness of inner-executive co-ordination since the MED Committee was involved in micro financing decisions while losing track of ensuring the 'coherence and consistency of strategic programming' (MEDA 1999: 39). A similar criticism was raised with regard to the time-consuming control by the MED Committee at the implementation stage, for example when deciding on tender procedures for individual projects (MEDA 1999: 47). While the Commission was closely controlled in its decision-making, member states were not, 'i.e. that Member States programmes be planned in co-ordination of complementarity with Commission programmes ... It would perhaps appear to be an infringement on the Member States' highly sensitive foreign policies' (MEDA 1999: 90).

It has been estimated that insufficient procedures within the MED Committee resulted in a delay of around one year with regard to the implementation of MEDA assistance (MEDA 1999: 57). This points to a problematic emphasis in the workload of both the Commission (preparing interim reports for the MED Committee) and the committee itself (dealing with too many details). A shift towards more co-operation on the strategic planning level seems the more justified since the rate of approval for projects suggested by the Commission is already high. Out of 87 projects throughout the Mediterranean region from 1995 to 1997, the committee approved 38 projects unanimously and another 39 with some qualified suggestions. Only nine projects had to be redrafted but were then approved. Only one project was turned down (COWI 1998: 33).

The strict requirements for financing projects were another factor in the implementation problems. The misuse and maladministration of funds during the protocol period explains why such a complex system as MEDA assistance was established. The problem of the new procedures, however, was that the Commission was now confronted with an even greater workload – negotiating financing provision with partner countries and communicating these negotiations to the MED Committee – without any real change in human resources at its disposal. A former head of delegation in the Middle East cynically summarized his experience about the workload in delegations as follows: 'There is an optimistic version that 95 per cent of our time was related to solving problems of implementation of the project cycle.'[30]

Besides the time delays and problems in co-ordination within the MED Committee, the workload of the Commission appears as a third issue related to implementation problems. The MEDA case actually shows that the Commission was faced with a dilemma resulting from the requirements of complex and time-consuming procedures and lack of human resources. These had to be balanced with expectations from partner countries for quick assistance, from member states in intense co-ordination and by Parliament in correct implementation.

The Commission was only able to employ additional staff for the implementation of the MEDA funds in 1998 when country-based MEDA Teams were formed (COWIE 1998: 41). While the MEDA Teams were useful in improving facilitating work on the operational and implementation level they could not contribute to a more effective approach with regard to the strategic level of planning. Even after the launch of MEDA assistance the Commission did little for the development of proper 'strategic planning instruments' (MEDA 1999: 32). The delegations were also cautious about adjusting projects to the new MEDA requirements. In the light of the complexities of inner-executive co-ordination and the absence of a 'programming-and-monitoring unit of the Commission', 'Delegation staff ... prefer to stick to what they know' (MEDA 1999: 73). The multi-annual programming of MEDA even supported these traditional working methods. Delegations felt under immense time pressure to inform the Directorate-General about projects for fund commitments because 'otherwise, the funds earmarked for MEDA could be "lost" for "their Country" by the end of the Financial Year' (MEDA 1999: 73).

To sum up, inner-executive co-ordination in foreign and interior policies is characterized by a tight overlap of executive powers between the different branches of the EU executive. This pattern of interaction has affected all stages of the policy-making process, namely the initiation of legislation, actual decision-taking and implementation. It was not so much the speed or the scope of decisions that were given the greatest importance but rather the emphasis on upholding consensual patterns of interaction within the executive.

Conclusion

This chapter has elaborated in greater detail on the way in which the executive/control divide in constituent policies has affected patterns of interaction between national and supranational actors in the policy-making process. It has provided several examples of how this relationship is characterized by a remarkable dominance of executive actors at the expense of parliamentary or judicial control. 'Control actors', most prominently Parliament, have often only been able to use rather confrontational means for asserting their role in policy-making. However, the use of these measures, such as recourse to the Court of Justice or even threats to seek the demise of the Commission, are costly for both sides and are no substitute for a permanent, balanced sharing of power between executive actors and 'control actors' in the policy-making process. Executive dominance does not, however, imply that the executive remains completely uncontrolled. A striking feature of the EU foreign and interior affairs system is that the executive is, in a sense, controlling itself. A complex system of inner-executive checks and balances ensures that action is usually only taken after a negotiated, consensual agreement among executive actors has been reached. While such patterns of interaction serve the functional requirement of ensuring a cautious approach to the integration of constituent policies, in particular through tight control of the Commission, it also brings with it several institutionally induced shortcomings regarding executive policy-making at all stages of the policy-making process.

The problems in effective parliamentary and judicial control and over-complex inner-executive co-ordination must, however, be balanced with the fundamental significance of integrating two areas as strongly linked to sovereignty as foreign and interior policies. Anything but a highly incremental, often painstakingly slow policy-making process in these areas would be surprising and arguably detrimental to integration. Such an argument should, however, not lower expectations to a point at which all deadlock is justified by the functional requirement of intense inner-executive co-ordination. However, what remains interesting about the political system of the EU from a comparative perspective is not so much the existence of such patterns of a consensus democracy ubiquitous in semi-sovereign states (Katzenstein 1987). What is striking is that these patterns of policy-making do not (only) relate to industrial relations, health issues or educational policies but to areas as closely linked with sovereignty as foreign and interior affairs.

8   Conclusion

This book has provided a thorough analysis of the policy-making dynamics in EU foreign and interior affairs and has in particular focused on the way in which the functional dynamics in these two areas have shaped the institutional and substantive processes of cross-pillarization in both policy areas. A key argument substantiated in the previous chapters has been that it is the *shared function* of both foreign and interior policies in equipping the EU with its own insider/outsider distinction that allows the conceptualization of both policy areas as constituting a distinct policy type. Hence, in both areas policy-making has the 'allocation function' of sustaining the distinction between an inside and an outside. Due to this sovereignty-related function, and based on the work of Theodore Lowi, this policy type has been referred to here as 'constituent policies'. Thus, rather than taking the three-pillar structure as the starting point of analysis, this book has argued, by drawing from sociological institutionalism, that policy-making dynamics in both areas relate to this shared 'functional frame' of an EU insider/outsider distinction. Notwithstanding the often meagre substantive outcomes in both areas and the nascent status of the EU's internal and external identity, this insider/outsider distinction functions as a 'focal point' which underpins policy-making in both areas and, as a result, the social construction of a distinct sovereignty dimension of the EU.

As this book has shown, since the Maastricht Treaty constituent policies have indeed become an integral part of the EU political system. As has been pointed out throughout the various chapters of this book, the specific focus on supranational actors in parts of this analysis does not mean that these actors hold the main sources of power in EU foreign and interior affairs. Thus, as a direct result of the close linkage of both areas with traditionally national prerogatives, the price that supranational actors have had to pay for their inclusion in policy-making processes in constituent policies has been their acceptance of the leadership of the (European) Council, the rotating Presidencies and, occasionally, individual member states. However, notwithstanding the importance of national governments and the Council in providing strategic and political leadership, policy-making processes in both areas cannot be understood from an intergovernmental perspective. As a result of the gradual centralization of constituent policies at the EU level, supranational actors have – to varying degrees – become increasingly involved in policy-making in foreign and interior affairs.

Based on the argument that the political significance of integration in foreign and interior policies relates to the specific value allocation of both areas for the political system of the EU, this book has provided a theoretical explanation for the gradual erosion of the three-pillar structure in day-to-day policy-making despite its formal continuation. More specifically, the previous chapters have identified three interrelated processes of cross-pillarization which shape the dynamics of policy-making in both areas. First, the book has emphasized the crucial role of the *functional dimension* of constituent policies (Chapter 2), more specifically the aforementioned function of 'constituent policies' in providing the EU with the distinction between insiders (EU/EU citizens) and outsiders (third countries/third-country nationals). Second, these functional characteristics of constituent policies help us to understand the *institutional dynamics* of cross-pillarization which have been discussed in Chapters 3 and 4. Thus, building upon Theodore Lowi's famous statement that *policies determine politics*, these shared functional features have led to the emergence of the cross-pillar institutional setting of EU foreign and interior policies. Notwithstanding the significance of the pillar divide at the formal Treaty level, the analysis in these chapters on the role of supranational actors has shown that the functional unity of both areas has allowed supranational actors to gain a strong foothold in both areas across the three pillars. Yet this analysis has also shown that there is a considerable institutional fragmentation in both areas that cross-cuts the pillar divide, as well as variance in the capabilities of supranational actors. Hence, a main feature of constituent policies is that the Council Secretariat and the Commission in particular – i.e. executive actors – have been delegated meaningful cross-pillar capabilities, whereas Parliament, the Court of Justice and the Court of Auditors draw mainly from their first-pillar powers. Chapter 5 then addressed cross-pillar linkages on the substantive dimension. It has offered a detailed analysis of the two case studies of EU Middle East and migration policies, showing how the functional and institutional cross-pillar linkages have been supplemented by processes of cross-pillarization on the level of substantive policies. Thus the years between the Maastricht Treaty and the Treaty of Nice have been characterized by a significant policy change. While EU policies were initially based on the distinction between policies in the first pillar and policies in the second and third pillar, over time EU policies were characterized by a blurring of the pillar distinction in day-to-day policy-making on the substantive level, including increasing linkages between foreign policies and justice and home affairs.

Chapters 6 and 7 then focused on how these functional, institutional and substantive dynamics of cross-pillarization have affected the patterns of policy-making in both areas from Maastricht to Nice. As Chapter 6 has shown, the preferences of supranational actors in the two areas vary considerably. Based on this observation, the assumption shared by both intergovernmentalist and supranational approaches that the main dividing line in EU politics is between national governments and supranational actors has been rejected here. Taken together, these characteristic features of constituent policies help to account for the dynamics of policy-making in foreign and interior policies. Thus, as Chapter 7 has argued, the dominant characteristic of policy-making is the distinction between executive actors, such as the Commission, the Council (and member states) and the Council Secretariat on the one hand, and 'control actors', such as Parliament, the Court of Justice and the Court of Auditors on the other. The relationship between executive actors and 'control actors' is subject to the remarkable dominance of the EU executive. However, these must not be treated as unified blocs. A look at inner-executive relations not only reveals a complex system of checks and balances but also brings to the fore deadlocks at all stages of the policy-making process.

The theoretical arguments of this book question the usefulness of those approaches in integration studies that continue to centre around the distinction between 'supranational' and 'intergovernmental' conceptualizations of European integration. This book argues instead that the integration of different policy areas and policy types increasingly renders the EU level the prime functional, institutional and substantive focal point to which actors (both national and supranational) relate. At the same time, this integration process does not, of course, mean that the emergence and consolidation of such a focal point would necessarily result in a 'supranationalization' of policies or a loss of power by member states or the Council. Hence, vertical integration leaves open the question of how the transfer of policy areas to the EU level affects the horizontal distribution of powers in the EU policy-making process. Any answer to this question thus requires concrete empirical analysis. Accordingly, this book has shown that both foreign and interior policies are indeed characterized by such a functionally induced integration process in which member states (most often acting as a collective unit) keep control of the main resources in policy-making, provide for political leadership and play an important role in ensuring the continuity of policy-making. Thus the European Council, the Council of Ministers, the Presidencies and, occasionally, individual member states remain the most powerful actors in EU foreign and interior policies across the pillars. Notwithstanding this argument, this book has at the same time provided ample evidence that centralization has not only led to an increased blurring of the pillar structure, which originally divided policy areas, but has also enabled supranational actors, in particular the Commission and the Council Secretariat, to have a significant role in policy-making in both areas across the three pillars. As far as foreign and interior policies are concerned, it is neither the allegedly intergovernmental nature of the second and third pillars nor the interests of member states alone that account for the dynamics of integration in the two areas. In a nutshell, institutions and preferences must be understood against the background of the specific functional frames to which both areas relate.

It is on this basis that this book has argued that EU foreign and interior policies have, since the Maastricht Treaty, indeed become key areas of EU policy-making. Moreover, both areas have been subject to a centralization process, albeit an incremental one. Given the slow process of centralizing foreign and interior policies at the EU level and the challenge this centralization ultimately poses to traditional understandings of sovereignty, any prognosis on future developments becomes inherently difficult. Thus the tension between functional unity and institutional fragmentation in EU foreign policies shows the difficulties – and some would argue the impossibility – of establishing single foreign and interior policies at the EU level, including issues of internal and external security. Thus, in contrast to other sovereignty-related policy areas such as monetary policies, there has still not even been a discussion on whether national foreign ministries, intelligence services, armies and (border) police should be replaced – rather than paralleled – by a single EU foreign ministry, an EU army, an EU intelligence service and an EU (border) police.

Notwithstanding its constitutional outlook, the Draft Constitutional Treaty (DCT) of the EU does not propose such a far-reaching centralization, but reflects the incremental dynamics of integration in EU foreign and interior policies which have already been operating in the years between Maastricht to Nice. While the negative referenda on the DCT in France and the Netherlands in 2005 make it questionable whether the Constitutional Treaty (in this form or another) will ever come into force, it might nevertheless be useful to ask from an analytical perspective what kind of changes the DCT proposed for foreign and interior policies and how these changes would relate to the general dynamics of policy-making in both areas – not least because the ideas generated by the DCT might provide a matrix for future reforms of EU foreign and interior policies both at the Treaty level and below.

From a legal perspective the DCT codifies the remarkable increase in cross-pillar dynamics in foreign and interior affairs and formally abolishes the pillar structure by leaving in place one organization (and legal personality) only, namely the EU. However, a more detailed look at the concrete provisions of the DCT shows that, at least with regard to foreign policies, the distinction between 'normal' areas of EU policy-making, on the one hand, and foreign policies, on the other, is actually strengthened (see also Cremona 2003). In that context it has to be mentioned that in the DCT neither foreign nor interior policies belong to the exclusive competencies of the EU. While interior policies – under the banner of the 'area of freedom, security and justice' – are part of the 'areas of shared competence' (Article 13.2), it is striking that the DCT has reserved a separate section for external affairs, to which 'all areas of foreign policy', i.e. CFSP and classical first-pillar areas, belong (see Article 15.1). Thus, surprisingly, foreign policies fall within the realm of neither exclusive nor shared competencies – without a specification of how this third category should logically be conceived of. Thus the DCT only makes vague reference to the 'achievement of an ever-increasing degree of convergence of Member States' action' in foreign affairs (Article 39.1).

This ambivalent status of foreign policies is clearly reflected in one of the major institutional innovations of the DCT, namely the establishment of the office of a 'Union Minister for Foreign Affairs' (Article 27 DCT). Thus the Union Minister, who would be appointed by qualified majority of the European Council and with the agreement of the Commission President, would replace the double structure of the High Representative for the CFSP (located in the Council Secretariat) and the Commissioner for Foreign Affairs. However, the DCT remains silent on how this innovation – the Union Minister being responsible to the Council in the context of the CFSP and a Vice-President of the Commission at the same time – would work in practice, in particular in cases of divergent interests between the Commission and the Council. Moreover, under the surface of the DCT looms the institutional fragmentation of foreign policies which was originally put in place by the pillar structure. Hence the Union Minister will carry out his or her activities 'as mandated by the Council of Ministers' (Article 27.2), while for all the tasks the Union Minister exercises for the Commission 'the Union Minister shall be bound by Commission procedures' (Article 27.3). This ambivalence in the way in which the DCT perceives the future integration of foreign policies at the EU level also relates to other institutional provisions. Thus, while the planned establishment of a 'European External Action Service' (EEAS) (Article III-197) and Union Delegations (Chapter VII) can be seen as a cautious step towards the greater centralization of EU foreign policies, neither the DCT nor the EU's Declaration on the EEAS attached to the DCT clarify what the precise relationship between national foreign ministries, the EEAS and Union Delegations would look like in practice and how this would contribute to greater convergence between national and EU foreign policies.

When looking at the various policy areas that the DCT refers to in its section on 'External Action', another example of path dependency can be detected. Thus, as has been the case since the Maastricht Treaty, the different institutional arenas of EU foreign policies relate to different legal bases and are internally fragmented. Thus, for the CFSP, defence issues, sanctions and the solidarity clause between member states, the DCT introduces a new legal instrument, namely 'European decision'. However, the legal status of European decisions is similar to the soft-law character of decisions in the context of the CFSP since the Maastricht Treaty and, consequently, the DCT refers to European decisions as 'non-legislative acts', some of which are made by unanimity, others by qualified majority and constructive abstention (Article 34). This weak legal status of the CFSP is underlined by the weak role of Parliament. Thus, Parliament would only be 'consulted on the main aspects and basic choices of the common foreign and security policy and shall be kept informed about how it evolves' (Article 39.6), i.e. Parliament would have no say on the precise shape of policies, thus ensuring the continuity of executive dominance in EU foreign policies. Moreover Article III-209 aims to keep the Court of Justice on the sidelines by stating that the ECJ has no jurisdiction in any decision taken in the context of the CFSP. In contrast, classical first-pillar areas such as developmental co-operation and the CCP would be governed by

European laws and framework laws. These would operate on the basis of the co-decision procedure (now referred to as the 'ordinary legislative procedure' of Article III-302 DCT) – with a single right of initiative for the Commission and a strong role for Parliament and the Court of Justice. In these areas, the Council would usually decide on the basis of a qualified majority, but there are exceptions such as a unanimity requirement for agreements in the field of trade in services (Article III-217.4) and most Association Agreements (Article III-221.3). For international agreements, Parliament's consent would be required and the Court of Justice would have jurisdiction to rule on whether 'an agreement envisaged is compatible with the provisions of the Constitution', including the Charter of Fundamental Human Rights. Overall, the DCT thus makes no major changes to decision-making structures when compared to the different institutional regimes outlined in the previous chapters. The ambivalent status of foreign policies in relation to other policy areas is then also replicated with regard to policy guidance. Thus the DCT confirms – and arguably strengthens – the established hierarchy in foreign policies, with the European Council setting the general policy guidelines and the Council of Ministers being responsible for translating these guidelines into concrete policies (Wessel 2004). While there are, thus, signs of the further incremental centralization of foreign policies at the EU level, most notably through the establishment of the office of the Union Minister and the establishment of Union Delegations and the EEAS, these reforms can hardly be seen as a major step forward. A short look at the various and internally fragmented institutional arenas in EU foreign policies already shows that, notwithstanding certain institutional innovations, the DCT has not succeeded in overcoming the institutional fragmentation of EU foreign policies that has characterized this policy area at the EU level since the Maastricht Treaty.

As far as interior policies in general, and migration policies in particular, are concerned, the DCT proposes a wholesale shift to the new legal basis of European laws and framework laws, thus ensuring that – at last – this policy area *in its entirety* is subject to the full participation of Parliament and the Court of Justice. However, being an area of shared competence, the provisions of Chapter IV DCT on the establishment of an 'area of freedom, security and justice' also point to the limits of integration. While it is true that the introduction of a single decision-making procedure in the form of co-decisions and the introduction of the full jurisdiction of the ECJ are significant developments, which confirm the incremental dynamics of integration in this area at the EU level since the Maastricht Treaty, the limits of integration lie on a more subtle level. Thus, to take the example of migration policies, these limits relate to the objective of developing common rather than single policies on migration and the strong focus on a 'fair sharing of responsibility' between member states on asylum and refugee policies. Arguably this provision can always serve as a pretext for national (security) considerations at the expense of the development of an explicit European approach to this policy area. Consequently, such security consideration are mentioned throughout Chapter IV DCT, for example, when referring to the task of member states in the context of the establishment of the 'area of freedom, security and justice', to maintain 'law and order and safeguarding internal security'. Ironically, 'internal' seems to refer here to member states rather than to the EU as such.

Seen from this perspective, the DCT is no major milestone but yet another example of path dependency in EU foreign and interior policies, in particular with regard to the on-going tension between the functional unity and the institutional fragmentation of both policy areas. The dynamics resulting from this tension favour an incremental process of integration in both areas, as outlined in the previous chapters. However, the fact that the DCT is no quantum leap in the history of European integration in foreign and interior policies does not come as a great surprise. Thus the focus in this book on policy-making dynamics in both policy areas at the EU level since the Maastricht Treaty has shown that the significance of integration cannot sufficiently be understood from a mere institutional perspective, which focuses on either Treaty reforms or (explicit or implicit) pillar divides and fragmented decision-making structures. As significant as these institutional provisions are, their analysis has to be supplemented by focusing on the way in which the dynamics of integration in constituent policies contribute to the consolidation of the 'functional frame' of an EU-specific insider/outsider distinction, which provides a powerful counter-weight to institutional fragmentation. Whether this 'functional frame' is the basis for securitizing or liberal policies cannot be determined in the abstract, but depends on concrete political decisions made in both areas. Seen from that perspective, the increase of parliamentary involvement and judicial overview in both areas since the Maastricht Treaty – as well as greater public awareness of the political significance of European decisions in both areas within the EU and beyond – might provide the best insurance against 'fortress Europe' mentalities in EU foreign and interior affairs.

Notes

1 Introduction

1 This book does not cover all parts of foreign and interior policies, such as defence policies or police and judicial co-operation. It would, however, be worthwhile to study the extent to which the concepts and arguments developed in this book also apply to these areas, in particular how they relate to issues of internal and external security. A case in point could be the study of emerging cross-pillar networks relating to Europol or the European Security and Defence Policy.

2 Another reason is, of course, the diverse sets of national actors involved in policy-making in both areas.

3 On the specific migration policy provisions of the Amsterdam Treaty see Chapter 3.

4 See also Chapters 3 and 4 in which the delegation of capabilities to the Council Secretariat is discussed in greater detail.

5 Prior to the Maastricht Treaty, the EPC Secretariat was clearly separated from the Council Secretariat. Although both Secretariats had been located within the same building since the establishment of the EPC Secretariat by the Single European Act (SEA), they remained detached from each other. Not only were they placed in different wings of the Council building, but the EPC Secretariat was separated from the Council Secretariat 'by doors with special locks on them' (M. E. Smith 2003: 168).

6 Notwithstanding the significance of this basic distinction between EU citizens on the one hand, and TCNs on the other, it should be emphasized that EU law provides for a multifaceted system of rights of TCNs (see Peers 2000).

7 In October 1999 the European Council meeting in Tampere decided that the Commission should closely follow the progress of developing an 'area of freedom, security and justice' in the legislative process. The Council asked the Commission to draw up a 'scoreboard' to review progress every six months, thereby assessing how the policy guidelines and objectives of the Tampere meeting and the Treaties in JHA were being fulfilled.

2 The construction of an EU insider/outsider distinction

1 Following the Greek temple metaphor, the overarching 'roof' of the European Union is carried by the three 'pillars' of the EC, the CFSP and JHA.

2 Foreign policies were for the first time linked with the EC in 1986 through the SEA. However, as opposed to the provisions of the Maastricht Treaty, the SEA did not provide for a 'single framework' covering all aspects of EC foreign policies. In contrast to the 'single institutional framework' referred to in the Maastricht Treaty, Article 30 3(a) SEA (Title III) only mentioned the 'framework of European Political Co-operation' and contained no overarching substantial linkage with the EC, save references to the Commission and the Parliament. Therefore, EPC 'was clearly separated from the provisions

of the Act which amended or related to the Community Treaties'. Consequently, 'EPC, pursuant to Title III, remained an intergovernmental process governed by international law' (MacLeod, Hendry and Hyett 1996: 411). On the SEA, see also Moravcsik (1991).

3 Given the variety of institutional arenas in the first pillar, the term 'classical' Community method should be regarded as an ideal type notion (Wallace and Wallace 2000). See Chapter 3 on the actual plurality of various institutional settings – also within the EC framework – in the areas of foreign and interior policies.

4 See, for example, the work of the Migration Policy Group (Brussels) or Statewatch (London) in the field of migration policies, or the Centre for European Policy Studies (Brussels) or the Euromesco Network (Lisbon) in foreign affairs.

5 See Lenaerts (1991) for an account of pre-Maastricht legal perspectives on the EC. See also Bardenhewer (1998); Barents (1997); Bogdandy and Ehlermann (1998); Curtin and Dekker (2002).

6 This legal unity thesis is not mere legal abstraction but has been applied by the ECJ in its *Airport Transit Visas* judgement on migration policies in 1997. This judgement will be analysed in greater detail in Chapter 6.

3 Authority delegation to supranational actors: primary capabilities

1 This chapter argues that even in the 'supranational' first pillar there is not one single institutional model that defines the capabilities of supranational actors. The so-called Community method has itself become increasingly hybrid and complex as EC coverage and competencies have widened. Therefore, the first pillar is also characterized by a multitude of institutional arenas.

2 The delegation of capabilities does also occur as a result of secondary decisions as part of day-to-day policy-making in the EU. These 'secondary capabilities' of supranational actors in foreign and interior policies will be dealt with in Chapter 4.

3 Agenda setting is understood here in the formal sense and refers to the initiation of legislation. Of course, the setting of the EU agenda does not depend on the Commission alone. Thus 'in treaties and reforms, the Council sets the long term policy goals of the EU', whereas 'the European Council (of heads of government) and certain other councils set the medium-term policy agenda' (Hix 1999: 25). Moreover, in the second and third pillars it has in particular been the rotating Presidencies which have often taken a lead in agenda setting by bringing their individual policy preferences to the formal EU agenda.

4 Interview with Director of Legal Service, Council Secretariat.

5 It should be mentioned that the Treaty provisions on the free movement of persons, which are of relevance for the analysis of interior policies, also make reference to the Economic and Social Committee as an institution involved in the legislative process. However, due to its overall insignificant role in foreign and interior policies, this book does not cover the activities of the Economic and Social Committee.

6 Interview with official from the Legal Service, Commission.

7 Interview with Head of Unit, Commission.

8 Interview with Deputy Head of Cabinet, Commission. However, when confronted with empirical findings this statement could be questioned. Cases such as the 'orange juice conflict' between the EU and Israel, or the debate on the relationship between EU assistance to the Palestinian Authority and corruption cases in Palestine, show that the Commission has not been reluctant to combine trade and politics if it is able to do so.

9 When arguing about the 'law-driven' character of EU politics, a member of the Commission's legal service, who was previously working for the Finnish Foreign Ministry, argued that the Commission has developed a particular 'initiative ethos'. Since national governments, which think much more in political terms, do not have such an institutional approach to EU politics, the Commission has a structural advantage in using

this instrument even when the right of initiative is shared. Interview with official from the Legal Service, Commission.

10 See Chapter 5 for more details on these agreements. The Commission failed when attempting to base those parts of the Association Agreements, which are decided internally by qualified majority, on Article 228 TEC. One example has been the free movement provisions in international agreements. Notwithstanding the Commission's efforts, the Council succeeded in ensuring that these provisions remained in the framework of mixed agreements which require a unanimous vote in the Council. Interview with Director, Legal Service, Council Secretariat.

11 An interesting side note is that Article 301 TEC is an example of a direct link between the first and the second pillars. Thus a decision on sanctions according to Article 301 TEC by qualified majority does actually require a prior decision in the framework of the CFSP on the basis of a joint action or a common decision. Note that these decisions require a unanimous vote in the Council. This equips all member states with a de facto veto on sanctions.

12 Moreover, in 1993 several parliamentarians recalled that the fourth financial protocol with Israel of 1992 contained a specific clause on the humanitarian situation in the Occupied Territories. Some Socialist members raised the issue of human rights violations in the Occupied Territories and brought up the possibility that Parliament could consider suspending the protocol or blocking the financing provisions therein (*Agence Europe*, 21 January 1993, No. 5902: 6). The relationship between parliamentary votes under the assent procedure, which confronts Parliament with a take-it-or-leave-it proposal, on the one hand, and the political situation in a conflict region on the other, is exemplified by the conclusion of the Association Agreements in the framework of the EMP. Thus, when the Middle East peace process seemed to be well under way, in 1996 Parliament gave its assent to the Association Agreement with Israel with the almost unanimous support of 265 to 2 with three abstentions (*Agence Europe*, 1 March 1996, No. 6678: 11). The 1997 Interim Association Agreement with the Palestine Liberation Organization (PLO) received a similar margin with 372 to 5 votes with four abstentions (*Agence Europe*, 10 April 1997, No. 6951: 3).

13 Interview with Desk Officer, Commission. Note that 'initiatives' in the second pillar differ from those in the first (and third) pillar due to differences between the requirement for flexibility in foreign policies and the need for codification in other areas. Most foreign policy issues do not involve legislation as such. This is one reason why parliamentary scrutiny is difficult in this field, not only at the European level. Taking note of this remark, initiatives are referred to here in a narrower (codified) sense than those second-pillar measures that are published as legal acts in the *Official Journal*.

14 Consider again the ability of Parliament to use its power of delay under the first pillar. When Parliament had to adopt a bilateral agreement which established scientific co-operation between the EU and Israel under the Fifth Framework Programme for Research and Development, a group of parliamentarians suggested (unsuccessfully) delaying the vote on this agreement until the outcome of the elections in Israel some three months later were known (*Agence Europe*, 12 February 1999, No. 7403: 13).

15 In order to make up for this dependence on the Council and the Commission, Parliament tried to establish close links with the Commission's delegations in Israel and Palestine in order to receive inside information from the region. Moreover, Parliament profited from the regular exchange with the Special Representatives to the Middle East peace process. One parliamentarian stated that the EU Special Representative to the Middle East peace process provided Parliament regularly with 'detailed briefings' and kept 'very good communication with Parliament'. Interviews with Desk Officer, Commission and MEP.

16 Interview with MEP.

17 When in 1996 the Commission initiated legislation on three directives aiming to establish the free movement of persons, the governments of the United Kingdom and

Portugal initially opposed these measures, arguing that they fell under the third pillar (*Agence Europe*, 28/29 May 1996, No. 6736: 7).

18 One of the provisions of ex-Article K.6 TEU was that Parliament should hold a yearly debate on progress in the third pillar. However, between 1993 and 1997 it was only in 1995 that Parliament received a prior report from the Council on the progress achieved in this area, pointing to the problems related to non-enforceable 'information rights' (*Agence Europe*, 3/4 June 1997, No. 6740: 8). Moreover, when reports were finally received, they often contained only a list of adopted decisions, not a detailed description of the Council's activities, as Parliament wished. Interview with Administrator, European Parliament.

19 Even after the Amsterdam Treaty came into force, Parliament was not consulted by the Council and the Commission on important decisions. Thus, prior to the Tampere European Council, Parliament was dissatisfied with the information it received from the Finnish Presidency (*Agence Europe*, 14 October 1999, No. 7572: 12). Also, with regard to the aforementioned 'progress reports', Title IV TEC did not lead to major changes. Thus, when drafting the progress report on this issue for the year 2000, one MEP was struck by the small amount of information received from the Council and the Commission. Interview with MEP.

20 Member states make use of their right of initiative, in particular when they hold the Presidency. Against this background it is interesting to note that the Swedish Presidency of 2001 made clear that it would not make use of its right of initiative under Title IV TEC and would instead co-ordinate its activities beforehand with the Commission. Interview with Head of Unit, Council Secretariat.

21 With regard to the ranking of the Commission's capabilities, more weight is given to 'qualified majority voting' than to 'right of initiative'. This is based on the assumption that unanimity automatically undermines the impact of the right of initiative since the Commission's ability to form alliances within the Council is severely undermined. In contrast, when there is a shared right of initiative, it has in several cases not been used by member states, which tend to rely on the Commission to propose legislation (see the following chapter). This has also been confirmed by the empirical research presented in this chapter.

22 If the Commission decides to do so. However, it often remains cautious about coming up with proposals. See Chapter 6, which discusses the Commission's preferences on migration policies.

23 There are always problems with indices and quantifying 'power'. Static figures cannot represent a dynamic process such as legislative politics in the EU. Therefore, the figures in Table 3.3 only aim to provide an indication of the diversity of the hybrid institutional regimes of EU foreign and interior policies, and to point to general ways in which the capabilities of the Commission and Parliament have developed rather than claiming to establish an exact statistical relationship.

24 Note that the co-decision procedure has been significantly changed with the Amsterdam Treaty. 'The reforms increased the powers of the EP' (Hix 1999: 66). In contrast, the role of the Commission in the reformed co-decision procedure is weaker than before. Since the indices in Table 3.3 do not relate to the six legislative procedures as far as the Commission is concerned, this (assumed) decrease in power is not included, but should be considered when interpreting the indices of Parliament vis-à-vis those of the Commission. Also the increase of Parliament's capabilities from Maastricht to Amsterdam, as indicated by the figures in Table 3.3, should be interpreted alongside the strengthening of Parliament's role in relation to the Commission in the co-decision procedure.

25 The capability indices are similar when looking at foreign and interior policies individually, thus indicating that the functional logic of constituent policies has translated into similar institutional rules in both areas, thus supporting the arguments made in Chapter 2.

26 As Cameron notes, this limitation with regard to the capabilities of Parliament in the area of foreign policies is not a unique characteristic of the EU political system. Thus Parliament's rights in the second pillar 'are akin to those of most national EU parliaments' (1998: 65). Moreover, in interior policies the 1990s led to a similar executive bias at the expense not only of the EP but also of member states' parliaments. Seen from that perspective, national governments can circumvent their national parliaments in legislation on interior policies by turning to the EU where parliamentary involvement had been low from the outset. Thus, since Maastricht, 'many of the Member States' parliaments encounter serious problems in exercising effective control' over interior policy at the EU level (Monar 1995: 249).

27 Comitology will be addressed in greater detail in Chapters 4 and 7.

28 Interview with Head of Delegation, Commission.

29 Interview with Desk Officer, Commission.

30 See Chapter 4 for more details on these secondary comitology provisions.

31 These reforms of the Nice Treaty further limit the Commission's autonomy in trade policies and foster the linkages within the executive. This follows the pattern which already characterized the trade policy provisions in the Amsterdam Treaty (Meunier and Nicolaïdis 1999).

32 Interview with Desk Officer, Council Secretariat.

33 Interview with Desk Officer, Commission.

34 An official from the Israeli Foreign Ministry stated in 2000 that Israel is 'putting a lot of emphasis on meetings with Solana' based on the observation that the new office of the High Representative is central to EU foreign policy-making. Interview with EU Desk Officer, Israeli Foreign Ministry.

35 Prior to the Amsterdam Treaty there was no clear Treaty base on the Troika. At this time, the Troika consisted of the Presidency together with the preceding and the following Presidency. An inclusion of the Commission in Troika or Presidency activities depended on the goodwill of the member states, and this sometimes led to tensions between the two institutions. For example, a visit of Council President Dick Spring to the Middle East in 1996 without any Commission involvement provoked an outcry within the Commission that such a move 'was in contradiction with the practice of visits by EU Troikas, in which the Commission also participates'. The reforms of the Amsterdam Treaty thus provided for a mechanisms that attempts to avoid 'institutional battles over this issue' (*Agence Europe*, 9 October 1996, No. 6828: 3).

36 The work of COREPER often leads to a 'doubling of activities, which is not always easy'. Thus, in the practice of foreign policy-making, both committees can demand proposals on specific issues from Council working groups. Interview with official from the Council Secretariat.

37 This linkage became visible when the Council President Jacques Poos wrote a letter to the Palestinian Authority Chairman Yasser Arafat stating that 'the European Union has decided to ask its representative in Tel Aviv to approach [Israeli] foreign Secretary Mr. Levy' in order to issue a protest from the EU against certain actions of the Israeli government. Note that Poos, a representative of a member state and the Council, refers to the head of the Commission Delegation in Israel as the EU's regional representative (*Agence Europe*, 9 August 1997, No. 7034: 1).

38 It can be debated to what extent budget really matters. But in the perspective of various participants in the policy-making process it does matter. This has been confirmed in several interviews with officials from the Council Secretariat, the Commission and Parliament. There are several concrete examples of Parliament's capabilities in the budgetary process (Monar 1997b). To mention just a few, during the 1994 budget readings Parliament succeeded in including in the budget a heading of €50 million on development projects in Palestine against the wish of the Council (*Agence Europe*, 13 November 1993, No. 6106: 3). Also the inclusion of human rights projects between Israel and Palestine in the framework of the EMP was the result of pressure from

Parliament on the Commission and the Council. Interview with official from the Commission.

39 It should be noted that executive dominance also characterizes foreign policies at the national level where the competencies of parliaments and courts are usually also less developed.

40 Peers, however, has cited the *Chernobyl* case of 1990 in which the Court of Justice accepted an appeal from Parliament on an alleged breach of its prerogatives, although such an appeal was excluded by the Treaties (2000: 47).

41 Due to this provision, Parliament's response to an alleged breach of its prerogatives on Association Agreements remained in the past declaratory. Thus, in 1995, the chair of the parliamentary committee on External Economic Relations accused the Commission of not consulting Parliament over the new agreement with Israel (*Agence Europe*, 27/28 November 1995, No. 6614: 11). The same problems were raised by Parliament on the lack of prior consultation on the Interim Association Agreement with the PLO (*Agence Europe*, 10 April 1997, No. 6951: 3). These accusations resemble the complaints from MEPs in the second pillar. As in the common foreign and security policies, judicial remedy on Association Agreements is not possible for Parliament until the entry into force of the Nice Treaty.

42 On developments in the case law of the Court of Justice in first-pillar areas related to the free movement of persons see Moore (2002).

43 In fact, prior to the Amsterdam Treaty, issues related to internal borders were brought to the Court of Justice and were hotly disputed within the EU. A famous case was settled with the *Wijsenbeek* judgement of the Court of Justice. Wijsenbeek, a Dutch national, argued that the deadline for the abolition of internal border controls as provided for by the Maastricht Treaty had direct effect. This perspective was also strongly advocated by Parliament. However, the Court of Justice argued that direct effect did not relate to this issue. The Court of Justice stressed that the deadline has a political not a legal meaning, thus supporting the point of view of member states as well as the Commission's 'diplomatic attitude' towards this issue (*Agence Europe*, 26 May 1993, No. 5987: 11 and 22 September 1999, No. 7556: 10). The judgement of the Court of Justice on *Wijsenbeek* was given after the entry into force of the Amsterdam Treaty, and therefore one can only speculate on the extent to which the Court of Justice has considered the provisions of Article 68(2) TEC, although this article was not mentioned in the judgement (Case C-378/97).

44 Article 68(3) TEC limits the Court of Justice's right to cases which have not become *res judicata,* i.e. the Court of Justice 'can only act on concrete situations and not on theoretical questions' in migration policies, thus further limiting the scope of its judgements. Interviews with officials from the Legal Service, Council Secretariat.

45 For more details see Laffan and Shackleton (2000) and Neunreither (1999).

46 Interviews with MEP (chair of committee) and administrator, European Parliament. According to a Commission official 'many projects in migration policies were put on us by Parliament' which made use of its budgetary powers. Interview with Deputy Head of Unit, Commission.

47 In this context one former Head of Delegation to the Palestinian Territories criticized the tendency of the Commission to rely mainly on its 'money spending culture' in relations to third parties. Such an approach is accompanied by a reluctance to act politically, for example by making greater use of the Commission's right of initiative in all the pillars. Therefore, he argued that the 'budget functions as an alternative to politics'. Interview with Deputy Head of Cabinet, Commission.

48 While this hybrid institutional setting provides for manifold linkages within the areas of foreign and interior policies, it is rather weak in formally linking the two 'inter-governmental' pillars with each other (for linkages between the second and third pillars that emerge in the policy-making process, see Lavenex 2004). Problems stemming from this division are discussed in Chapters 6 and 7.

49 Interview with Director, Legal Service, Council Secretariat.

4   Authority delegation in between Treaty reforms: the secondary capabilities of supranational actors

1 The decisions on migration policies comprise the legislative acts directly related to EU migration policies as well as those provisions of the Schengen *acquis* that deal with migration policy, and which have become part of the European Union's migration policy *acquis* following the Amsterdam Treaty.
2 Prior to the Amsterdam Treaty the official title of the Special Representative for the Middle East peace process was Special Envoy. This book uses the term 'Special Representative' except for quotations from official documents or secondary literature and for those references that relate to the mandate prior to 1999.
3 Statement of Commission President Jacques Delors reported by *Agence Europe*, No. 5972, 1 May 1993: 13.
4 An informal Council meeting in Thessaloniki in May 1994 discussed all aspects of the Communication but suggested concentrating in the actual decision-making on the third-pillar elements therein; *Agence Europe*, No. 6224, 5 May 1994: 7.
5 In a Council Resolution of 1994 on the admission of third-country nationals, direct reference is made to a regulation on the freedom of movement for workers, while a decision of 1996 on burden-sharing calls for a co-ordination of measures under this decision with the Commission's action in the area of humanitarian aid (Council 1994b; 1996a). This is also an early example of cross-pillar linkages between foreign and interior policies.
6 For example, the concept of full association also comprised the integration of the Commission in multilateral meetings at the ministerial level. Thus, from 1993 onwards, the Commissioner responsible for migration policies attended meetings of the so-called Berlin Group (later the Budapest Group) of West and East European migration ministers (*Agence Europe*, No. 5922, 18 February 1993: 15). However, in most international organizations dealing with migration policy issues the Commission is not represented alongside member states; also the Council Secretariat participates in more such international fora than the Commission (Guiraudon 2000: 255).
7 See below in this chapter for more details on these committees.
8 The first scoreboard was published by the Commission in April 2000 and from then onwards biannually. The preferences of the Commission, as they appear in the six scoreboards until December 2002 will be analysed in detail in the following chapter.
9 The High-Level Working Group is an interesting example of linkages between EU interior and foreign affairs settings. While cross-pillar linkages are omnipresent within these two areas, linkages between the two settings of foreign and interior policies have only developed in very small steps. The fact that over time they have apparently mushroomed points to the functional dynamics inherent in the integration of constituent policies at large (see, for example, for the European Neighbourhood Policy and the integration of JHA therein, Lavenex 2004).
10 From the project initiation perspective, however, the ERF is characterized by a hierarchical dominance of member states, which propose to the Commission the projects to be funded, leaving the Commission little room for manoeuvre.
11 Note that the ERF allocates a fixed amount to each member state each year and the Commission's leverage to choose projects applies only to allocating funds *within* each member state.
12 Note that the actual negotiating mandate was transferred to the Commission by the Council voting under the unanimity requirement, *Agence Europe*, No. 7287, 27 August 1998: 2–3.
13 Such a linkage between EC measures and 'intergovernmental' settings was already

established in some areas of foreign policies during the EPC period. The Euro-Arab dialogue could be mentioned as an example (Rhein 1999: 692).

14 The view that it has been the Commission which is the main actor behind the creation of EMP is raised by Commission officials in particular – accordingly member states tend to emphasize their pivotal role.

15 Only the Joint Action of April 2002, on the temporary reception of Palestinians who were involved in the siege of the Church of the Nativity in Bethlehem, contains no reference to the Commission (Council 2002a).

16 Also the organization of visits of members of the European Parliament to the region belongs to the 'logistical support tasks' of the Commission Delegations. Interview with official from the European Commission.

17 EC–Israel: Cooperation Committee, Press Release: Brussels (28 November 1997), Press 370. The dispute has centred around false export certificates for Israeli oranges, which in fact originated from Brazil. The government of Israel says that 'administrative cooperation' between Israel and the EU would have sufficed to settle the issue. The publication of a note to exporters within the *Official Journal* by the Commission was seen as a political step. *Agence Europe*, No. 7107, 26 November 1997: 7. This interpretation has also been confirmed in several interviews with EU officials.

18 Interview with Head of Unit, European Commission.

19 Interview with Desk Officer, European Commission.

20 Although there are regular meetings between the Commission and the EIB, the Commission was dissatisfied in particular with the co-ordination of policies by the EIB. 'They had problems sticking to the plans. MEDA II also provides for changes to that.' Interview with Desk Officer, European Commission.

21 See below in this chapter on the committee rules in MEDA II.

22 See Chapter 7 on the actual implementation problems of MEDA.

23 Interview with Desk Officer, Council Secretariat.

24 CIREA is the Centre for Information, Discussion and Exchange on Asylum, CIREFI stands for Centre for Information, Discussion and Exchange on the Crossing of Borders and Immigration.

25 It should also be emphasized that the Schengen Secretariat has been integrated into the Council Secretariat and not into the Commission; *Agence Europe*, No. 7202, 17 April 1998: 4–5. The decision to integrate the Schengen personnel into the Council Secretariat was made by the Council voting with qualified majority with a negative vote from France which insisted that the number of posts exceeded the actual needs of the Secretariat (*Agence Europe*, No. 7458, 4/5 May 1999: 15). The integration has not only led to tensions between the Commission and Parliament – both of which preferred an integration of the Secretariat into the Commission – on the one hand, and the Council on the other, it has also led to tensions between the Council Secretariat and the Council since the Council's Staff Committee feared that the new personnel would undermine the position of long-standing Council Secretariat officials. The Secretary-General of the Council Secretariat even suggested letting the row be decided by the Court of Justice. In order to avoid such recourse to the Court of Justice, the Schengen personnel was then integrated into the Council Secretariat as trainees only and not as officials (*Agence Europe*, 12/13 April 1999: 16).

26 Since 2003 the EU has had a new Special Representative, namely Marc Otte, who followed Miguel Angel Moratinos, the Special Representative from 1996 to 2003.

27 According to a member of staff of the Special Representative, it was easier to get accepted by Israeli and Palestinian officials than by Americans. 'It is difficult to deal with them, they never call.' Interview with Desk Officer, Council Secretariat.

28 See Chapter 7.

29 Of course, Parliament has been involved in the decision-making process in all first-pillar secondary decisions in migration and Middle East policies due to its role as one of the two legislative chambers of the EU.

30　Thus, from all documents the Council Secretariat had dealt with from the Maastricht to the Amsterdam Treaty, 21 per cent related to the third pillar and 15 per cent to the second pillar. Interview with Director, Legal Service, Council Secretariat.

5　Substantive cross-pillar linkages in foreign and interior affairs: the cases of EU Middle East and migration policies

1　On (neo-)functionalism and the role of Community-building see, among others, Deutsch (1957), Hass (1958), Sandholtz and Stone Sweet (1998) and Stone Sweet and Sandholtz (1997).
2　On the role of the EU as an international actor in the years following the Maastricht Treaty see, for example, Ginsberg (1999), Jørgensen (1998), Rosecrance (1998) or M. Smith (1996). From a theoretical perspective this issue is covered by Jupille (1999).
3　It should be noted that talking about the 'classical' EC pillar is only an ideal typical notion. In practice, the first pillar is characterized by a variety of institutional regimes, as discussed in previous chapters.
4　As discussed further in Chapter 6, the concept of a strict legal separation between the pillars has been undermined by the Court of Justice in its *Airport Transit Visas* judgement.
5　See also, for policy instruments of the EU in the area of foreign affairs, K. E. Smith (1998).
6　Data calculated from Regelsberger (1997: 70).
7　The Commission attempted to revitalize REDWG by organizing a meeting of the REDWG steering committee in Moscow in January 2000. However, the decisions of this meeting was not able to unblock the deadlock of REDWG co-operation caused by the stalemate of the peace process (European Union 2000).
8　Interview with former official of the Israeli Defence Force.
9　During the Barak administration, EU member states were, among other European states, responsible for incorporating Israel into the West European country group of the United Nations, thus putting an end to Israel's previously non-aligned status within the UN.
10　Interview with representative from Legal Service, Commission.
11　See Chapter 7.
12　In the light of the freezing of transactions by Israel of custom duty revenues since the beginning of the Al-Aqsa Intifada, the EU decided to transfer direct budgetary support of €10 million a month to the Palestinian Authority. These transactions started in July 2001 and document the changing prioritization of the EU from project funding towards government stabilization. Investigations by the weekly *Die Zeit* have revealed that these transactions have been used by the Palestinian leadership to support terrorist activities. This accusation has, however, been strongly rejected by the Palestinian Authority and the Commission (Kleine-Brockhoff and Schirra 2002).
13　It is quite interesting to note that the Common Strategy also provides for linkages between foreign and interior policies. Thus an entire section of the Common Strategy deals with the issue of Justice and Home Affairs and how these policies relate to EU Mediterranean policies. This corresponds with the increased focus of Euro-Mediterranean conferences on this area, such as at the 2002 Valencia meeting, which 'has firmly implanted the JHA dimension within the third chapter of the Barcelona process' (Gillespie 2002: 111).
14　Trevi was 'cryptically named after its first chairman, A. R. Fonteijn, and the Trevi fountain in Rome (where its first meeting was convened)' (den Boer 1996: 394.).
15　The special provisions on the application of Title IV TEC and Schengen provisions for the UK, Ireland and Denmark can be related to debates on variable geometry and differentiation within specific policy areas (Cullen 1995; Ehlermann 1998).
16　Due to the development of positive law on migration policies in the formal EU setting

of the third and first pillars after the Maastricht Treaty, and due to the increasing number of EU member states participating in the Schengen co-operation even before the formal integration of Schengen into the EU framework in 1999, there has been a de facto approximation between the two settings prior to the Amsterdam Treaty.

17 The slow ratification process can be related to reservations in some member states on the exclusion of burden-sharing provisions on the one hand, and the limited role of the Court of Justice on the other. See also *Agence Europe*, No. 6436, 9 March 1995: 6, and *Agence Europe*, No. 6610, 22 November 1995: 10–11.

18 The first pillar act on visa policies was formally adopted by the Council in 1995, but was subsequently annulled by the Court of Justice due to procedural shortcomings relating to the consultation of the European Parliament. This case will be discussed in Chapter 6.

19 For a detailed discussion of these two cases see Chapter 6.

20 Some initial drafts of the Austrian Presidency met with vigorous criticism from non-governmental organizations and some member states, because Austria made no reference to the Geneva Convention, raising doubts about whether a future EU migration policy regime would be based on this provision. In subsequent meetings the reference to the Geneva Convention was again introduced in official EU papers (*Agence Europe*, No. 7332, 29 October 1998: 7–8). It should, however, also be noted that the Geneva Convention was already explicitly referred to in the Amsterdam Treaty, thus already documenting its relevance for the EU migration regime.

21 For all data on foreign policy expenditure referred to in this chapter, the appropriations for funding enlargement have been excluded. Enlargement expenditure appears in the foreign policy chapter of the EC budget; it does not really regulate the EU's relations with the outside world but rather with future insiders.

6 The divergent policy preferences of supranational actors in foreign and interior policies: tackling the myth of supranational unity

1 The same applies to the preferences of national governments, which are not analysed in this chapter.

2 There was, of course, an EC history for both areas prior to the Maastricht Treaty. However, it was only in 1993 that both areas were formally integrated into the 'single institutional setting'. Thus, while supranational actors had already developed specific preferences on the two areas prior to the Maastricht Treaty, the Treaty allowed these preferences to unfold within and become directed towards a functionally unified setting, albeit an institutionally highly fragmented one.

3 Officials from the Council Secretariat and the Commission confirmed in various interviews that they have a regular and permanent exchange. They also know each other personally. Officials from both institutions, however, pointed out that they hardly ever meet their counterparts in Parliament.

4 In the early years of the peace process the Commission regarded the multilateral track and its own impact on the Regional Economic Development Working Group as a key to EU influence. Expectations of REDWG were high. Thus the Commission was quite enthusiastic about the relaunch of REDWG at a multilateral Steering Group meeting in Moscow in February 2000 (European Union 2000). However, these expectations did not materialize and although REDWG formally still exists it has not moved from institutionalization to concrete joint action by Israel, Palestine, Jordan and Egypt (*Agence Europe*, No. 6055, 2 September 1993: 5–6).

5 *Agence Europe*, No. 6095, 28 October 1993: 7.

6 Interview with Advisor to Special Representative, Council Secretariat.

7 Arguably a similar dynamic could then be observed in the context of the 'Wider Europe' programme of the Prodi Commission, which met strong opposition on semantics in the Council. The Commission had to accept that this initiative was

officially launched with a more neutral policy frame, under the guidance of the European Council, namely the 'neighbourhood frame' of the European Neighbourhood Policy (ENP).

8 The Commission was less concerned about Parliament's role and proposed the introduction of consultation only.

9 Note that the Council issued an official statement on the Commission communication. This is different from the two 1991 proposals by the Commission on migration policies, which were not even discussed in the Council. This points to the argument that over time the Commission was gradually accepted within the previously intergovernmental club (*Agence Europe*, No. 5972, 1 May 1993: 13).

10 It was in the Maastricht Treaty that the Commission announced that it would only make cautious use of its (shared) right of initiative in this area (*Agence Europe*, No 6018, 9 July 1993: 5).

11 This is underlined by the importance the Commission attached to studying national interests prior to publishing the first scoreboard. In a tour to all national capitals the Commissioner responsible explored the possibilities and constraints and only then did the Commission publish its own approach.

12 Interviews with Deputy Head of Unit, Commission and Head of Unit, Commission.

13 Interview with former Head of Unit, Commission.

14 Take, for example, the database of the *Frankfurter Allgemeine Zeitung*. The High Representative is referred to in 642 articles from 1 May 1999 until the end of 2002. The Special Representative is referred to in 85 articles from 1996 until 2002.

15 Interview with Advisor to the Special Representative, Council Secretariat.

16 Interview with Desk Officer CFSP, Council Secretariat.

17 Interview with Desk Officer CFSP, Council Secretariat.

18 Interview with Advisor to the Special Representative, Council Secretariat.

19 Interview with Advisor to the Special Representative, Council Secretariat.

20 Interview with Advisor to the Special Representative, Council Secretariat.

21 Interview with Advisor to the Special Representative, Council Secretariat.

22 Interview with Advisor to the Special Representative, Council Secretariat.

23 Interview with Advisor to the Special Representative, Council Secretariat.

24 Interview with Advisor to the Special Representative, Council Secretariat. In 2003 this close linkage became a problem for the second Special Representative, Marc Otte, after the Israeli government decided to initiate a boycott of those foreign politicians meeting Arafat.

25 Interview with former Israeli army official. See also, on the subject of the EU Special Advisor, a British national, MacAskill (2002).

26 Interviews with Advisor to the Special Representative, Council Secretariat. The work of the task forces is covered by the CFSP budget. It is a small budget of approximately €60,000 which is mainly spent on reports.

27 Interview with Desk Officer CFSP, Council Secretariat.

28 Interview with Desk Officer CFSP, Council Secretariat.

29 The non-acceptance of the EU as a 'player' in Middle East policies by the Israeli government is often referred to as a major hindrance to the EU for a greater role in the peace process. Yet the actions of the EU Special Advisor seem to tell another story and point to the way in which, without the glare of publicity, there are manifold attempts from both sides to deepen EU–Israeli relations.

30 In 1993 the Israeli Foreign Minister Shimon Peres had already suggested that Israeli should be an associate member of the EU (*Agence Europe*, No. 6116).

31 Interview with Head of Unit, Legal Service, Council Secretariat.

32 Interview with Head of Unit, Council Secretariat.

33 Interview with Head of Unit, Legal Service, Council Secretariat.

34 Interview with Head of Unit, Legal Service, Council Secretariat.

35 Interview with Head of Unit, Council Secretariat.

36 Interview with Head of Unit, Legal Service, Council Secretariat.

37 When the Maastricht Treaty came into force Parliament started to publish annual human rights reports (*Agence Europe*, No. 5936, 10 March 1993: 5). When looking at reports dealt with in the foreign affairs committee another interesting observation comes to the fore. Since the Maastricht Treaty Parliament has laid greater emphasis on the scrutiny of policy-making in the first pillar than in the second pillar. Most reports adopted by this committee have thus dealt with either first-pillar or cross-pillar issues, such as Association Agreements, accession treaties or financial assistance, rather than mere second-pillar areas.

38 In the academic debate there is also some scepticism whether the EMP has embarked on the right agenda to develop, through economic and security policies, a stable Middle East. See on this debate, among others, Al-Khouri (2000); Bertelsmann Group (1999, 2000); Erzan (1999); Halbach (1995); Kienle (1998) and Vasconcelos and Joffé (2000).

39 MEDA Democracy has been integrated into the MEDA budget line.

40 Interview with MEP.

41 Interview with MEP, Vice-President of the European Parliament.

42 Interview with MEP, Head of Inter Group.

43 Interview with MEP, Head of Inter Group.

44 Interviews with two MEPs, Heads of Inter Group.

45 Interview with MEP.

46 This links up to the description of EU migration policies as creating a 'fortress Europe'. This notion was particularly popular in the 1990s when positive integration was seen as being primarily focused on restrictive policies rather than a 'comprehensive' approach to migration and integration policies (Geddes 2000; Huysmans 2000; Peers 1998; Morris 1997a). See Chapter 2 on this debate on the underlying securitization/liberalization discourses in both foreign and interior policies.

47 An argument has emerged between Parliament and the Commission on this issue. Parliament accused the Commission of not taking action in this area. It even threatened to go to the Court of Justice. Ultimately, the Commission presented the three Directives on this issue (*Agence Europe*, No. 6772, 17 July 1996: 11–12). The Commission occasionally threatened member states that it would take legal action, but refrained from doing so (*Agence Europe*, No. 5991, 2 June 1993: 5). The belief of most member states that there was no direct effect in the free movement provisions of the TEC was supported by the Court of Justice in the *Wijsenbeek* judgement (*Agence Europe*, No. 7556, 22 September 1999: 10).

48 Interview with MEP.

49 As one interviewee noted, the only 'influence we have' is the budget, where, for example, Parliament claims ownership for budget lines such as the ERF budget or budget line B7–677 on support measures for third countries on migration matters. Interview with Administrator, European Parliament.

50 On the 1996 IGC see also Bieber (1995) and van Outrive (1995).

51 Interview with MEP.

52 Interview with Administrator, European Parliament.

53 Interview with MEP.

54 Interview with MEP.

55 This has been confirmed by several interviewees from Parliament, the Commission and the Council Secretariat.

56 The case has become even more problematic since a close personal relationship between the Commissioner and the firm to which implementation had been delegated was disclosed.

57 SCR was later renamed as EuropeAid.

58 It is in this context that the Joint Actions on the mandate of the Special Representative have contained specific budgetary clauses only since the year 2000.

59 Judgement of the Court of 9 July 1987, *Meryem Demirel* v. *Stadt Schwäbisch Gmünd*, Case C-12/86.

60 Judgement of the Court of 10 June 1997, *European Parliament* v. *Council of the European Union: Nationals of third countries – Visas – Legislative Procedure – Consultation of the European Parliament*, Case C-392/95 and opinion of Mr Advocate-General Fennelly delivered on 20 March 1997 (Court of Justice 1997).

   Judgement of the Court of 12 May 1998, *Commission of the European Communities* v. *Council of the European Union: Act of the Council – Joint action regarding airport transit visas – Legal basis*, Case C-170/1996 and opinion of Mr Advocate-General Fennelly delivered on 5 February 1998 (Court of Justice 1998).

61 The Advocate-General put it fairly clear. While Article M TEU excluded jurisdiction, Article L TEU reintroduced it. Hence, he argued that 'the power of judicial review which the Court enjoys under the jurisdictional clauses of each of the Community Treaties is extended by Article L'.

62 Interviews with members of the Legal Service, Council Secretariat. See also cases T-349/99 *Moroslav Miskovic* v. *Council of the European Union* and T-350/99 *Bogoljub Karic* v. *Council of the European Union*. Cited in Wessel (2004: 128).

7 Patterns of policy-making in EU foreign and interior policies: executive dominance and co-ordination problems

1 Interviews with members of Legal Service, Council Secretariat.
2 Interview with Head of Unit, Commission.
3 Interviews with Advisor to the Special Representative, Council Secretariat and Desk Officer, Commission.
4 Interview with Head of Unit, Council Secretariat.
5 Interviews with members of the Legal Service, Council Secretariat.
6 Interview with Director, Legal Service, Council Secretariat.
7 Interview with MP, House of Commons.
8 Interview with MEP.
9 See *Agence Europe*, various issues.
10 Interview with Head of Unit, Commission.
11 Interview with MEP, Head of Inter Group.
12 Interview with Desk Officer, Commission.
13 Interview with MEP, Head of Inter Group.
14 Interview with Administrator, European Parliament.
15 Interview with Desk Officer, Commission.
16 Interview with Desk Officer, Commission.
17 Interview with Deputy Head of Unit, Commission.
18 Interview with Deputy Head of Unit, Commission.
19 Interview with Desk Officer, Commission.
20 Interview with Administrator, European Parliament.
21 Interviews with members of the Legal Service, Council Secretariat.
22 Interview with Administrator, European Parliament.
23 Interviews with members of the Legal Service, Council Secretariat.
24 Interview with former Director, Commission.
25 Interview with Desk Officer, Council Secretariat.
26 Interview with Advisor to Special Representative, Council Secretariat.
27 Interviews with members of the Legal Service, Council Secretariat.
28 Interview with Desk Officer, Commission.
29 It must also be mentioned that the implementation of policies in the framework of the EMP was not only problematic regarding financial assistance. Progress relating to other policies or other 'baskets' of the EMP was also lagging behind schedule, such as, for example, on the EMP security charter, on the conclusion of some Association Agreements or on the establishment of a Euro-Mediterranean Free Trade Area, including flanking measures such as the rules of origin provisions.
30 Interview with Deputy Head of Cabinet, Commission.

Bibliography

Agreement (1997a) 'Euro-Mediterranean Interim Association Agreement on trade and cooperation between the European Community, of the one part, and the Palestine Liberation Organization (PLO) for the benefit of the Palestinian Authority of the West Bank and the Gaza Strip, of the other part', *Official Journal*, L 187, 16 July 1997: 3–135.

——(1997b) 'Agreement between the European Community and the State of Israel on procurement by telecommunications operators – Article 1 (6) side letters – Agreed minutes', *Official Journal*, L 202, 30 July 1997: 74–84.

——(1997c) 'Agreement between the European Community and the State of Israel on government procurement', *Official Journal*, L 202, 30 July 1997: 85–8.

——(1999a) 'Agreement on scientific and technical cooperation between the European Community and the State of Israel – Joint Declaration – Annex A: Principles on the allocation of intellectual property rights – Annex B: Financial rules governing the financial contribution of Israel referred to in Article 7 of this Agreement', *Official Journal*, L 83, 27 March 1999: 51–61.

——(1999b) '99/662/EC: Council Decision of 19 July 1999 concerning the conclusion of the Agreement on mutual recognition of OECD principles of good laboratory practice (GLP) and compliance monitoring programmes between the European Community and the State of Israel', *Official Journal*, L 263, 09 October 1999: 6.

——(2000) 'Euro-Mediterranean Agreement establishing an association between the European Communities and their Member States, of the one part, and the State of Israel, of the other part', *Official Journal*, L 147, 21 June 2000: 3–171.

——(2001) 'Agreement concluded by the Council of the European Union and the Republic of Iceland and the Kingdom of Norway concerning the latters' association with the implementation, application and development of the Schengen acquis – Final Act', *Official Journal*, L 176, 10 July 1999: 36–62.

Ahiram, E. and Tovias, A. (eds) (1995) *Whither EU–Israeli Relations? Common and Divergent Interests*, Frankfurt: Peter Lang.

Albert, M. (2005) 'Politik der Weltgesellschaft und Politik der Globalisierung: Überlegungen zur Emergenz von Weltstaatlichkeit', in B. Heintz, R. Münch and H. Tyrell (eds) *Zeitschrift für Soziologie*, special edition on '*Weltgesellschaft: Theoretische Zugänge und empirische Problemlagen*'.

Al-Khouri, R. (2000) 'Reconsidering the Economic Benefits of a Stable Middle East', in Behrendt and Hanelt (2000).

Allen, D. (1998) '"Who Speaks for Europe?": The Search for an Effective and Coherent External Policy', in Peterson and Sjursen (1998).

Alpher, J. (1998) 'The Political Role of the European Union in the Arab–Israeli Peace Process: An Israeli Perspective', *The International Spectator*, 33: 77–86.

——(2000) 'The Political Role of the EU in the Middle East: Israeli Aspirations', in Behrendt and Hanelt (2000).

Alter, K. J. (1998) 'Who are the "Masters of the Treaty"?: European Governments and the European Court of Justice', *International Organization*, 52: 121–47.

Anderson, J. (1999) 'The European Union: Time for a Place at the Table?', *Middle East Policy*, 6: 160–6.

Aoun, E. (2003) 'European Foreign Policy and the Arab–Israeli Dispute: Much Ado About Nothing', *European Foreign Affairs Review*, 8: 289–312.

Asseburg, M. (2001) 'Der Nahost-Friedensprozess und der Beitrag der EU – Bilanz und Perspektiven', *Die Friedens-Warte – Journal of International Peace and Organization*, 76: 257–88.

——(2002a) 'Arafat vor dem Aus – und dann?', SWP-Aktuell, 37, Berlin: Stiftung Wissenschaft und Politik.

——(2002b) 'Ein Neuanfang im Nahost-Friedensprozeß? Innere Reformen und internationales Engagement', SWP-Aktuell, 17, Berlin: Stiftung Wissenschaft und Politik.

Association Council (2000) 'Decision No.1/2000 of the EU–Israel Association Council of 13 June 2000 adopting its rules of procedure', *Official Journal*, L 151, 24 June 2000: 12–15.

Baldwin-Edwards, M. (1997) 'The Emerging European Immigration Regime: Some Reflections on Implications for Southern Europe', *Journal of Common Market Studies*, 35: 497–519.

Baldwin-Edwards, M. and Schain, M. A. (1994) 'The Politics of Immigration: Introduction', *West European Politics*, 17: 1–16.

Balibar, E. (1998) 'The Borders of Europe', in P. Cheah and B. Robins (eds) *Cosmopolitics: Thinking and Feeling Beyond the Nation*, Minneapolis, MN: University of Minnesota Press.

Ballmann, A., Epstein, D. and O'Halloran, S. (2002) 'Delegation, Comitology, and the Separation of Powers in the European Union', *International Organization*, 56: 551–74.

Barbé, E. (1998) 'Balancing Europe's Eastern and Southern Dimension', in Zielonka (1998a: 117–30).

Bardenhewer, A. (1998) 'Die Einheitlichkeit der Organisationsstruktur der Europäischen Union', in Bogdandy and Ehlermann (1998).

Barents, R. (1997) 'Some Observations on the Treaty of Amsterdam', *Maastricht Journal of European and Comparative Law*, 4: 332–45.

Barnett, M. and Finnemore, M. (1999) 'The Politics, Power, and Pathologies of International Organizations', *International Organization*, 53: 699–732.

Barnett, M. and Coleman, L. (2005) 'Designing Police: Interpol and the Study of Change in International Organizations', *International Studies Quarterly*, 49: 593–619.

Beck, M. (1997) 'Can Financial Aid Promote Regional Peace Agreements? The Case of the Arab–Israeli Conflict', *Mediterranean Politics*, 2: 49–70.

Behrendt, S. and Hanelt, C.-P. (eds) (1999) *Security in the Middle East*, Munich: Bertelsmann Foundation.

——(eds) (2000) *Bound to Co-operate: Europe and the Middle East*, Gütersloh: Bertelsmann Foundation.

Bertelsmann Group (1999) 'Europe and the Middle East and North Africa – Steps Towards Comprehensive Stability', discussion paper presented by the Bertelsmann Group for Policy Research – Center for Applied Policy Research, Munich, to the V. Kronberg Talks, December 1999.

—— (2000) 'Reshaping European Policy in the Middle East and North Africa', discussion paper presented by the Bertelsmann Group for Policy Research – Center for Applied Policy Research, Munich, to the VI. Kronberg Talks, October 2000.

Bieber, R. (1995) 'The Third Pillar and the 1996 Intergovernmental Conference. What Could and What Should Be on the Agenda?', in Bieber and Monar (1995).

Bieber, R. and Monar, J. (eds) (1995) *Justice and Home Affairs in the European Union: The Development of the Third Pillar*, Brussels: European University Press.

Bogdandy, A. v. (1999) 'The Legal Case for Unity: The European Union as a Single Organization with a Single Legal System', *Common Market Law Review*, 36: 887–910.

Bogdandy, A. v. and Ehlermann, C.-D. (eds) (1998) 'Konsolidierung und Kohärenz des Primärrechts nach Amsterdam', *Europarecht*, Beiheft, 2.

Branch, A. P. and Øhrgaard, J. C. (1999) 'Trapped in the Supranational-Intergovernmental Dichotomy: A Response to Stone Sweet and Sandholtz', *Journal of European Public Policy*, 6: 123–43.

Brynen, R. (2000) *A Very Political Economy: Peacebuilding and Foreign Aid in the West Bank and Gaza*, Washington, DC: United States Institute of Peace Press.

Budget (1993) 'European Commission: Financial Report 1993', Luxembourg: Office for Official Publications of the European Communities, 1995.

—— (1994) 'European Commission: Financial Report 1994', Luxembourg: Office for Official Publications of the European Communities, 1996.

—— (1995) 'European Commission: Financial Report 1995', Luxembourg: Office for Official Publications of the European Communities, 1996.

—— (1996) 'European Commission: Financial Report 1996', Luxembourg: Office for Official Publications of the European Communities, 1997.

—— (1997) 'European Commission: Financial Report 1997', Luxembourg: Office for Official Publications of the European Communities, 1998.

—— (1998) 'European Commission: Financial Report 1998', Luxembourg: Office for Official Publications of the European Communities, 1999.

—— (1999) 'European Commission: Financial Report 1999', Luxembourg: Office for Official Publications of the European Communities, 2001.

—— (2000) 'European Commission: Financial Report 2000', Luxembourg: Office for Official Publications of the European Communities, 2001.

—— (2001) 'European Commission: Financial Report 2001', Luxembourg: Office for Official Publications of the European Communities, 2002.

—— (2002) 'European Commission: General Budget of the European Union for the Financial Year 2002: The Figures', Luxembourg: Office for Official Publications of the European Communities, 2002.

—— (2003) 'European Commission: General Budget of the European Union for the Financial Year 2003: The Figures', Luxembourg: Office for Official Publications of the European Communities, 2003.

Bulmer, S. J. (1998) 'New Institutionalism and the Governance of the Single European Market', *Journal of European Public Policy*, 5: 365–86.

Butt Philip, A. (1994) 'European Union Immigration Policy: Phantom, Fantasy or Fact?', *West European Politics*, 17: 168–91.

Buzan, B., Wæver, O. and deWilde, J. (1998) *Security: A New Framework for Analysis*, Boulder, CO: Lynne Rienner.

Callovi, G. (1992) 'Regulation of Immigration in 1993: Pieces of the European Community Jig-Saw Puzzle', *International Migration Review*, 26: 353–72.

Cameron, F. (1998) 'Building a Common Foreign Policy: Do Institutions Matter?', in Peterson and Sjursen (1998).

Caporaso, J. A. (1996) 'The European Community and Forms of State: Westphalian, Regulatory, or Post-Modern?', *Journal of Common Market Studies*, 34: 29–52.

Caviedes, A. (2004) 'The Open Method of Co-ordination in Immigration Policy: A Tool for Prying Open Fortress Europe?', *Journal of European Public Policy*, 11: 289–310.

Cederman, L.-E. (ed.) (2000) *Constructing Europe's Identity: The External Dimension*, Boulder, CO: Lynne Rienner.

Chalmers, D. (1998) 'Bureaucratic Europe: From Regulating Communities to Securitising Unions', unpublished manuscript, London School of Economics and Political Science.

Checkel, J. T. (1999) 'Social Construction and Integration', *Journal of European Public Policy*, 6: 545–60.

Checkel, J. T. and Moravcsik, A. (2001) 'A Constructivist Research Program in EU Studies?', *European Union Politics*, 2: 219–49.

Christiansen, T. (2002) 'The Role of Supranational Actors in EU Treaty Reform', *Journal of European Public Policy*, 9: 33–53.

Christiansen, T., Jørgensen, K. E. and Wiener, A. (eds) (2001) *The Social Construction of Europe*, London: Sage Publications.

Collinson, S. (1994) *Europe and International Migration*, London: Pinter Publishers.

——(1996) 'Visa Requirements, Carrier Sanctions, "Safe Third Countries" and "Readmission": The Development of an Asylum "Buffer Zone" in Europe', *Transactions (Journal of the Institute of British Geographers)*, 21: 76–90.

Commission (1993a) 'Communication from the Commission: Future relations and cooperation between the Community and the Middle East', COM(93) 375 final, Brussels, 8 September 1993.

——(1993b) 'Communication from the Commission to the Council and the European Parliament: EC support to the Middle East peace process', COM(93) 458 final, Brussels, 29 September 1993.

——(1994a) 'Communication from the Commission to the Council and the European Parliament: On immigration and asylum policies', COM(94) 23 final, Brussels, 23 February 1994.

——(1994b) 'Communication from the Commission to the Council and the European Parliament: Strengthening the Mediterranean Policy of the European Union: Establishing a Euro-Mediterranean Partnership', COM(94) 427 final, Brussels, 19 October 1994.

——(1995a) 'Communication from the Commission to Parliament and the Council on the possible application of Article K.9 of the Treaty on European Union', COM(95) 966 final. Brussels, 30 January 1995.

——(1995b) 'Report on the operation of the Treaty on European Union (presented by the Commission)', SEC(1995) 731 final, Brussels, 10 May 1995.

——(1996) 'Commission opinion: "Reinforcing political union and preparing for enlargement"', COM(96) 90 final, Brussels: 28 February 1996.

——(1998a) 'Towards an area of freedom, security and justice', unpublished document.

——(1998b) 'Communication from the Commission: The role of the European Union in the peace process and its future assistance to the Middle East', COM(98) 715 final, Brussels, 16 January 1998.

——(2000a) 'Communication from the Commission to the Council and the European Parliament: Scoreboard to review progress on the creation of an "Area of freedom, security and justice" in the European Union', COM(2000) 167/2, Brussels, 13 April 2000.

——(2000b) 'Commission communication: A Basic Treaty for the European Union', COM(2000) 434 final, Brussels, 12 July 2000.

——(2000c) 'Communication from the Commission to the Council and the European Parliament: Concerning the development of the external service', COM(2000) 456 final, Brussels, 18 July 2000.

——(2000d) 'Communication from the Commission to the Council and the European Parliament: To prepare the fourth meeting of Euro-Mediterranean Foreign Ministers: "Reinvigorating the Barcelona Process"', COM(2000) 497 final, Brussels, 6 September 2000.

——(2000e) 'Communication from the Commission to the Council and the European Parliament: Biannual update of the scoreboard to review progress on the creation of an "Area of freedom, security and justice" in the European Union', COM(2000) 782 final, Brussels, 30 November 2000.

——(2001a) 'Communication from the Commission to the Council and the European Parliament: The development of the external service', COM(2001) 381 final, Brussels, 3 July 2001.

——(2001b) 'Communication from the Commission to the Council and the European Parliament: On an open method of coordination for the Community immigration policy', COM(2001) 387 final, Brussels, 11 July 2001.

——(2001c) 'Communication from the Commission to the Council and the European Parliament: On the common asylum policy, introducing an open coordination method: First report by the Commission on the application of Communication COM(2000) 755 final of 22 November 2000', COM(2001) 710 final, Brussels, 28 November 2001.

——(2002a) 'For the European Union: Peace, freedom, solidarity: Communication of the Commission on the institutional architecture', COM(2002) 728 final, Brussels, 4 December 2002.

——(2002b) 'Communication from the Commission to the Council and the European Parliament: Biannual update of the scoreboard to review progress on the creation of an "Area of freedom, security and justice" in the European Union, second half of 2002', COM(2002) 738 final, Brussels, 16 December 2002.

Convention (1997) 'Convention determining the State responsible for examining applications for asylum lodged in one of the Member States of the European Communities – Dublin Convention', *Official Journal*, C 254, 19 August 1997: 1–12.

Convey, A. and Kupiszewski, M. (1995) 'Keeping Up with Schengen: Migration and Policy in the European Union', *International Migration Review*, 29: 939–63.

Council (1994a) '94/276/CFSP: Council Decision of 19 April 1994 on a joint action adopted by the Council on the basis of Article J (3) of the Treaty on European Union, in support of the Middle East peace process', *Official Journal*, L 119, 7 May 1994: 1–2.

——(1994b) 'Council Resolution of 20 June 1994 on limitation on admission of

third-country nationals to the territory of the Member States for employment',
Official Journal, L 274, 19 September 1996: 3–6.

—— (1994c) 'Council Conclusions of 20 June 1994 concerning the possible application
of Article K.9 of the Treaty on European Union to asylum policy', *Official Journal*,
C 274, 19 September 1996: 34.

—— (1994d) 'Council Conclusions of 20 June 1994 on the Commission communication on immigration and asylum policies', *Official Journal*, C 274, 19 September
1996: 49.

—— (1994e) 'Council Conclusions of 30 November 1994 on the organization and
development of the Centre for Information, Discussion and Exchange on the Crossing of Frontiers and Immigration (Cirefi)', *Official Journal*, C 274, 19 September
1996: 50–1.

—— (1995a) '95/205/CFSP: Council Decision of 1 June 1995 supplementing Deci-
sion 94/276/CFSP on a joint action adopted by the Council on the basis of Article
J.3 of the Treaty on European Union, in support of the Middle East peace process',
Official Journal, L 130, 14 June 1995: 1.

—— (1995b) 'Council Resolution of 20 June 1995 on minimum guarantees for
asylum procedures', *Official Journal*, C 274, 19 September 1996: 13–17.

—— (1995c) '95/403/CFSP: Council Decision of 25 September 1995 supplementing
Decision 94/276/CFSP on a joint action adopted by the Council on the basis of
Article J.3 of the Treaty on European Union, in support of the Middle East peace
process, concerning the observation of elections to the Palestinian Council and the
coordination of the international operation for observing the elections', *Official
Journal*, L 238, 6 October 1995: 4–7.

—— (1996a) 'Council Decision of 4 March 1996 on an alert and emergency procedure
for burden-sharing with regard to the admission and residence of displaced persons
on a temporary basis', *Official Journal*, L 63, 13 March 1996: 10–11.

—— (1996b) 'Council Regulation (EC) No. 1488/96 of 23 July 1996 on financial and
technical measures to accompany (MEDA) the reform of economic and social structures in the framework of the Euro-Mediterranean partnership', *Official Journal*,
L 189, 30 July 1996: 1–9.

—— (1996c) '96/637/JHA: Joint Action of 28 October 1996 adopted by the Council
on the basis of Article K.3 of the Treaty on European Union introducing a programme of training, exchanges and cooperation in the field of identity documents
("Sherlock")', *Official Journal*, L 287, 8 November 1996: 7–9.

—— (1996d) '96/676/CFSP: Joint Action of 25 November 1996 adopted by the
Council on the basis of Article J.3 of the Treaty on European Union in relation to
the nomination of an EU special Envoy for the Middle East peace process', *Official
Journal*, L 315, 4 December 1996: 1–2.

—— (1996e) '96/706/EC: Council Decision of 6 December 1996 concerning the
adoption of the guidelines for the indicative programmes concerning financial and
technical measures to accompany the reform of economic and social structures in
the framework of the Euro-Mediterranean partnership (MEDA)', *Official Journal*,
L 325, 14 December 1996: 20–6.

—— (1996f) '97/11/JHA: Joint Action of 16 December 1996 adopted by the Council
on the basis of Article K.3 of the Treaty on European Union concerning a uniform
format for residence permits', *Official Journal*, L 7, 10 January 1997: 1–4.

—— (1997a) '97/289/CFSP: Joint Action of 29 April 1997 adopted by the Council on
the basis of Article J.3 of the Treaty on European Union on the establishment of a

European Union assistance programme to support the Palestinian Authority in its efforts to counter terrorist activities emanating from the territories under its control', *Official Journal*, L 120, 12 May 1997: 2–3.

——(1997b) 'Council Decision of 26 May 1997 on the exchange of information concerning assistance for the voluntary repatriation of third-country nationals', *Official Journal*, L 147, 5 June 1997: 3–4.

——(1997c) '97/420/JHA: Council Decision of 26 June 1997 on monitoring the implementation of instruments adopted concerning asylum', *Official Journal*, L 178, 7 July 1997: 6–7.

——(1997d) 'Council Resolution of 26 June 1997 on unaccompanied minors who are nationals of third countries', *Official Journal*, C 221, 19 July 1997: 23–7.

——(1997e) 'Council Decision of 22 July 1997 continuing the application of Joint Action 96/676/CFSP adopted by the Council on the basis of Article J.3 of the Treaty on European Union in relation to the nomination of an EU special Envoy for the Middle East peace process', *Official Journal*, L 205, 31 July 1997: 1.

——(1997f) '97/477/JHA: Joint Action of 22 July 1997 adopted by the Council on the basis of Article K.3 of the Treaty on European Union, concerning the financing of specific projects in favour of displaced persons who have found temporary protection in the Member States and asylum-seekers', *Official Journal*, L 205, 31 July 1997: 3–4.

——(1997g) '97/478/JHA: Joint Action of 22 July 1997 adopted by the Council on the basis of Article K.3 of the Treaty on European Union, concerning the financing of specific projects in favour of asylum-seekers and refugees', *Official Journal*, L 205, 31 July 1997: 5–6.

——(1997h) 'Council Resolution of 18 December 1997 laying down the priorities for cooperation in the field of justice and home affairs for the period from 1 January 1998 to the date of entry into force of the Treaty of Amsterdam', *Official Journal*, C 11, 15 January 1998: 1–4.

——(1998a) '98/244/JHA: Joint Action of 19 March 1998 adopted by the Council on the basis of Article K.3 of the Treaty on European Union, introducing a programme of training, exchanges and cooperation in the field of asylum, immigration and crossing of external borders (Odysseus programme)', *Official Journal*, L 99, 31 March 1998: 2–7.

——(1998b) '98/304/JHA: Joint Action of 27 April 1998 adopted by the Council on the basis of Article K.3 of the Treaty on European Union, concerning the financing of specific projects in favour of displaced persons who have found temporary protection in the Member States and asylum-seekers', *Official Journal*, L 138, 9 May 1998: 6–7.

——(1998c) '98/305/JHA: Joint Action of 27 April 1998 adopted by the Council on the basis of Article K.3 of the Treaty on European Union, concerning the financing of specific projects in favour of asylum-seekers and refugees', *Official Journal*, L 138, 9 May 1998: 8–9.

——(1998d) '98/608/CFSP: Council Decision of 26 October 1998 modifying Joint Action 96/676/CFSP adopted by the Council on the basis of Article J.3 of the Treaty on European Union in relation to the nomination of an EU Special Envoy for the Middle East peace process', *Official Journal*, L 290, 29 October 1998: 4.

——(1999a) 'Council Regulation (EC) No.574/1999 of 12 March 1999 determining the third countries whose nationals must be in possession of visas when crossing the external borders of the Member States', *Official Journal*, L 72, 18 March 1999: 2–5.

——(1999b) '1999/290/JHA: Joint Action of 26 April 1999 adopted by the Council on the basis of Article K.3 of the Treaty on European Union, establishing projects and measures to provide practical support in relation to the reception and voluntary repatriation of refugees, displaced persons and asylum seekers, including emergency assistance to persons who have fled as a result of recent events in Kosovo', *Official Journal*, L 114, 1 May 1999: 2–5.

——(1999c) '1999/440/CFSP: Council Decision of 6 July 1999 concerning the extension of joint action 97/289/CFSP on the establishment of a European Union assistance programme to support the Palestinian Authority in its efforts to counter terrorist activities emanating from the territories under its control', *Official Journal*, L 171, 7 July 1999: 1.

——(1999d) 'Council Regulation (EC) of 28 June 1999 laying down the procedures for the exercise of the implementing powers conferred upon the Commission', *Official Journal*, L 184, 17 July 1999: 23.

——(1999e) '1999/664/CFSP: Council Joint Action of 11 October 1999 amending Joint Action 96/676/CFSP in relation to the nomination of an EU Special Envoy for the Middle East Peace Process', *Official Journal*, L 264, 12 October 1999: 1.

——(1999f) '1999/870/EC: Council Decision of 17 December 1999 authorising the Deputy Secretary-General of the Council of the European Union to act as representative of certain Member States for the purpose of concluding contracts relating to the installation and the functioning of the communication infrastructure for the Schengen environment, "SISNET", and to manage such contracts', *Official Journal*, L 337, 30 December 1999: 41–42.

——(1999g) '1999/843/CFSP: Council Joint Action of 17 December 1999 extending and amending Joint Action 96/676/CFSP in relation to the nomination of an EU Special Envoy for the Middle East peace process', *Official Journal*, L 326, 18 December 1999: 71.

——(2000a) 'Council Decision of 27 March 2000 on the improved exchange of information to combat counterfeit travel documents', *Official Journal*, L 81, 1 April 2000: 1–3.

——(2000b) '2000/265/EC: Council Decision of 27 March 2000 on the establishment of a financial regulation governing the budgetary aspects of the management by the Deputy Secretary-General of the Council, of contracts concluded in his name, on behalf of certain Member States, relating to the installation and the functioning of the communication infrastructure for the Schengen environment, "Sisnet"', *Official Journal*, L 85, 6 April 2000: 12–20.

——(2000c) '2000/298/CSFP: Council Joint Action of 13 April 2000 on a European Union assistance programme to support the Palestinian Authority in its efforts to counter terrorist activities emanating from the territories under its control', *Official Journal*, L 97, 19 April 2000: 4–5.

——(2000d) '2000/596/EC: Council Decision of 28 September 2000 establishing a European Refugee Fund', *Official Journal*, L 252, 6 October 2000: 12–18.

——(2000e) 'Council Regulation (EC) No.2698/2000 of 27 November 2000 amending Regulation (EC) No. 1488/96 on financial and technical measures to accompany (MEDA) the reform of economic and social structures in the framework of the Euro-Mediterranean partnership', *Official Journal*, L 311, 12 December 2000: 1–8.

——(2000f) 'Council Regulation (EC) No. 2725/2000 of 11 December 2000 concerning the establishment of "Eurodac" for the comparison of fingerprints for the effective application of the Dublin Convention', *Official Journal*, L 316, 15 December 2000: 1–10.

——(2000g) '2000/794/CFSP: Council Joint Action of 14 December 2000 appointing the European Union Special Representative for the Middle East peace process and repealing Joint Action 96/676/CFSP', *Official Journal*, L 318, 16 December 2000: 5–6.

——(2001a) 'Council Directive 2001/55/EC of 20 July 2001 on minimum standards for giving temporary protection in the event of a mass influx of displaced persons and on measures promoting a balance of efforts between Member States in receiving such persons and bearing the consequences thereof', *Official Journal*, L 212, 7 August 2001: 12–23.

——(2001b) '2001/800/CFSP: Council Joint Action of 19 November 2001 extending the mandate of the European Union Special Representative for the Middle East peace process', *Official Journal*, L 303, 20 November 2001: 5–6.

——(2001c) 'Council Regulation (EC) No. 2424/2001 of 6 December 2001 on the development of the second generation Schengen Information System (SIS II)', *Official Journal*, L 328, 13 December 2001: 4–6.

——(2001d) 'Note from Presidency to General Affairs Council / European Council: Evaluation of the conclusions of the Tampere European Council', 14926/01, LIMITE, JAI 166, Brussels: 6 December 2001.

——(2002a) 'Council Common Position of 21 May 2002 concerning the temporary reception by Member States of the European Union of certain Palestinians', *Official Journal*, L 138, 28 May 2002: 33–4.

——(2002b) 'Council Regulation (EC) No. 1030/2002 of 13 June 2002 laying down a uniform format for residence permits for third-country nationals', *Official Journal*, L 157, 15 June 2002: 1–7.

——(2002c) '2002/463/EC: Council Decision of 13 June 2002 adopting an action programme for administrative cooperation in the fields of external borders, visas, asylum and immigration (ARGO programme)', *Official Journal*, L 161, 19 June 2002: 11–15.

——(2004) '2004/927/EC: Council Decision of 22 December 2004 providing for certain areas covered by Title IV of Part Three of the Treaty establishing the European Community to be governed by the procedure laid down in Article 251 of that Treaty', *Official Journal*, L 396, 31 December 2004: 45–6.

Council Secretariat (1998) 'The Evolution of European Union Common Foreign and Security Policy', lecture by Special Representative Moratinos, at the Helmut Kohl Institute for European Studies, Hebrew University of Jerusalem, 11 January 1998.

——(2002a) 'Summary of the address by Javier Solana, EU High Representative for the Common Foreign and Security Policy (CFSP): "Europe's Place in the World: The Role of the High Representative"', Stockholm, 25 April 2002, S0078/02, Brussels, 25 April 2002.

——(2002b) 'Summary of the intervention by Javier Solana, EU High Representative for the Common Foreign and Security Policy (CFSP): Plenary Session of the European Parliament, Strasbourg, 15 May 2002: Debate on the Reform of the Council', S0090/02, Brussels, 15 May 2002.

Court of Auditors (1996) 'Special Report No.1/96 on the MED programmes together with the Commission's replies', *Official Journal*, C 240, 19 August 1996: 1–32.

——(1997) 'Special Report No. 2/97 concerning humanitarian aid from the European

Union between 1992 and 1995 together with the Commission's replies', *Official Journal*, C 143, 12 May 199: 1–65.

—— (1998) 'Special Report No. 1/98 in respect of bilateral financial and technical cooperation with non Mediterranean Countries together with the Commission's replies', *Official Journal*, C 98, 31 March 1998: 1–37.

—— (2000) 'Special Report No. 19/2000 on the management by the Commission of the programme of assistance to Palestinian society together with the Commission's replies', *Official Journal*, C 32, 31 January 2001: 1–23.

—— (2001a) 'Special Report No. 21/2000 on the management of the Commission's external aid programme (in particular on country programming, project preparation and the role of Delegations), together with the Commission's replies', *Official Journal*, C 57, 22 February 2001: 1–24.

—— (2001b) 'Special Report No. 13/2001 on the management of the common foreign and security policy (CFSP), together with the Council's replies and the Commission's replies', *Official Journal*, C 338, 30 November 2001: 1–40.

Court of Justice (1995) 'Report of the Court of Justice on Certain Aspects of the Application of the Treaty on European Union', Luxembourg, May 1995, available at: www.europa.eu.int/en/agenda/igc-home/eu-justice/cj_rep.html.

—— (1997) 'Judgement of the Court of 10 June 1997, European Parliament v. Council of the European Union: Nationals of Third Countries: Visas: Legislative Procedure: Consultation of the European Parliament, Case C-392/1995', European Court Reports 1997: I-3213.

—— (1998) 'Judgement of the Court of 12 May 1998, Commission of the European Communities v. Council of the European Union: Act of the Council: Joint Action Regarding Airport Transit Visas: Legal Basis, Case C-170/1996', European Court Reports 1998: I-2763.

COWI (1998) 'Evaluation of Aspects of EU Development Aid to the MED-Region, Final Synthesis Report', COWI Consulting Engineers and Planners (Denmark) in association with Netherlands Economic Institute (Netherlands) and Andante (Sweden), available at: www.europa.eu.int/comm/europeaid/evaluation/program/medrep.htm.

Cram, L., Dinan, D. and Nugent, N. (eds) (1999) *Developments in the European Union*, Houndsmill: Macmillan.

Cremona, M. (2003) 'The Draft Constitutional Treaty: External Relations and External Action', *Common Market Law Review*, 40: 1347–66.

Cullen, D. (1995) 'Variable Geometry and Overlapping Circles: In Search of a Suitable Model for Justice and Home Affairs', in Bieber and Monar (1995).

Curtin, D. M. and Dekker, I. F. (2002) 'The Constitutional Structure of the European Union: Some Reflections on Vertical Unity-In-Diversity', in P. Beaumont, C. Lyons and N. Walker (eds) *Convergence and Divergence in European Public Law*, Oxford: Hart.

D'Alançon, F. (1994) 'The EC Looks to a New Middle East', *Journal of Palestine Studies*, 23: 41–51.

den Boer, M. (1996) 'Justice and Home Affairs', in Wallace and Wallace (1996).

—— (1997) 'Justice and Home Affairs Cooperation in the Treaty on European Union: More Complexity Despite Communitarization', *Maastricht Journal of European and Comparative Law*, 4: 310–16.

den Boer, M. and Wallace, W. (2000) 'Justice and Home Affairs: Integration Through Incrementalism?', in Wallace and Wallace (2000).

Denza, E. (2002) *The Intergovernmental Pillars of the European Union*, Oxford: Oxford University Press.

Dessus, S. and Suwa, A. (eds) (2000) *Regional Integration and Internal Reforms in the Mediterranean Area*, Paris: OECD.

Deutsch, K. W. *et al.* (1957) *Political Community and the North-Atlantic Area: International Organization in the Light of Historical Experience*, New York: Greenwood Press Publishers.

Diez, T. (2002) 'Postmoderne Konflikttheorien', in T. Bonacker (ed.) *Sozialwissenschaftliche Konflikttheorien*, Opladen: Leske + Budrich.

——(2004) 'Europe's Other and the Return of Geopolitics', *Cambridge Review of International Affairs*, 17: 319–35.

Diez, T., Stetter, S. and Albert, M. (2006) 'The European Union and Border Conflicts: The Transformative Power of Integration', *International Organization*, 60: 563–93.

DiMaggio, P. J. and Powell, W. W. (eds) (1991) *The New Institutionalism in Organizational Analysis*, Chicago, IL: University of Chicago Press.

Dowding, K. (2000) 'Institutionalist Research on the European Union: A Critical Review', *European Union Politics*, 1: 125–44.

Drüke, L. (1995) 'Harmonization of Asylum Law and Judicial Control Under the Third Pillar', in Bieber and Monar (1995).

Duff, A. (ed.) (1997) *The Treaty of Amsterdam: Text and Commentary*, London: Federal Trust.

Economic Co-operation Foundation (2002) 'International Involvement: Workshop Summary', Ma'alee Ha-Chamischa, Israel, 29–30 September 2002.

Edis, R. (1998) 'Does the Barcelona Process Matter?', *Mediterranean Politics*, 3: 93–105.

Ehlermann, C. D. (1998) 'Differentiation, Flexibility, Closer Cooperation: The New Provisions of the Amsterdam Treaty', working paper of the Robert Schuman Centre, Florence: European University Institute.

Erzan, R. (1999) 'Regionalism and Globalization in the Context of Euro-Mediterranean Agreements', *Mediterranean Politics*, 4: 23–35.

Eurobarometer (2003) 'Latest Survey Shows Growing Support for Key EU Policies in Acceding Countries', IP/03/1366, Brussels, 10 October 2003.

European Council (1994) 'Presidency Conclusions: Essen Summit, 9 December 1994', available at: http://ue.eu.int/presid/conclusions.htm.

——(1998) 'Vienna Action Plan on the implementation of the area of freedom, security and justice', *Official Journal*, C 91, 23 January 1999: 1–15.

——(1999a) 'Presidency Conclusions: Berlin Summit, 25 March 1999', available at: http://ue.eu.int/presid/conclusions.htm.

——(1999b) 'Presidency Conclusions: Tampere Summit, 16 October 1999', available at: http://ue.eu.int/presid/conclusions.htm.

——(2000) '2000/458/CFSP: Common Strategy of the European Council of 19 June 2000 on the Mediterranean region', *Official Journal*, L 183, 22 July 2000: 5–11.

——(2001) 'Presidency Conclusions: Laeken Summit, 15 December 2001', available at: http://ue.eu.int/presid/conclusions.htm.

European Parliament (1995) 'Resolution on the functioning of the Treaty on European Union with a view to the 1996 Intergovernmental Conference – Implementation and development of the Union', *Official Journal*, C 151, 19 June 1995: 56.

——(1996a) 'Report on the Commission Communication to the Council and the

European Parliament on future European Union economic assistance to the West Bank and the Gaza Strip', Rapporteur Per Gahrton (Greens, Sweden), A4–0129/1996, 25 April 1996.

——(1996b) 'Report on the proposal for a Council Directive on the elimination of controls on persons crossing internal frontiers', Rapporteur Glyn Ford (PES, UK), A4–0219/1996, 27 June 1996.

——(1996c) 'Report on the draft Resolution on minimum guarantees for asylum procedures', Rapporteur Hedy d'Ancona (PES, Netherlands), A4–0315/96, 10 October 1996.

——(1996d) 'Report on the Communication from the Commission to the European Parliament and the Council concerning the possible application of Article K.9 on the Treaty on European Union', Rapporteur Irini Lambraki (PES, Greece), A4–0349/96, 4 November 1996.

——(1996e) 'Report on the Middle East peace process', Rapporteur Luigi Alberto Colajanni (PES, Italy), A4–0351/1996, Brussels, 4 November 1996.

——(1997a) 'Report on the functioning and future of Schengen', Rapporteur Anne van Lancker (PES, Belgium), A4–0014/97, Brussels, 22 January 1997.

——(1997b) 'Report on the joint report by the Presidency of the Council and the Commission on Mediterranean policy: follow-up to the Barcelona Conference', Rapporteur Jannis Sakkelariou (PES, Germany), A4–0027/97, 29 January 1997

——(1997c) 'Report on the Draft Council Act drawing up the Convention on the European Information System (EIS)', Rapporteur Anna Terrón I Cusí (PES, Spain), A4–0062/97, Brussels, 27 February 1997.

——(1997d) 'Report on improving the impact of Joint Actions', Rapporteur Enrique Barón Crespo (PES, Spain), A4–0133/1997, Brussels, 16 April 1997.

——(1997e) 'Report on setting up a single coordinating structure within the European Commission responsible for human rights and democratisation', Rapporteur Marlene Lenz (EPP, Germany), A4–0393/1997, 4 December 1997.

——(1997f) 'Report on the draft Council Act drawing up the Convention concerning the establishment of "Eurodac" for the comparison of fingerprints of applicants for asylum and the Convention drawn up on the basis of Article K.3 of the Treaty on European Union, concerning the establishment of "Eurodac" for the comparison of fingerprints of applicants for asylum', Rapporteur Hedy d'Ancona (PES, Netherlands), A4–401/1997, Brussels, 10 December 1997.

——(1998) 'Report on the harmonisation of forms of protection complementing refugee status in the European Union', Rapporteur Michèle Lindeperg (PES, France), A4–0450/98, Brussels, 26 November 1998.

——(1999a) 'Report on the Commission Communication "The role of the European Union in the Middle East peace process and its future assistance to the Middle East"', Rapporteur Luigi Alberto Colajanni (PES, Italy), A5–0042/989, Brussels, 2 February 1999.

——(1999b) 'Report I. on the proposal for a Council Act drawing up a Protocol to the Convention concerning the establishment of "Eurodac" for the comparison of fingerprints of applicants for asylum; and II. on the draft Protocol drawn up on the basis of Article K.3 of the Treaty on European Union, to the Convention concerning the establishment of "Eurodac" for the comparison of fingerprints of applicants for asylum', Rapporteur Hubert Pirker (EPP, Austria), A5–0138/1999, Brussels, 18 March 1999.

——(1999c) 'Report on the influx of migrants from Iraq and the neighbouring region: EU action plan adopted by the Council on 26 January 1998 (Hughes Procedure)', Rapporteur Anna Terrón i Cusí (PES, Spain), A4–0079/99, 23 February 1999.

——(1999d) 'Report containing the European Parliament's proposal for a recommendation to the Council on the European Union's Mediterranean policy', Rapporteur Jannis Sakellariou (PSE, Germany), A4–0095/1999, 25 February 1999.

——(1999e) 'Working Paper: The Middle East peace process and the European Union', Directorate General for Research, Political Series, POLI-115 EN, 05–999.

——(2000a) 'Report on asylum-seekers and migrants – action plans for countries of origin or transit – High Level Working Group', Rapporteur Jorge Salvador Hernández Mollar (EPP, Spain), A5–0057 final, Brussels, 29 February 2000.

——(2000b) 'Report on the European Parliament's proposals for the Intergovernmental Conference', Rapporteur Giorgos Dimitrakopoulos (EPP, Greece) and Jo Leinen (PES, Germany), A5–0086 final, Brussels, 27 March 2000.

——(2000c) 'Report on the convening of the Intergovernmental Conference', Rapporteurs Girogos Dimitrakopoulos (EPP, Greece) and Jo Leinen (PES, Germany), A5–0018 final, Brussels, 27 January 2000.

——(2000d) 'Report on the Commission's Staff Working Paper "Towards common standards on asylum procedures"', Rapporteur Ingo Schmitt (EPP, Germany), A5–0123/2000 final, Brussels, 19 April 2000.

——(2000e) 'Report on the initiative of the Republic of Finland in view of the adoption of a Council Regulation determining obligations as between the Member States for the readmission of third-country nationals', Rapporteur Anna Karamanou (PES, Greece), A5–0110/2000 final, Brussels, 25 April 2000.

——(2000f) 'Report on a common Community diplomacy: A Common Diplomacy for the European Union', Rapporteur Gerardo Galeote Quecedo (EPP, Spain), A5–0210/2000, Brussels, 24 July 2000.

——(2000g) 'Report on the proposal for a Council Regulation (EC) concerning the establishment of "Eurodac" for the comparison of the fingerprints of applicants for asylum and certain other aliens – (reconsultation)', Rapporteur Hubert Pirker (EPP, Austria), A5–0219/2000 final, 1 September 2000.

——(2000h) 'Report I. on the initiative of the French Republic with a view to the adoption of a Council Directive defining the facilitation of unauthorised entry, movement and residence (10675/2000 – C5–0427/2000 – 2000/0821 (CNS)); II. on the initiative of the French Republic with a view to the adoption of a Council Framework Decision on the strengthening of the penal framework to prevent the facilitation of unauthorised entry and residence (10676/2000 – C5–0426/00 – 2000/0820(CNS))', Rapporteur Ozan Ceyhun (PES, Germany), A5–0315/2000 final, Brussels, 25 October 2000.

——(2001a) 'Parliament's position on the preliminary draft Constitutional Treaty', available at: http://europarl.eu.int/comparl/conv/documents/working_documents_en.htm.

——(2001b) 'Report on the Common Strategy of the European Union on the Mediterranean region, as laid down by the Feira European Council of 19 June 2000', Rapporteur Cristina Muscardini (Europe of the Nations, Italy), A5–0008/2001 final, Brussels, 22 January 2001.

——(2001c) 'Report on the Commission Communication on relations between the EU and the Mediterranean region: reinvigorating the Barcelona process', Rapporteur

Sami Naïr (European United Left / Nordic Green Left, France), A5–0009/2001 final, Brussels, 22 January 2001.

——(2001d) 'Report on the Commission communication on the development of the external service (Hughes procedure)', Rapporteur Gerardo Galeote Quecedo (EPP, Spain), A5–0199/2001, Brussels, 30 May 2001.

——(2001e) 'Report on the proposal for a Council directive on minimum standards on procedures in Member States for granting and withdrawing refugee status', Rapporteur Graham Watson (Group of the European Liberal, Democrat and Reform Party, UK), A5–0029/2001, 31 August 2001.

——(2001f) 'Report on the progress achieved in the implementation of the common foreign and security policy', Rapporteur Elmar Brok (EPP, Germany), A5–0332/2001, 11 October 2001. Rapporteur Elmar Brok (EPP, D), A5–0332/2001, 11 October 2001.

——(2002a) 'Situation in the Middle East, European Parliament resolution on the Middle East', P5–TA(2002)0173, Brussels, 10 April 2002.

——(2002b) 'Report on the proposal for a Council directive laying down minimum standards on the reception of applicants for asylum in Member States', Rapporteur Jorge Salvador Hernández Mollar (EPP, Spain), A5–0112 final, Brussels, 15 April 2002.

——(2002c) 'Report on asylum: common procedure and internal security', Rapporteur Robert Evans (PES, UK), A5–0257/2002 final, Brussels, 22 July 2002.

——(2002d) 'Report on the progress achieved in the implementation of the common foreign and security policy', Rapporteur Elmar Brok (EPP, Germany), A5–0296/2002 final, 11 September 2002.

European Union (2000) 'Middle East Peace Process: Multilateral Steering Group: Moscow, 31 January/1 February 2000, REDWG', Report from the European Union.

Favell, A. (1998) 'The Europeanisation of Immigration Policy', *European Integration Online Papers*, 2, available at: http://eiop.or.at/eiop/texte/1998-010a.htm.

Finnemore, M. and Sikkink, K. (1998) 'International Norm Dynamics and Political Change', *International Organization*, 52: 887–917.

Fligstein, N. and Mara-Drita, I. (1996) 'How to Make a Market: Reflections on the Attempt to Create a Single Market in the European Union', *American Journal of Sociology*, 102: 1–33.

Fligstein, N. and McNichol, J. (1998) 'The Institutional Terrain of the European Union', in Sandholtz and Stone Sweet (1998).

Fligstein, N. and Stone Sweet, A. (2002) 'Constructing Polities and Markets: An Institutionalist Account on European Integration', *American Journal of Sociology*, 108: 1206–43.

Forster, A. and Wallace, W. (2000) 'Common Foreign and Security Policy: From Shadow to Substance?', in Wallace and Wallace (2000).

Fortescue, J. A. (1995) 'First Experiences with the Implementation of the Third Pillar Provisions', in Bieber and Monar (1995).

Franchino, F. (2000) 'Control of the Commission's Executive Functions: Uncertainty, Conflict and Decision Rules', *European Union Politics*, 1: 63–92.

Galal, A. and Hoekman, B. (eds) (1997) *Regional Partners in Global Markets: Limits and Possibilities of the Euro-Med Agreements*, London: CEPR/ECES.

Garrett, G. (1995) 'From the Luxembourg Compromise to Codecision: Decision-making in the European Union', *Electoral Studies*, 14: 289–308.

Garrett, G. and Weingast, B. R. (1993) 'Ideas, Interests, and Institutions: Construct-ing the European Community's Internal Market', in J. Goldstein and R. O. Keohane (eds) *Ideas and Foreign Policy: Beliefs, Institutions and Political Change*, Ithaca, NY: Cornell University Press.

Garrett, G. and Tsebelis, G. (1996) 'An Institutionalist Critique of Intergovern-mentalism', *International Organization*, 50: 269–99.

Gatsios, K. and Seabright, P. (1989) 'Regulation in the European Community', *Oxford Review of Economic Policy*, 5: 37–60.

Geddes, A. (1995) 'Immigrant and Ethnic Minorities and the EU's "Democratic Deficit"', *Journal of Common Market Studies*, 33: 197–217.

—— (2000) *Immigration and European Integration: Towards Fortress Europe?*, Manchester: Manchester University Press.

Giammusso, M. (1999) 'Civil Society Initiatives and Prospects of Economic Develop-ment: The Euro-Mediterranean Decentralized Co-operation Network', *Mediterranean Politics*, 4: 25–52.

Giersch, H. (ed.) (1980) *The Economic Integration of Israel in the EEC*, Tübingen: J. C. B. Mohr.

Gillespie, R. (2002) 'The Valencia Conference: Reinvigorating the Barcelona Process?', *Mediterranean Politics*, 7: 105–14.

Gillespie, R. and Youngs, R. (2002) 'Themes in European Democracy Promotion', *Democratization*, 9: 1–16.

Ginsberg, R. H. (1999) 'Conceptualizing the European Union as an International Actor: Narrowing the Theoretical Capability–Expectations Gap', *Journal of Common Market Studies*, 37: 429–54.

Gomez, R. (1998) 'The EU's Mediterranean Policy: Common Foreign Policy by the Back Door?', in Peterson and Sjursen (1998).

Goodin, R. E. (2000) 'Institutional Gaming', *Governance*, 13: 523–33.

Greilsammer, I. and Weiler, J. H. H. (1988) *Europe's Middle East Dilemma: The Quest for a Unified Stance*, Boulder, CO: Westview Press.

Grunert, T. (1997) 'The Association of the European Parliament: No Longer the Under-dog in EPC?', in Regelsberger, Schoutheete de Tervarent and Wessels (1997a).

Guéhenno, J.-M. (1998) 'A Foreign Policy in Search of a Polity', in Zielonka (1998a).

Guild, E. (ed.) (1996) *The Developing Immigration and Asylum Policies of the European Union: Adopted Conventions, Resolutions, Recommendations, Decisions and Conclusions*, The Hague: Kluwer Law International.

Guiraudon, V. (2000) 'European Integration and Migration Policy: Vertical Policy-Making as Venue Shopping', *Journal of Common Market Studies*, 38: 251–71.

—— (2003) 'The Constitution of a European Immigration Policy Domain: A Political Sociology Approach', *Journal of European Public Policy*, 10: 263–82.

Haas, E. B. (1958) *The Uniting of Europe: Political, Social, and Economic Forces, 1950–1957*, Stanford: Stanford University Press.

Haas, P. (1992) 'Introduction: Epistemic Communities and International Policy Co-ordination', *International Organization*, 46: 1–35.

Hadar, L. t. (1996) 'Meddling in the Middle East? Europe Challenges U.S. Hegemony in the Region', *Mediterranean Quarterly*, 7: 40–54.

Hailbronner, K. (1995) 'Migration Law and Policy within the Third Pillar of the Union Treaty', in Bieber and Monar (1995).

—— (1998) 'European Immigration and Asylum Law under the Amsterdam Treaty', *Common Market Law Review*, 35: 1047–67.

——(2000) *Immigration and Asylum Law and Policy of the European Union*, The Hague: Kluwer Law International.

Hailbronner, K. and Thiery, C. (1997) 'Schengen II and Dublin: Responsibility for Asylum Applications in Europe', *Common Market Law Review*, 34: 957–89.

Hakura, F. S. (1998) 'The External EU Immigration Policy: The Need to Move Beyond the Orthodoxy', *European Foreign Affairs Review*, 3: 115–34.

Halbach, A. (1995) *New Potentials for Cooperation and Trade in the Middle East: An Empirical Analysis*, Munich: Weltforum Verlag.

Hayes-Renshaw, F. and Wallace, H. (1997) *The Council of Ministers*, London: Macmillan.

Heller, M. A. (ed.) (1997) *Europe and the Middle East: New Tracks to Peace?*, Herzliya: Friedrich-Ebert-Stiftung.

Heusgen, C. (2003) 'Eine gemeinsame Außen-und Sicherheitspolitik der Europäischen Union', *Politische Meinung*, 4: 19–26.

Hill, C. (1993) 'The Capability–Expectations Gap, or Conceptualizing Europe's International Role', *Journal of Common Market Studies*, 31: 305–28.

——(ed.) (1996) *The Actors in Europe's Foreign Policy*, London: Routledge.

——(1997) 'The Actors Involved: National Perspectives', in Regelsberger, Schoutheete de Tervarent and Wessels (1997a).

——(1998a) 'Convergence, Divergence and Dialectics: National Foreign Policies and the CFSP', in Zielonka (1998a).

——(1998b) 'Closing the Capability–Expectations Gap?', in Peterson and Sjursen (1998).

——(2004) 'Renationalizing or Regrouping? EU Foreign Policy Since 11 September 2001', *Journal of Common Market Studies*, 42: 143–63.

Hix, S. (1995) 'The 1996 Intergovernmental Conference and the Future of the Third Pillar', CCME Briefing Paper, 20, Brussels: Churches Commission for Migrants in Europe.

——(1999) *The Political System of the European Union*, London: Macmillan.

Hix, S. and Niessen, J. (1996) 'Reconsidering European Migration Policies. The 1996 Intergovernmental Conference and the Reform of the Maastricht Treaty', Brussels: Migration Policy Group.

Hodson, D. and Maher, I. (2001) 'The Open Method as a New Mode of Governance: The Case of Soft Economic Policy Co-ordination', *Journal of Common Market Studies*, 39: 719–46.

Holland, M. (1999) 'The Common Foreign and Security Policy', in Cram, Dinan and Nugent (1999).

Hollis, R. (1994) 'The Politics of Israeli–European Economic Relations', *Israel Affairs*, 1: 118–34.

——(1997) 'Europe and the Middle East: Power by Stealth?', *International Affairs*, 73: 15–29.

——(2000) 'Barcelona's First Pillar: An Appropriate Concept for Security Relations?', in Behrendt and Hanelt (2000).

House of Commons (2002) 'Adaptation to the Common Consular Instructions, Draft Decisions on the Adaptation of Part III and the Creation of an Annex 16 to the Common Consular Instructions, 23056 and 23057', London: House of Commons.

House of Lords (1999) 'Nineteenth report, 27 July 1999, By the Select Committee appointed to consider Community proposals, whether in draft or otherwise, to obtain all necessary information about them, and to make reports on those which, in the opinion of the Committee, raise important questions of policy or principle, and on other questions to which the Committee considers that the special attention of the House should be drawn, ordered to report prospects for the Tampere European Council', London: House of Lords.

——(2001) 'Ninth report, 14 March 2001, By the Select Committee appointed to consider European Union documents and other matters relating to the European Union, ordered to report the Common Mediterranean Strategy', London: House of Lords.

Huysmans, J. (2000a), 'European Identity and Migration Policy', in Cederman (2000).

——(2000b) 'The European Union and the Securitization of Migration', *Journal of Common Market Studies*, 38: 751–77.

Hyde-Price, A. (2003) 'Interests, Institutions and Identity in the Study of European Union Foreign Policy', in Tonra and Christiansen (2003).

Inter-institutional Agreement (1997) 'Resolution on the proposal for an Inter-institutional Agreement between the European Parliament, the Council and the European Commission on provisions regarding the financing of the Common Foreign and Security Policy', *Official Journal*, C 286, 22 September 1997: 80–1.

——(1999) 'Inter-institutional Agreement of 6 May 1999 between the European Parliament and the Commission on budgetary discipline and improvement of the budgetary procedure', *Official Journal*, C 172/1, 18 June 1999: 1–22.

Jachtenfuchs, M. and Kohler-Koch, B. (eds) (1996a) *Europäische Integration*, Opladen: Leske + Budrich.

Jamal, A. (2001) 'State-Building, Institutionalization and Democracy: The Palestinian Experience', *Mediterranean Politics*, 6: 1–30.

Joffé, G. (ed.) (1999) *Perspectives on Development: The Euro-Mediterranean Partnership*, London: Frank Cass.

Jørgensen, K. E. (1998) 'The European Union's Performance in World Politics: How Should We Measure Success?', in Zielonka (1998a).

Jupille, J. (1999) 'The European Union and International Outcomes', *International Organization*, 53: 409–25.

Katzenstein, P. (1987) *Policy and Politics in West Germany: The Growth of a Semi-Sovereign State?*, Philadelphia, PA: Temple University Press.

Kienle, E. (1998) 'Destabilization through Partnership? Euro-Mediterranean Relations after the Barcelona Declaration', *Mediterranean Politics*, 3: 1–20.

Kiewiet, D. R. and McCubbins, M. D. (1991) *The Logic of Delegation: Congressional Parties and the Appropriation Process*, Chicago, IL: University of Chicago Press.

Kiso, J. O. (1997) 'COREPER and the Political Committee: Damaging for CFSP?', *Cambridge Review of International Affairs*, 10: 141–54.

Kleine-Brockhoff, T. and Schirra, B. (2002) 'Arafat bombt, Europa zahlt', *Die Zeit*, 24, available at: www.zeit.de/2002/24/Politik/200224_arafat_haupttext.html.

Klos, C. (1998) *Rahmenbedingungen und Gestaltungsmöglichkeiten der europäischen Migrationspolitik*, Konstanz: Hartung-Gorre Verlag.

Korella, G. D. and Twomey, P. M. (eds) (1993) *Towards a European Immigration Policy*, Brussels: European Inter-university Press.

Koser, K. and Black, R. (1999) 'Limits to Harmonization: The "Temporary Protection" of Refugees in the European Union', *International Migration*, 37: 521–43.

Kostakopoulou, T. (1998) 'Is There an Alternative to "Schengenland"?', *Political Studies*, 46: 886–902.

——(2000) 'The "Protective Union": Change and Continuity in Migration Law and Policy in Post-Amsterdam Europe', *Journal of Common Market Studies*, 38: 497–518.

Kuijper, P. J. (2000) 'Some Legal Problems Associated with the Communitarization of Policy on Visas, Asylum and Immigration Under the Amsterdam Treaty and Incorporation of the Schengen Acquis', *Common Market Law Review*, 37: 345–66.

Laffan, B. (1996) 'The Budget', in Wallace and Wallace (1996).

Laffan, B. and Shackleton, M. (2000) 'The Budget: Who Gets What, When, and How', in Wallace and Wallace (2000).

Lapid, Y. (2001) 'Introduction: Identities, Borders, Orders: Nudging International Relations Theory in a New Direction', in M. Albert, D. Jacobsen and Y. Lapid (eds) *Identities, Borders, Orders: Rethinking International Relations Theory*, Minneapolis, MN: University of Minnesota Press.

Lavenex, S. (2004) 'EU External Governance in "Wider Europe"', *Journal of European Public Policy*, 11: 680–700.

Leitner, H. (1997) 'Reconfiguring the Spatiality of Power: The Construction of a Supranational Migration Framework for the European Union', *Political Geography*, 16: 123–43.

Lenaerts, K. (1991) 'Some Reflections on the Separation of Powers in the European Community', *Common Market Law Review*, 28: 11–35.

Lewis, J. (2000) 'The Methods of Community in EU Decision-Making and Administrative Rivalry in the Council's Infrastructure', *Journal of European Public Policy*, 7: 261–89.

Licari, J. (1998) 'The Euro-Mediterranean Partnership: Economic and Financial Aspects', *Mediterranean Politics*, 3: 1–20.

Lijphart, A. (1984) *Democracies: Patterns of Majoritarian and Consensus Government in Twenty-one Countries*, New Haven, CT: Yale University Press.

Lindberg, L. N. (1969) 'The European Community as a Political System: Notes Toward the Construction of a Model', *Journal of Common Market Studies*, 5: 344–87.

Lobkowicz, W. d. (1994) 'Intergovernmental Cooperation in the Field of Migration: From the Single European Act to Maastricht', in Monar and Morgan (1994).

Lowi, T. J. (1964) 'American Business, Public Policy, Case-Studies, and Political Theory', *World Politics*, 16: 677–715.

——(1972) 'Four Systems of Policy, Politics and Choice', *Public Administration*, 32: 300–10.

McGoldrick, D. (1997) *International Relations Law of the European Union*, London: Longman.

Macleod, I., Hendry, I. D. and Hyett, S. (1996) *The External Relations of the European Communities: A Manual of Law and Practice*, Oxford: Oxford University Press.

Mahoney, J. (2000) 'Path Dependence in Historical Sociology', *Theory and Society*, 29: 507–48.

Majer, D. (1999) 'Europa zwischen Integration und Kooperation: Einheitsstiftende und koordinative Elemente in den Rechtsgrundlagen der Gemeinsamen Außen- und Sicherheitspolitik (GASP) sowie der Gemeinsamen Innen-und Rechtspolitik (GIRP): Eine Normenanalyse', *Politische Vierteljahresschrift*, 40: 116–30.

Majone, G. (1996) *Regulating Europe*, London: Routledge.

Manners, I. (2002) 'Normative Power Europe: A Contradiction in Terms?', *Journal of Common Market Studies*, 40: 235–58.

Manners, I. and Whitman, G. (2003) 'The "Difference Engine": Constructing and

Representing the International Identity of the European Union', *Journal of European Public Policy*, 10: 380–404.

March, J. G. and Olson, J. P. (1989) *Rediscovering Institutions: The Organisational Basis of Politics*, New York: Free Press.

Marr, P. (1994) 'The United States, Europe, and the Middle East: An Uneasy Triangle', *Middle East Journal*, 48: 211–25.

Mattli, W. and Slaughter, A.-M. (1998) 'Revisiting the European Court of Justice', *International Organization*, 52: 177–209.

Maurer, A. and Parkes, R. (2006) 'Asylum Policy and Democracy in the European Union from Amsterdam towards the Hague Programme', Working Paper FG1, 2006/01, Berlin: Stiftung Wissenschaft und Politik.

MEDA (1999) 'Evaluation of the MEDA Regulation, final report', by W. Euchner, N. Garrigue and N. Petropoulos, available at: www.europa.eu.int/comm/europeaid/evaluation/program/medrep.htm.

MEDA Democracy (1999) 'Evaluation of the MEDA Democracy Programme 1996–98, final report', by N. Karkutli and D. Bützler, available at: www.europa.eu.int/comm/europeaid/evaluation/program/medrep.htm.

Meunier, S. and Nicolaïdis, K. (1999) 'Who Speaks for Europe? The Delegation of Trade Authority in the EU', *Journal of Common Market Studies*, 37: 477–501.

Mitchell, M. and Russell, D. (1996) 'Immigration, Citizenship and the Nation-State in the New Europe', in B. Jenkins and S. A. Sofos (eds) *Nation and Identity in Contemporary Europe*, London: Routledge.

Monar, J. (1995) 'Democratic Control of Justice and Home Affairs: The European Parliament and the National Parliaments', in Bieber and Monar (1995).

——(1997a) 'The European Union's Foreign Affairs System after the Treaty of Amsterdam: A "Strengthened Capacity for External Action"?', *European Foreign Affairs Review*, 2: 413–36.

——(1997b) 'The Finances of the Union's Intergovernmental Pillars: Tortuous Experiments with the Community Budget', *Journal of Common Market Studies*, 35: 57–78.

——(1998) 'Institutional Constraints of the European Union's Mediterranean Policy', *Mediterranean Politics*, 3: 39–60.

——(2000) 'Institutional Constraints of the European Union's Middle Eastern and North African Policy', in Behrendt and Hanelt (2000).

——(2001) 'The Dynamics of Justice and Home Affairs: Laboratories, Driving Factors and Costs', *Journal of Common Market Studies*, 39: 747–64.

Monar, J. and Morgan, R. (eds) (1994) *The Third Pillar of the European Union: Cooperation in the Fields of Justice and Home Affairs*, Brussels: European University Press.

Moore, M. (2002) 'Freedom of Movement and Migrant Workers' Social Security: An Overview of the Case Law of the Court of Justice, 1997–2001', *Common Market Law Review*, 39: 807–39.

Moravcsik, A. (1991) 'Negotiating the Single European Act: National Interests and Conventional Statecraft in the European Community', *International Organization*, 45: 19–56.

——(1993) 'Preferences and Power in the European Community: A Liberal Inter-governmentalist Approach', *Journal of Common Market Studies*, 31: 473–524.

——(1998) *The Choice for Europe: Social Purpose and State Power from Messina to Maastricht*, London: UCL Press.

Moravcsik, A. and Nicolaïdis, K. (1998) 'Keynote Article: Federal Ideals and

Constitutional Realities in the Treaty of Amsterdam', *Journal of Common Market Studies*, 36, Annual Review: 13–38.

——(1999) 'Explaining the Treaty of Amsterdam: Interests, Influence, Institutions', *Journal of Common Market Studies*, 37: 59–85.

Morris, L. (1997a) 'A Cluster of Contradictions: The Politics of Migration in the European Union', *Sociology*, 31: 241–59.

——(1997b) 'Globalization, Migration and the Nation-State: The Path to a Post-National Europe?', *British Journal of Sociology*, 48: 192–209.

Mörth, U. (2003) *Organizing European Co-operation: The Case of Armaments*, Lanham, MD: Rowman and Littlefield.

Mörth, U. and Britz, M. (2004) 'European Integration as Organizing: The Case of Armaments', *Journal of Common Market Studies*, 42: 957–73.

Müller-Graff, C.-P. (1995) 'The Dublin Convention. Pioneer and Lesson for Third-Pillar-Convetions', in Bieber and Monar (1995).

Musgrave, R. A. and Musgrave, P. B. (1959) *Public Finance in Theory and Practice*, second edition, New York: McGraw-Hill.

Musu, C. (2003) 'European Foreign Policy: A Collective Policy or a Policy of "Converging Parallels"', *European Foreign Affairs Review*, 8: 35–49.

Myers, P. (1995) 'The Commission's Approach to the Third Pillar: Political and Organizational Elements', in Bieber and Monar (1995).

Nanz, K.-P. (1995) 'The Schengen Agreement: Preparing the Free Movement of Persons in the European Union', in Bieber and Monar (1995).

Nassehi, A. (2002) 'Politik des Staates oder Politik der Gesellschaft? Kollektivität als Problemformel des Politischen', in K.-U. Hellmann and R. Schmalz-Bruns (eds) *Theorie der Politik: Niklas Luhmanns politische Soziologie*, Frankfurt: Suhrkamp.

Nathanson, R. and Stetter, S. (2005) *The Israeli European Policy Network Reader*, Herzliya: Friedrich-Ebert-Stiftung.

Neumann, I. B. (2000) 'European Identity, EU Expansion, and the Integration/Exclusion Nexus', in Cederman (2000).

Neumann, I. B. and Welsh, J. M. (1991) 'The Other in European Self-Definition: An Addendum to the Literature on International Society', *Review of International Studies*, 17: 327–48.

Neunreither, K. (1999) 'The European Parliament', in Cram, Dinan and Nugent (1999).

Neuwahl, N. A. E. M. (1995) 'Judicial Control in Matters of Justice and Home Affairs: What Role for the Court of Justice?', in Bieber and Monar (1995).

Niemeier, M. (1995) 'The K.4 Committee and its Position in the Decision Making Process', in Bieber and Monar (1995).

Niessen, J. (1996) 'Introduction: The European Union's Migration and Asylum Policies', in Guild (1996).

Nugent, N. (1999) 'Decision-Making', in Cram, Dinan and Nugent (1999).

Nuttall, S. J. (2000) *European Foreign Policy*, Oxford: Oxford University Press.

Oliveiro, Á. (1999) 'Case Law: A. Court of Justice: Case C-170/96, Commission of the European Communities v. Council of the European Union, judgement of 12 May 1998, [1998] ECR I-2763', *Common Market Law Review*, 99: 149–55.

Paasivirta, E. (1999) 'EU Trading with Israel and Palestine: Parallel Legal Frameworks and Triangular Issues', *European Foreign Affairs Review*, 4: 305–26.

Peers, S. (1998) 'Building Fortress Europe: The Development of EU Migration Law', *Common Market Law Review*, 35: 1235–72.

—— (2000) *EU Justice and Home Affairs Law*, Harlow: Longman.

Peres, S. (1996) *Die Versöhnung: Der neue Nahe Osten*, Munich: Goldmann.

Perthes, V. (ed.) (2002a) *Germany and the Middle East*, Berlin: Heinrich-Böll-Stiftung and Stiftung Wissenschaft und Politik.

—— (2002b) 'The Advantages of Complementarity: US and European Policies towards the Middle East Peace Process', in Perthes (2002a: 90–107).

Peters, J. (1996) *Pathways to Peace: The Multilateral Arab–Israeli Peace Talks*, London: Royal Institute of International Affairs.

—— (1998) 'The Arab–Israeli Multilateral Peace Talks and the Barcelona Process: Competition or Convergence?', *The International Spectator*, 33: 63–76.

—— (2000) 'Europe and the Arab–Israeli Peace Process: The Declaration of the European Council of Berlin and Beyond', in Behrendt and Hanelt (2000).

Peterson, J. (1998) 'Introduction: The European Union as a Global Actor', in Peterson and Sjursen (1998).

Peterson, J. and Sjursen, H. (eds) (1998) *A Common Foreign Policy for Europe: Competing Visions of the CFSP*, London: Routledge.

Pierson, P. (1996) 'The Path to European Integration: A Historical Institutionalist Analysis', *Comparative Political Studies*, 29: 123–63.

—— (1998) 'The Path to European Integration: A Historical Institutionalist Analysis', in Sandholtz and Stone Sweet (1998).

—— (2000a) 'Increasing Returns, Path Dependence, and the Study of Politics', *American Political Science Review*, 94: 251–67.

—— (2000b) 'The Limits of Design: Explaining Institutional Origins and Change', *Governance*, 13: 475–99.

Pollack, M. A. (1997) 'Delegation, Agency, and Agenda Setting in the European Community', *International Organization*, 51: 99–134.

Regelsberger, E. (1997) 'The Institutional Setup and Functioning of EPC/CFSP', in Regelsberger, Schoutheete de Tervarent and Wessels (1997a).

—— (ed.) (1993) *Die Gemeinsame Außen-und Sicherheitspolitik der Europäischen Union: Profilsuche mit Hindernissen*, Bonn: Europa Union Verlag.

Regelsberger, E. and Wessels, W. (1996) 'The CFSP Institutions and Procedures: A Third Way for the Second Pillar', *European Foreign Affairs Review*, 1: 29–54.

Regelsberger, E., Schoutheete de Tervarent, P. and Wessels, W. (eds) (1997a) *Foreign Policy of the European Union: From EPC to CFSP and Beyond*, Boulder, CO: Lynne Rienner.

—— (1997b) 'From EPC to CFSP: Does Maastricht Push the EU Toward the Role as a Global Power', in Regelsberger, Schoutheete de Tervarent and Wessels (1997a).

Rhein, E. (1999) 'Europa und der Mittelmeerraum', in W. Weidenfeld (ed.) *Europa-Handbuch*, Gütersloh: Verlag Bertelsmann Stiftung.

Richardson, J. (ed.) (1996a) *European Union: Power and Policy-Making*, London: Routledge.

—— (1996b) 'Policy-making in the EU: Interests, Ideas and Garbage Cans of Primeval Soup', in Richardson (1996a).

Ries, M. (2000) *Oslo: Tor zum Frieden in Nahost?*, Idstein: Meinhardt.

Robin, P. (1997) 'Always the Bridesmaid: Europe and the Middle East Peace Process', *Cambridge Review of International Affairs*, 10: 69–83.

Rosecrance, Richard (1998) 'The European Union: A New Type of International Actor', in Zielonka (1998a).

Rumelili, B. (2004) 'Constructing Identity and Relating to Difference: Understanding the EU's Mode of Differentiation', *Review of International Studies*, 30: 27–47.

Rummel, R. and Wiedemann, J. (1998) 'Identifying Institutional Paradoxes of CFSP', in Zielonka (1998a).

Salamé, G. (1994) 'Torn Between the Atlantic and the Mediterranean: Europe and the Middle East in the Post-Cold War Era', *Middle East Journal*, 48: 226–49.

Sandholtz, W. and Stone Sweet, A. (eds) (1998) *European Integration and Supranational Governance*, Oxford: Oxford University Press.

——(1999) 'European Integration and Supranational Governance: Rejoinder to Branch and Øhrgaard', *Journal of European Public Policy*, 6: 144–54.

Santiso, C. (2002) 'Promoting Democracy by Conditioning Aid? Towards a More Effective EU Development Assistance', *International Politics and Society*, 3: 107–33.

Sassen, S. (1996) 'The De-Facto Transnationalizing of Immigration Policy', Jean Monnet Chair Papers, 35, Florence: Robert Schuman Centre at the European University Institute.

Schael, C. (ed.) (2002) *Israel's Way to the European Union: Documentation of the Activities of the Israel–EU Forum at Tel Aviv University from its Establishment in Spring 2000 until June 2002*, Tel Aviv: Israel–EU Forum, Tel Aviv University and Friedrich-Ebert-Stiftung, Israel Office.

Scharpf, F. W. (1997) *Games Real Actors Play: Actor-Centered Institutionalism in Policy Research*, Boulder, CO: Westview Press.

Schengen Executive Committee (1997) 'The Schengen acquis – Decision of the Executive Committee of 25 April 1997 on awarding the contract for the SIS II preliminary study (SCH/Com-ex (97) 2, rev. 2)', *Official Journal*, L 239, 22 September 2000: 44.

——(1998) 'The Schengen acquis – Decision of the Executive Committee of 16 September 1998 setting up a Standing Committee on the evaluation and implementation of Schengen (SCH/ Com-ex (98) 26 def.)', *Official Journal*, L 239, 22 September 2000: 138–43.

Schimmelfennig, F. and Wagner, W. (eds) (2004) 'Symposium: External Governance in the European Union', *Journal of European Public Policy*, 11: 655–758.

Schumacher, T. (2005) *Die Europäische Union als internationaler Akteur im südlichen Mittelmeerraum: Zum Verhältnis von 'Actor Capability' und EU-Mittelmeerpolitik*, Baden-Baden: Nomos.

Sebenius, J. K. (1992) 'Challenging Conventional Explanations of International Cooperation: Negotiation Analysis and the Case of Epistemic Communities', *International Organization*, 46: 323–65.

Smith, K. E. (1998) 'The Instruments of European Union Foreign Policy', in Zielonka (1998a).

Smith, M. (1996) 'The EU as an International Actor', in Richardson (1996a).

——(1998) 'Does the Flag Follow Trade?: "Politicisation" and the Emergence of a European Foreign Policy', in Peterson and Sjursen (1998).

——(2003) 'The Framing of European Foreign and Security Policy: Towards a Post-Modern Policy Framework?', *Journal of European Public Policy*, 10: 556–75.

Smith, M. E. (1998) 'Rules, Transgovernmentalism, and the Expansion of European Political Cooperation', in Sandholtz and Stone Sweet (1998).

——(2001) 'Diplomacy by Decree: The Legalization of EU Foreign Policy', *Journal of Common Market Studies*, 39: 79–104.

——(2003) *Europe's Foreign and Security Policy: The Institutionalization of Cooperation*, Cambridge: Cambridge University Press.

Stavridis, S. (2001) 'The Democratic Control of the EU's Foreign and Security Policy after Amsterdam and Nice', *Current Politics and Economics of Europe*, 10: 289–311.

Stavridis, S. and Hutchence, J. (2000) 'Mediterranean Challenges to the EU's Foreign Policy', *European Foreign Affairs Review*, 5: 35–62.

Sterzing, C. and Böhme, J. (2002) 'German and European Contributions to the Israeli–Palestinian Peace Process', in Perthes (2002a).

Stetter, S. (1997) 'Promoting Trade in the Middle East: The Regional Economic Development Working Group (REDWG) and its Contribution to Stable Economic Relations between Israel and its Arab Neighbors', unpublished manuscript, Hebrew University of Jerusalem.

——(2000) 'Regulating Migration: Authority Delegation in Justice and Home Affairs', *Journal of European Public Policy*, 7: 80–103.

——(2003) 'Democratization without Democracy? The Assistance of the European Union for Democratization Processes in Palestine', *Mediterranean Politics*, 8: 153–73.

——(2004) 'Cross-Pillar Politics: Functional Unity and Institutional Fragmentation in EU Foreign Policies', *Journal of European Public Policy*, 11: 720–39.

——(2005) 'The Politics of De-Paradoxification in Euro-Mediterranean Relations: Semantics and Structures of "Cultural Dialogue"', *Mediterranean Politics*, 10: 331–48.

Stone Sweet, A. and Sandholtz, W. (1997) 'European Integration and Supranational Governance', *Journal of European Public Policy*, 4: 297–317.

——(1998) 'Integration, Supranational Governance, and the Institutionalization of the European Polity', in Sandholtz and Stone Sweet (1998).

Stone Sweet, A. and Caporaso, J. A. (1998) 'From Free Trade to Supranational Polity: The European Court and Integration', in Sandholtz and Stone Sweet (1998).

Tallberg, J. (2000) 'The Anatomy of Autonomy: An Institutional Account of Variation in Supranational Influence', *Journal of Common Market Studies*, 38: 843–64.

——(2002) 'Delegation to Supranational Institutions: Why, How, and with What Consequences?', *West European Politics*, 25: 23–46.

Tonra, B. and Christiansen, T. (eds) (2004) *Rethinking European Union Foreign Policy*, Manchester: Manchester University Press.

Tovias, A. (1997) 'The Economic Impact of the Euro-Mediterranean Free Trade Area Initiative on Mediterranean Non Member Countries', *Mediterranean Politics*, 2: 113–28.

——(2003) 'Mapping Israel's Policy Options Regarding its Future Institutionalised Relations with the European Union', CEPS Working Papers, 3.

Tovias, A. and Bacaria, J. (eds) (1999) 'Euro-Mediterranean Free Trade Areas: Commercial Implications', *Mediterranean Politics*, special issue, 4, 2.

Tsebelis, G. (1994) 'The Power of the European Parliament as a Conditional Agenda Setter', *American Political Science Review*, 88: 128–42.

Uçarer, E. (1999) 'Cooperation on Justice and Home Affairs', in Cram, Dinan and Nugent (1999).

Ugur, M. (1995) 'Freedom of Movement vs. Exclusion: A Reinterpretation of the "Insider"-"Outsider" Divide in the European Union', *International Migration Review*, 29: 964–99.

Van Krieken, P. J. (ed.) (2000) *The Asylum Acquis Handbook: The Foundation for a Common European Asylum Policy*, The Hague: T. M. C. Asser Press.

Van Outrive, L. (1995) 'Commentary on the Third Pillar and the 1996 Intergovernmental Conference. What Could and What Should Be on the Agenda?', in Bieber and Monar (1995).

Vasconcelos, Á. and Joffé, G. (eds) (2000) 'The Barcelona Process: Building a Euro-Mediterranean Regional Community', *Mediterranean Politics*, special issue, 5, 1.

Veit, W. and Münster, K. v. (2002) 'Conflict Management and Prevention through Dialogue: The Middle East from the Perspective of Civil Society', Forum Israel, Friedrich Ebert Stiftung, Israel Office: Herzliya.

Viola, D. M. (2000) *European Foreign Policy and the European Parliament in the 1990s: An Investigation into the Role and Voting Behaviour of the European Parliament's Political Groups*, Aldershot: Ashgate.

Wagner, W. (2004) 'Why the EU's Common and Security Policy Will Remain Intergovernmental: A Rationalists Institutionalist Choice Analysis of European Crisis Management Policy', *Journal of European Public Policy*, 10: 576–95.

Wallace, H. (1996) 'The Institutions of the EU: Experience and Experiments', in Wallace and Wallace (1996).

——(2000) 'The Institutional Setting: Five Variations on a Theme', in Wallace and Wallace (2000).

Wallace, H. and Wallace, W. (eds) (1996) *Policy-Making in the European Union*, third edition, Oxford: Oxford University Press.

——(eds) (2000) *Policy-Making in the European Union*, fourth edition, Oxford: Oxford University Press.

Wallace, W. (1982) 'Europe as a Confederation: The Community and the Nation-State', *Journal of Common Market Studies*, 21–2: 57–68.

——(1999) 'The Sharing of Sovereignty: the European Paradox', *Political Studies*, 47: 503–21.

——(2000) 'Collective Governance: The EU Political Process', in Wallace and Wallace (2000).

Walters, W. (2002) 'The Power of Inscription: Beyond Social Construction and Deconstruction in European Integration Studies', *Millennium: Journal of International Studies*, 31: 83–108.

Watzal, L. (1995) 'Hilfreiche Konkurrenz? Die Nahost-Politik der USA und der EU im Vergleich', *Internationale Politik*, 7: 37–42.

Weber, M. (1988) *Gesammelte Politische Schriften*, fifth edition, Tübingen: Mohr.

Weber-Panariello, P. A. (1995) 'The Integration of Matters of Justice and Home Affairs into Title VI of the Treaty on European Union: A Step towards more Democracy?', EUI Working Paper RSC 95/32, Florence: European University Institute.

Weidenfeld, W. (ed.) (1998) *Amsterdam in der Analyse: Strategien für Europa*, Gütersloh: Verlag Bertelsmann Stiftung.

Weiler, J. H. H. (1997) 'The Reformation of European Constitutionalism', *Journal of Common Market Studies*, 35: 97–131.

Wessel, R. A. (2000) 'The Inside Looking Out: Consistency and Delimitation in EU External Relations', *Common Market Law Review*, 37: 1135–71.

——(2004) 'Fragmentation in the Governance of the EU External Relations: Legal Institutional Dilemmas and the New Constitution for Europe', in J. W. de Zwaan, J. H. Jans, F. A. Nelissen and S. Blockmans (eds) *The European Union: An Ongoing Process of Integration*, The Hague: T. M. C. Asser Press.

Wessels, W. (1998) 'Comitology: Fusion in Action: Politico-Administrative Trends in the EU System', *Journal of European Public Policy*, 5: 209–34.

Wessels, W. and Rometsch, D. (eds) (1996) *The European Union and the Member States: Towards Institutional Fusion?*, Manchester: Manchester University Press.

West Bank and Gaza (2000) 'Evaluation of the European Community's Programme of Assistance to the West Bank and Gaza Strip', available at: http://ec.europa.eu/comm/europeaid/evaluation/evinfo/1999/951403_ev.pdf.

Wiener, A. (2001) 'Zur Verfassungspolitik jenseits des Staates: Die Vermittlung von Bedeutung am Beispiel der Unionsbürgerschaft', *Zeitschrift für Internationale Beziehungen*, 8: 73–104.

—— (2003) 'Finality vs. Enlargement: Constitutive Practices and Opposing Rationales in the Reconstruction of Europe', in J. H. H. Weiler and M. Wind (eds) *European Constitutionalism Beyond the State*, Cambridge: Cambridge University Press.

World Society Research Group (2000) 'Introduction. World Society', in M. Albert, L. Brock and K. D. Wolf (eds) *Civilizing World Politics. Society and Community beyond the State*, Lanham, MD: Rowman and Littlefield.

Youngs, R. (2002) 'The European Union and Democracy Promotion in the Mediterranean: A New or Disingenuous Strategy?', *Democratization*, 9: 40–62.

—— (2004) 'Normative Dynamics and Strategic Interests in the EU's External Identity', *Journal of Common Market Studies*, 42: 415–35.

Zaafrane, H. and Mahjoub, A. (2000) 'The Euro-Mediterranean Free Trade Zone: Economic Challenges and Social Impacts on the Countries of the South and East Mediterranean', *Mediterranean Politics*, 5: 9–32.

Zaim, F. (1999) 'The Third Generation of Euro-Mediterranean Association Agreements: A View from the South', *Mediterranean Politics*, 4: 36–52.

Zielonka, Jan (ed.) (1998a) *Paradoxes of European Foreign Policy*, The Hague: Kluwer Law International.

—— (1998b) 'Constraints, Opportunities and Choices in European Foreign Policy', in Zielonka (1998a).

Index

Note: page numbers in **bold** refer to an illustration.

T - #0020 - 270225 - C0 - 234/156/14 [16] - CB - 9780415414913 - Gloss Lamination